11 00

D0563156

Race, Campaign Politics, and the Realignment in the South

Race, Campaign Politics, and the Realignment in the South

James M. Glaser

Yale University Press   *New Haven and London*

Designed by Rebecca Gibb. Set in Bell type by Keystone
Typesetting, Inc. Printed in the United States of America by
Edwards Brothers, Inc., Ann Arbor, Michigan.

Library of Congress Cataloging-in-Publication Data

Glaser, James M., 1960–
    Race, campaign politics, and the realignment in the South /
James M. Glaser.
        p.   cm.
    Includes bibliographical references and index.
    ISBN 0-300-06398-9 (cloth: alk. paper)
            0-300-07723-8 (pbk.: alk. paper)
    1. Southern States—Politics and government—1961–
2. United States. Congress—Elections.   3. Elections—Southern
States.   4. Party affiliation—Southern States.   5. Political
parties—Southern states.   6. Southern States—Race relations.
I. Title.
JK2683.G58   1996
324.975'043—dc20   95-32636
                                                            CIP

A catalogue record for this book is available from the British
Library.

The paper in this book meets the guidelines for permanence and
durability of the Committee on Production Guidelines for Book
Longevity of the Council on Library Resources.

10 9 8 7 6 5 4 3 2

To my parents, Harold and Judith Glaser,
and to my grandmother Mae Kramer,
with love and thanks

Contents

Illustrations

Figures

Tables

Preface

"EXACTLY WHAT ARE YOU DOING HERE?" asked an Alabama campaign manager back in 1989. "*Rashomon*," I responded. The man looked at me blankly. "You know," I explained, "the Kurosawa movie where he shows the same event from the perspective of everybody who participates in it." He rolled his eyes: "I don't know no *Rashomon*."

My answer, which made some sense when I first uttered it as a graduate student in a Berkeley coffeehouse, did not go over well in this Anniston, Alabama, coffeeshop. It was a rookie mistake. Still, over all these years the metaphor has guided me. The point of this classic Japanese movie, which shows an attack on a couple from the very different perspectives of the attacker, the man and woman who are attacked, and an "objective" observer, is that the truth is to be found by putting together all their accounts (the objective observer also is shown to have biases that shape his point of view). Likewise, my purpose has been to gather the perspectives of many different actors on the same events, some congressional elections in the South, to construct some narratives of these elections, adding my own observations, and to analyze and interpret them.

The result is a book that is quite different from most other work on southern political behavior. This is not to say that analyses of public opinion data or electoral data are not of value. There are any number of good, detailed quantitative studies of southern voters. Understanding southern politics, however, comes also from knowing about the context in which mass political decisions are made, and that is the purpose of what follows.

Much of the work on southern politics, going back several decades now, starts with the assumption that the changes that took place in politics and society in the 1960s would lead inexorably to Republican domination in the region. In particular, changes in race relations and the infusion of blacks into the electorate—and into the Democratic party, at that—have long been viewed as fueling Republican growth and providing for the party's very promising future. Although the Republican party has grown enormously since the 1960s, it has not achieved the full-scale electoral success many expected. Even in the 1980s, Republicans did not come to dominate in the South except at the presidential level. Only after the midterm elections of 1994, thirty years after passage of the Voting Rights Act, have they achieved even partisan balance at the congressional level. Most indications point to continued and perhaps dramatic Republican congressional success. The fact remains that it has been a surprisingly slow development.

This book on the choices offered to southern voters in congressional elections will shed light on why Republican success in presidential elections in the South has been so slow in translating to lower-level electoral success. One major argument I make is that the Democratic party's fate was not sealed by the civil rights movement and the political changes it engendered. Democrats, in fact, adjusted well to the dramatic changes in the political environment, including the racial changes in this environment, and political strategy surrounding race actually helped the Democratic party keep its tenacious hold on many lower-level positions in the South. In the decades after the passage of major civil and voting rights legislation, Democrats were better at reading and understanding the requirements of the campaign, the constraints that the racial balance in the South posed, and the opportunities it provided. Moreover, they were better able to construct biracial coalitions in race-sensitive environments. In the thirty years following the Voting Rights Act, they stayed in political contention and even dominated at the congressional level on down for a variety of reasons. But this ability to manage the challenges of race in the South certainly was vital to their success. They must continue to manage these challenges if they are to continue to hold off Republican domination at all levels of southern politics.

It has been exciting putting this story together and writing it. Much of the pleasure of doing this work came from the people I encountered along the way, and I wish to thank them here. I talked with many people, some at great length, about their experiences in the campaigns described in the upcoming pages. In many cases, these interviews came during the heat of the campaign, when time was very valuable. In some cases, the interviews came with a ride to the next campaign event and even assistance in getting into that event. For their time, their candor, and in many cases their kindness, I want to thank James Anderson, C. F. Appleberry, Linda Arey, Sam Attlesey, Edith Back, Unita Blackwell, Betty Jo Boyd, Bob Boyd, Glen Browder, Sarah Campbell, Jim Chapman, William Coleman, Joe Colson, Dave Cooley, Chris Crowley, Dwayne Crump, Hayes Dent, Wayne Dowdy, Pat Duncan, Thom Ferguson, C. J. Fogle, Johnny Ford, Sheila Gilbert, Dylan Glenn, Jerome Gray, Reed Guice, Edd Hargett, Charlie Horhn, Paul Houghton, Lee Howard, Jim Humlicek, Craig James, Ron Jensen, David Jordan, Tom King, Jim Merrill, Pat Murphy, David Murray, Trudy Nichol, L. F. Payne, Clarke Reed, Ken Reid, Chip Reynolds, John Rice, George Shipley, Brent Shriver, Christopher Smith, Mike Smith, Sharon Souther, Carolyn Stuckett, Gene Taylor, Worth Thomas, Bennie Thompson, Charles Tisdale, Cora Tucker, Bobby Vincent, Steve

Walton, Jim Warren, Jim Yardley, Lauren Ziegler, and Bill Zortman. I owe an additional thank you to Tom Anderson, Unita Blackwell, Glen Browder, Hayes Dent, John Rice, Gene Taylor, and Bennie Thompson for opening their campaigns to me and permitting me to attend their campaign events.

Many organizations helped me through the lengthy process of writing this book. My visits to Alabama, Mississippi, and Washington, D.C., were expensive, and without support from these different sources I would not have been able to do this research. I am most grateful for the financial support I received as a graduate student at the University of California at Berkeley. The Department of Political Science, the Institute of Governmental Studies, the Berkeley Chapter of Phi Beta Kappa, and the Dean of Graduate Studies at Berkeley all provided me with funding that made it possible to write a dissertation that has evolved into this book. I also received funding later in the process, which enabled me to return to Mississippi in 1993 and to complete this project. I would like to thank the Political Science Department at Tufts University and the University Faculty Research Award Committee for their generous support. I also received funding from the American Political Science Association Small Grant Program and wish to thank Michael Brintnall, director of professional affairs at the APSA, for helping me obtain permission to use some of that grant for this project when the opportunity to go to Mississippi arose.

I am especially grateful to Raymond Wolfinger, who, as my dissertation chair and mentor, originally encouraged me to do this research and helped me plan a research design that eventually would yield so much wonderful material. I have greatly valued his guidance, his wisdom, and his friendship. Paul Sniderman gave me sage advice throughout this process as well. He has contributed so much to my thinking and my development as a political scientist, more than he even knows, and I feel fortunate to have linked up with him early in my graduate career. I also thank Jack Citrin, Martin Gilens, Marissa Martino Golden, Michael Hagen, Michael Hout, and Jonathan Krasno, who read and critiqued several early chapters of this book (Professors Citrin and Hout as members of my dissertation committee). Jon Krasno deserves a special thank you for helping me enormously at a critical point in this process. More recently, David Mayhew read and critiqued the manuscript for Yale University Press. His very smart observations and advice were invaluable to me as I worked to improve it. Jeffrey Berry, Pamella Endo, and Kent Portney also read later versions of the manuscript and helped me to make it better. My colleagues, particularly Professors Berry, Portney, and Frances Hagopian, and the staff of the Political Science Department, Lidia Bonaventura, Paula Driscoll, and Jini Kelly, have been very supportive of me during my years at Tufts, and I am thankful.

In the final stages of this project, I was lucky to have connected with John Covell. He and his staff at Yale University Press have made this a most pleasant experience. Lawrence Kenney, the manuscript editor, did a superb job preparing it for publication.

Most of all, I thank my wife, Pamella Endo, for her love, her understanding, and her encouragement from beginning to end, and my daughter Alison, who came along in the middle of this process. They were my inspiration.

Race, Campaign Politics, and the Realignment in the South

1 The Puzzles of the Southern Realignment

"I never should have been a Democrat. People like me made the Democratic party strong." *Alabama State Senator John Rice (Rep.—Lee County)*

"I'm a Democrat, but I vote for the man. All the men are Republicans though." *Former Democratic county chairman, Mississippi*

THROUGHOUT THE SOUTH, a lot of old Democrats are finding themselves at various stages of conversion to the Republican party. Born Democratic, raised Democratic, they have had difficulty letting go of their old affiliation, which in many cases was burned into them. "Daddy would have whipped me if I was anything but a Democrat," said one former Democratic county chairman from East Texas. "There's no rhyme or reason for [my being a Democrat] anymore, except it's all I know" (Taylor 1985a). Still, he and many other white southerners slowly are working their way toward a new identity.

People like this have made the South competitive territory, but it has been a painfully slow process, slow not just in the conversion of old Democrats, but also in the Republican realization of the fruits of their efforts. Republicans have yet to experience full-fledged success in the South, though many have been expecting it for years, indeed decades. What has impeded Republican progress and how the Democrats have held back the future is, in fact, the subject of this book.

V. O. Key and the Politics of the Old South

The story begins in the Old South, where a political system based on segregation and the subjugation of blacks flourished. V. O. Key, in his classic work *Southern Politics in State and Nation* (1949), describes the southern political system and the relation of race to politics in the region.[1] His analysis is based upon the contention that race had been and continued to be the fundamental structuring force of southern politics. Almost every feature of southern politics—the peculiar electoral rules and regulations, the practices, rhetoric, and styles of politicians, the concentration of political power in black belt whites, the nature of public opinion, the unity among southern representatives in Congress—fit into his scheme. Writes Key in 1949, "In its grand outlines the politics of the South revolves around the position of the Negro. It is at times interpreted as a politics of cotton, as a politics of free trade, as a politics of agrarian poverty, or as a politics of planter and plutocrat. Although such interpretations have a superficial validity, in the last analysis the major peculiarities of southern politics go back to the Negro. Whatever phase of the southern political process one seeks to understand, sooner or later the trail of inquiry leads to the Negro" (5).

My interest in V. O. Key is his argument that the nature of the party system, if it can be called that, rested on the power of racial issues. Democrats reigned supreme because the "race issue," the issue or set of issues of segregation, eclipsed any other issue that could possibly generate a cleavage in the electorate and upset the prevailing partisan situation. As Key writes, "The maintenance of southern Democratic solidarity has depended fundamentally on a willingness to subordinate to the race question all great social and economic issues that tend to divide people into opposing parties" (315–16). So long as this issue remained atop the political agenda, there was little to split the Democratic party.

The leadership of the Democratic party, according to Key, thus worked hard to keep the race issue festering. It is hardly surprising that this leadership was dominated by conservative black belt whites and that their fears, concerns, and priorities on the race question permeated the politics of the entire region.[2] As Key argues, these "black belt whites succeeded in imposing their will on their states" (11) and were the most important southern voices in national politics as well. Key also documents a strong relation between black populations and white support for these types of politicians. Blacks in the most heavily black counties of the South were the most shut out of politics, and whites in these counties were most supportive of keeping it that way. The Solid South was white supremacist and solidly Democratic, two tendencies that reinforced each other.

Given this status quo, Republicans, as "the party of Lincoln," were unable to gain a foothold in the electorate except in a few remote places in the hill country of the region.[3] In a party system whose genesis lay in the Civil War and Reconstruction, they had no natural constituency to appeal to, particularly as blacks were disenfranchised. As Democrats were not about to yield the overwhelming advantage the racial issue gave them, the situation was bleak for the Republican party. Southern Republican leaders, however, accommodated themselves to this situation rather well. Many were, as Key describes them, "patronage farmers" and "palace politicians" whose "chief preoccupation [was] not with voters but with maneuvers to gain and keep control of the state party machinery" (292). Although not all Republican leaders fit this description, Key's point is that Republican leaders, having no divisive issue to call upon, were ill equipped and in many cases not even inclined to challenge Democratic dominance.

One of the important consequences of this partisan situation was that class issues were, for the most part, kept off the political agenda. Appeals to racial hatred were designed to distract lower-class whites from challenging the prevailing economic order. By keeping emotions high on racial issues, elites were able to minimize the possibility of a class-based political movement emerging. Of course, there was (and is) a populist strain in southern political culture, and southern political history is peppered with characters like Huey Long and the Georgia radical Tom Watson. But these populist figures are notable as exceptions, not as the rule.[4] Class-based politics was largely subordinated to a race-based politics in the South, and southern Democrats worked hard to keep it that way.

Key's interpretation of the politics of the Old South ties together the one-party system, the black belt domination of politics, and the subordination of class issues to racial issues. The South he describes is the baseline from which all political change is measured, and since Key wrote his famous book, much has happened to change politics, society, and the economy in the South.

Most notably, the civil rights movement abolished de jure segregation, a set of events that altered southern politics forever. The civil rights movement and the passage of civil rights and voting rights legislation represented the death knell of the old political system as the basis upon which it rested—the disenfranchisement and officially sanctioned subjugation of blacks—crumbled in the years to follow. These pieces of legislation had profound and inevitable consequences for the southern political system as blacks entered the electorate in large numbers and became an important new constituency and as the defenders of the Old South lost the most potent issue in their political arsenal.

The civil rights movement and the changes it brought to the South are not the only reasons the old southern political system began to change. Changes in the economy had some bearing on partisan change in the region. Through the 1950s, a growing, prosperous urban and suburban middle class, for instance, gave the Republicans a new and important base of support (Bartley and Graham 1975, 185). Industrialization and the desire to attract northern investment to the region led to some new political priorities (Wright 1986) and placed power in a different set of elites.

Changes within the national parties starting in 1948 were also partly responsible for the decay of the old southern political system. In that year, skirmishing in Congress over President Truman's new civil rights policy was followed by a southern walkout from the Democratic national convention. The Dixiecrats bolted over a civil rights plank in the Democratic party platform and ran their own ticket throughout the South in the presidential elections of 1948. Their rebellion (which cost the Democrats thirty-seven electoral votes in the South) made clear that the partnership of southern and northern Democrats was the source of potentially large problems.

There was little change in the racial positions of the parties through most of the 1950s. The Democrats managed to balance the programmatic wing of the party and the southern Democrats, and the Republican position on racial change was not clarified by the actions of the Eisenhower administration. Although the administration did little to advance civil and voting rights during the decade, the president did call out federal troops to resolve the Little Rock school crisis. Moreover, as Sundquist (1983) notes, "The white South could not forget that it was a Republican chief justice, appointed by Eisenhower—Earl Warren—who molded the unanimous Supreme Court decision outlawing the South's segregated schools" (357). A transformation in party positions on race really can be traced to the end of Eisenhower's term. In the congressional elections of 1958, liberal Democrats defeated several prominent liberal Republicans (including some active civil rights supporters), and the complexion of both national parties began to change considerably (Carmines and Stimson 1989). When the Kennedy and Johnson administrations started to take a more active role in advancing civil rights in the South and when Barry Goldwater partially based his presidential campaign in 1964 on his opposition to the Civil Rights Act of 1964, a polarization of the national parties over race began to set. Though this polarization was certainly not complete, particularly in the South, the parties became distinguishable on racial issues.

At about this time, many important political analysts started predicting a new party system in the South, one predicated on this different racial cleavage. Philip Converse (1966), for instance, wrote, "Of the current issues on the American scene, the Negro problem comes closest [in the South, but not elsewhere] to showing those characteristics necessary if a political issue is to form the springboard to large-scale partisan realignment" (240). In their book on the "new" southern politics, Donald R.

Matthews and James W. Prothro (1966) said, "One or two more presidential campaigns like that of 1964, in which the Republicans appealed explicitly to the racial prejudices of the white South, and an abrupt and thoroughgoing party realignment might well be brought about" (474). And Samuel Lubell (1966) described Republican opportunities this way: "In nearly every Southern state racial emotions were—and still are—sufficiently powerful to constitute the balance of voting power. When these racial feelings lie bedded down, the political balance favors the Democrats. But a popular recoil against efforts to enforce desegregation could swing much of the South out of the Democratic fold" (172). Though all these analysts were predictably careful in their predictions, they saw the challenge to the racial status quo as a potentially great boon to the Republican party.

The Republican political strategist Kevin Phillips was even bolder. Noting that as blacks entered the electorate, they would become almost completely incorporated into the Democratic fold, he enthusiastically argued that realignment was imminent. "Negroes are slowly but surely taking over the apparatus of the Democratic party in a growing number of Deep South Black Belt counties," he wrote. "This cannot help but push whites into the alternative major party structure—that of the GOP" (1969, 287). As Phillips predicted, the entry of blacks into politics did have profound implications for the Republican party. So long as blacks were denied access to politics, the Democrats could continue to speak for southern conservatism. Blacks' full entry into the political system and inevitably into the Democratic party put white Democratic politicians in a new and different situation. The play of events was certain to work in the Republican party's favor, and Phillips urged the GOP to work with, not against, these trends.

The Republicans essentially followed the plan sketched out by Kevin Phillips. As the party began to be associated with racial conservatism and as the Democratic party incorporated blacks into its ranks, the Republican party in the South began to grow and become a viable political force in the region. Perhaps it was because the Republican party was becoming more racially conservative than the Democratic party. Perhaps the social and political events of the late 1950s and early 1960s simply released many conservative southern whites from a race-based allegiance to the Democratic party, enabling them to connect with the party that most appealed to their other conservative political beliefs. Perhaps *liberalism* lost its New Deal connotation and became associated with social engineering and the presence of the federal government in changing the racial status quo. Whatever the case—all three explanations are plausible and not mutually exclusive—there was no returning to anything resembling the Solid South described by V. O. Key.

The Republican party has grown considerably since the civil rights era, and a new party system now defines the politics of the region. But some aspects of this growth and this new party system are perplexing. Given the strong possibility of a "thoroughgoing," "large-scale" realignment and given commonly held assumptions about the long-standing nature of southern politics, there have been some surprises. In the remainder of this chapter, I discuss two of these surprises, two puzzles that arise from a study of Republican growth in the South since the 1950s and most notably since Ronald Reagan's election in 1980. This book is structured around these puzzles.

The Puzzle of Mixed Republican Success

Whatever one attributes Republican growth to, it clearly has not been an overnight phenomenon. From 1952 to the present, the Republicans have gained steadily. But, as noted at the beginning of this chapter, the process has been slow and, in fact, it is likely not over.

The growing strength of Republicanism is apparent in the partisan affiliations of southerners over time (fig. 1.1). In 1952, fully 83 percent of all southerners were Democrats; only 14 percent were Republicans, and a fair proportion of these people were black.[5] Democratic affiliation dipped to 64 percent in 1960, but actually rose to 73 percent in 1964, as blacks were driven into the Democratic camp. In spite of a Republican presidential campaign that attracted many southern whites, only 19 percent of southerners counted themselves as Republicans in 1964. The Republicans have made almost continuous gains in the years since. From that

Figure 1.1   Party Identification of Southerners, 1952–1992

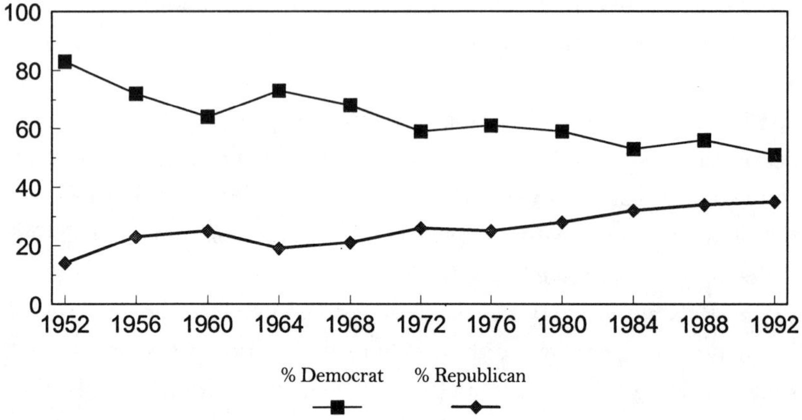

% Democrat   % Republican

Source: American National Election Studies, 1952–1992

low, Republicans have come to comprise 35 percent of the southern population (as of 1992), and this growth of 16 percentage points has been almost monotonic.

Republican gains, of course, have come at the expense of the Democratic party. The Democrats have lost 22 percentage points in the years between 1964 and 1992. Their losses have been marked by dramatic dips and mild recoveries rather than a steady, monotonic decline. As of 1992, Democrats comprised 51 percent of the southern population. There is little doubt that there has been a major change in the aggregate party balance. Yet, perhaps the most important point here is that, as of 1992, in spite of the attrition the Democrats had experienced, they still held an advantage—a 16-percentage-point advantage—in partisan identification in the South. Although things look promising for the Republican party, they are still the minority party in the region.

If one looks at blacks and whites separately, the picture is sharpened somewhat. By the election of 1964, southern blacks had almost all turned to the Democratic party. This shift had started earlier as blacks became part of the New Deal coalition put together by Franklin Roosevelt (Weiss 1983). But a good many blacks, particularly southern blacks, still felt a tie to the Republican party, the party of Lincoln and the party of their parents. Of course, prior to the election of 1964, not all that many southern blacks were registered to vote. About one-quarter of southern blacks voted in the presidential election of 1960, up from 13 percent in 1952 (Jaynes and Williams 1989, 230). As they entered the electorate in much more significant numbers, the civil rights movement, the Goldwater campaign, and the Democratic response to these two developments led many blacks to align themselves with the Democratic party. By 1964, more than 86 percent of southern blacks were Democratic, up from 60 percent in 1960. Since then, southern black support for the Democratic party has continued to be close to complete. Throughout the 1980s, southern black Democratic support fluctuated quite a bit from year to year, but still ranged between 76 and 94 percent. The percentage of blacks identifying themselves as Republican through the entire time period is quite small, at no time greater than 12 percent.

While blacks have moved almost entirely into the Democratic camp, many southern whites are now in the other camp. If one looks only at the partisanship levels of whites (fig. 1.2), the shift toward Republicanism is dramatic. In the early 1950s, about 85 percent of white southerners called themselves Democrats, 13 percent Republicans. Democratic affiliation fell significantly in the 1950s and early 1960s to 65 percent, but rebounded some in 1964 (70 percent versus 22 percent for the GOP). Since then, conversions and generational replacement have had a steady effect on party balance. Perhaps in response to Wallace's independent campaign, many white Democrats left the fold in 1968, though they were not yet prepared to call themselves Republican. Republican gains that year did not amount to even half the Democratic attrition. Republican growth and Democratic decline among southern whites continued through 1972 but then held steady through the decade, the trend likely retarded by Jimmy Carter's candidacy and presidency. Republican growth among southern whites resumed in the 1980s, and by 1992, 43 percent of white southerners were Republicans compared to 42 percent calling themselves Democrats. Among whites, the Republicans had finally caught up.

Republican gains in the electorate mean little unless they can be con-

Figure 1.2   Party Identification of White Southerners, 1952–1992

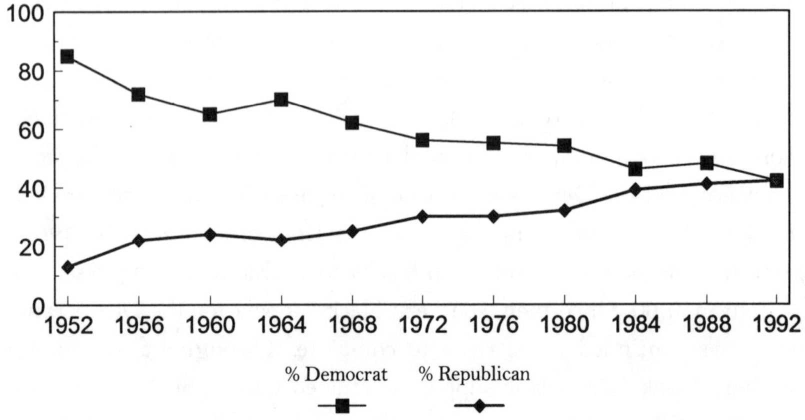

Source: American National Election Studies, 1952–1992

verted into electoral victories, into Republicans in office. The South has contributed to Republicans in one office in particular—the presidency. In recent elections, the South, with one exception, has gone overwhelmingly for the Republican ticket (see fig. 1.3), a fact that has been very important to the party's national chances. Black and Black (1992) even call the region the Vital South, the key to Republican success in the electoral college. A Solid South accounts for almost two-thirds of the electoral votes required to win the presidency. And although the Republican lock on the electoral college failed in 1992, it was not because of the South. Almost two-thirds of President Bush's electoral vote came from the region.

Even before the civil rights movement, the Republican ticket was competitive in electoral votes and in popular votes in the South. In 1952 and 1956, Dwight Eisenhower picked up about half the electoral votes in the South, even breaking through in the Deep South in 1956 with a victory in Louisiana. Richard Nixon won more than one-quarter of southern electoral votes in the election of 1960, taking the peripheral southern states of Florida, Tennessee, and Virginia. But the election in 1964 saw the biggest breakthrough. Although Lyndon Johnson and the Democrats

Figure 1.3   Presidential Electoral Vote in the South, 1952–1992

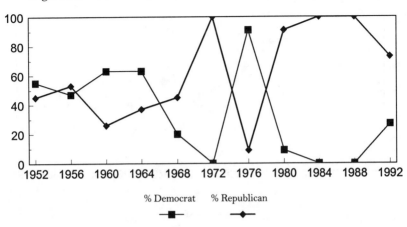

again won eighty-one electoral votes (as they had in 1960), Barry Gold-water won forty-seven electoral votes, reaping rewards for his staunchly conservative, anti–civil rights campaign and sweeping the Deep South. In 1968, George Wallace's candidacy complicated the election in the South. In spite of Wallace, Nixon won a plurality of the popular vote (35 percent compared to Wallace's 33 percent and Hubert Humphrey's 31 percent) and of the electoral vote. Nixon won five states for fifty-seven electoral votes while Wallace took five states for forty-six electoral votes. Humphrey won only Texas's twenty-five electoral votes.

Since then, with the exception of 1976, Republicans have overwhelmingly dominated the presidential contest. In 1972, 1984, and 1988, the patently conservative Republican candidate completely shut out the unmistakably liberal Democrat in the electoral count. What is more, Nixon took a whopping 71 percent of the southern vote in 1972, while Ronald Reagan and George Bush won 63 percent and 59 percent, respectively. In 1976, Jimmy Carter won 54 percent of the southern vote, but took more than 90 percent of the electoral vote, losing only Virginia to Gerald Ford. In 1980, the situation was reversed, Reagan taking 51 percent of the popular vote and all but Georgia's twelve electoral votes. Even in 1992, when the Democrats fielded a ticket of two southerners, they won only

Figure 1.4   Percent of Southern Democrats in Congress, 1952–1992

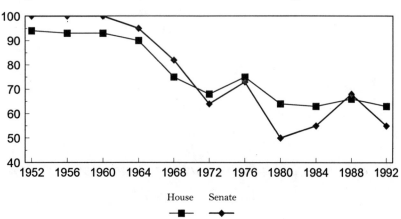

their standard-bearers' home states (Arkansas and Tennessee), Louisiana, and Georgia.

If the Republicans have been inordinately successful in winning recent presidential elections in the South, their congressional fortunes have not been nearly as good. From the 1950s, prior to the demise of Jim Crow, through 1994, Democrats held a large advantage in congressional seats (see fig. 1.4). Only with the 1994 elections did the Republicans catch up. It is striking that through the 1970s, 1980s, and early 1990s, a time Republican presidents were exceedingly popular and electorally successful in the South, southern congressional seats continued to turn over to Democrats.

Republicans did not hold any Senate seats as recently as 1960. Over the next few decades, they made some progress, and by 1980, when several conservative Republican candidates—Paula Hawkins in Florida, Jeremiah Denton in Alabama, Mack Mattingly in Georgia, and John East in North Carolina—won narrow victories, the partisan balance of southern senators was fifty-fifty. Between 1980 and 1992, however, Republicans were unable to protect their gains. In 1986, the Democrats defeated Hawkins, Denton, and Mattingly and recaptured the seat won by East, who died in the middle of his term. With these victories, the Democrats restored their two-to-one advantage in the southern Senate contingent. In 1992, Republicans won back the Georgia and North Carolina seats (and added a Texas seat), but the Democrats still held a twelve to ten advantage. Only with the loss of two Tennessee seats and the defection of Richard Shelby in 1994 have the Republicans finally captured a majority of southern Senate seats. But it was an awfully long time coming.

In the House, the trend lines are similar. Through the 1950s to 1960, Democrats held about 93 percent of the congressional seats. By the time of Reagan's victory in 1980, Democrats held 64 percent of southern congressional seats, a decline to be sure, but still a convincing majority. The Republican House contingent, however, did not continue to grow in the Reagan-Bush years. In 1980, Republicans held 36 percent of southern congressional seats; after the elections in 1992, they held 37 percent of them. Again, 1994 appears to have been a watershed year, with Republicans winning sixteen new seats and holding a small majority (51 percent) of seats in the region.[6] Again, even after the 1994 elections, the difference between Republican congressional and presidential success in the South is still marked. After all, from 1980 to 1992, Ronald Reagan and George Bush won 71 percent of southern congressional districts in their presidential contests.

It is quite noteworthy that southern Democrats weathered the Reagan-Bush years so well. Lest Democratic congressional success be interpreted as simply the result of entrenched incumbents, *open seat* elections in the South show how successful the Democrats were at the congressional level in these years.[7] From the 1980 elections to the 1992 elections, Democrats won a sizable majority (62 percent) of the 109 open seat House elections. Because Democrats had more seats to defend, they could still have been experiencing a net loss. This, however, was not the case. Democrats held a steady percentage of House seats because they were slightly more successful than Republicans at defending their own open seats. In open elections in which a Democratic incumbent retired, died, or was defeated in a primary, Democrats retained the seat 79 percent of the time. Republicans retained their seats 69 percent of the time.[8]

The weakness of congressional Republicans in this period is striking when one compares Ronald Reagan's performance in these same districts in 1984. Of seventy-nine open seat elections, only twelve were held in districts that Reagan had lost in 1984.[9] Democrats won ten of these contests. The other sixty-seven open seat elections were held in districts won by Reagan, and Democrats won thirty-eight (57 percent) of them. Where Reagan won a district by more than 60 percent, Republicans took 68 percent of the open seat contests, but this represented only twenty-eight elections.

Democratic congressional dominance is reflected further in the size and scope of these open seat victories. For one thing, when Democrats won, they won more convincing victories than Republicans. Of the sixty-eight Democratic open seat victories, 60 percent were won with at least 60 percent of the vote. Only 20 percent of the forty-one Republican open seat victories were convincing by this standard. On the other hand, 42 percent of Republican victories were narrow, with winning percentages of 52 percent or less. Only 16 percent of Democratic victories fell into this category.

The geographic scope of Democratic victories in these open seat elections is impressive as well. Democrats won at least half of the open seat elections in every state but one, the exception being Florida. The Republican party has enjoyed notable success in this state, mostly because of a burgeoning population fed by several million migrants from the North and from Latin America. Many of these northern migrants have brought their Republican identities with them. The large Cuban community in Florida also is strongly allegiant to the Republicans, the party that appeals most to their strong anti-Communist, anti-Castro sentiments. These new constituencies have helped the Republicans win twelve of Florida's twenty-two open seat elections. Although the party is doing well in this important, rapidly growing state, Florida is the least characteristically southern state in the entire region, given its diverse and rapidly changing population. Removing Florida from the picture and looking only at the other ten states of the region, one discovers that Democrats have taken 67 percent of the open seat contests. Why, in the Reagan-Bush

Figure 1.5 Percent of Democrats in Southern State Legislatures, 1952–1992

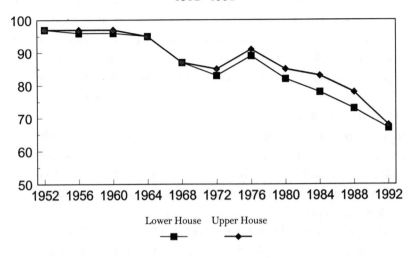

years, a period of popular Republican administrations, a period in which Republicans won 91 percent of southern electoral votes in four presidential elections, and a period of high Republican hopes in the South, were Republicans not very successful in winning congressional elections when their chances were best, that is, when seats opened up because of retirement or death?[10]

Republican gains have been even more limited in state legislative elections than in congressional elections (fig. 1.5).[11] As recently as 1964, Democrats held 96 percent of the seats in the lower houses of the South, a remarkable total. Through the sixties and seventies, the Democratic percentage of state house seats never dipped lower than 83 percent. In the 1980s, the Republicans did much better, and following the 1994 elections Democrats still held 63 percent of state house seats, though down from 82 percent in 1980 and 67 percent in 1992.

The story is much the same in the upper houses of the South. Democrats held almost every senate seat (95 percent of them) as late as 1964. Democratic dominance continued through the next three decades, falling to a low of 59 percent in 1994, down from 83 percent in 1984. Although the recent gains are encouraging for Republicans, the dominance of the Democrats in the state legislatures of the South is still quite impressive.

In the parlance of the literature, the realignment in the South has been slow to filter down. This review of partisanship and office holding in the region shows plainly that Republican success has not been fully achieved. The obvious question is, why not? How come so many southern whites still identify with the Democratic party? Why is it that the Republicans have so dominated at one level and that the Democrats have defended themselves so effectively at lower levels? Thirty years is a long time in political terms. Why has it taken so long for Republicans to build a party, wait out incumbents, recruit quality candidates, and see the realignment work its way down?

These questions lead to the first puzzle of this book. The region is decidedly conservative in its opinions on a great variety of issues (Nie, Verba, and Petrocik 1979; Black and Black 1987), which by all accounts should have given the Republicans a great advantage. Yet low-level Republican politicians have not fully harnessed this advantage. And if Republican presidential candidates, particularly since 1980, have provided some sort of demonstration as to how elections can be won in the region with standard conservative themes and have given lower-level Republican candidates a clear connection to conservatism, the long period of Republican mixed success is especially perplexing. Why was this connection not worth more? Even putting aside the ideological advantage, how come overwhelmingly popular figures at the top of the ticket did not do more for the rest of the party's candidates? To sum up the first puzzle, it seems the GOP should have gained more of an advantage from winning presidential elections than they did. How was this advantage spent and why did it not materialize?

The Puzzle of Race and the Realignment

If part of the Republican advantage in the South has been an ideological one, a second presumed advantage Republicans have held over Democrats is the race issue. Many have interpreted the rise of the Republican party in the region as a racial phenomenon. They link Republican growth to racial issues and to the steady flow of southern whites (both former Democrats and those new to the electorate) to a Republican party that best represents their views on race.

From this perspective, the southern realignment has been a continuation of the past. Issues of race defined and maintained the one-party system for decades in the South. By this view, the political salience of such issues did not change. They still held a powerful grip on southern whites and still influenced their political behavior. What changed was the positions the parties took on these issues and how people perceived the parties on such issues. Realignment was thus not the result of a new issue redefining the political landscape. It was the result of a new cleavage on an old issue.

As to the first element of this argument, there has been a change in the character of the race issue. Racial attitudes in the South have become markedly more progressive since the early 1960s (Schuman, Steeh, and Bobo 1985). This is not to say that racist attitudes have disappeared from the region. Only a small minority of southern whites, however, cling to segregationist views, and their numbers continue to dwindle with generational change.

What has changed since the civil rights movement is the nature of the dialogue over racial issues (as well as the issues themselves). In the face of these changes, racial attitudes have become informed by conservative ideology, not only in the South but, of course, in the country as a whole. The racial attitudes of many whites still may be characterized as conservative, reflecting resistance to government assistance to blacks as a group and applying individualistic notions and standards to the situation of blacks in this country. Some social scientists argue that much contemporary hostility to black interests stems from anti-black prejudice, which is dressed up in new ways and combined with this conservative logic (Kinder and Sears 1981; Kinder 1986). Others argue that it is simply conservative values that guide positions on racial issues (Sniderman and Hagen 1985, 110–12). Whatever one's position in this debate, it is indisputable that this racially conservative constellation of attitudes is

Table 1.1 Southern White Attitudes on Racial Questions

Generations of slavery and discrimination have created conditions that make it difficult for blacks to work their way out of the lower class.

	Southern Whites	Northern Whites
% disagreeing	43	35
% agreeing	45	53
% neither disagreeing nor agreeing	12	11
Base N	(855)	(2,316)

It's really a matter of some people not trying hard enough; if blacks would only try harder they could be just as well off as whites.

	Southern Whites	Northern Whites
% agreeing	69	56
% disagreeing	16	30
% neither agreeing nor disagreeing	16	14
Base N	(857)	(2,312)

Some people feel that the government in Washington should make every effort to improve the social and economic position of blacks. Others feel that the government should not make any special effort to help blacks because they should help themselves. Where would you place yourself [on this scale]?

	Southern Whites	Northern Whites
% saying blacks should help themselves	62	49
% saying the government should make effort	16	20
% at midpoint of scale	22	31
Base N	(819)	(2,197)

Most blacks who receive money from welfare programs could get along without it if they tried.

	Southern Whites	Northern Whites
% agreeing	76	54
% disagreeing	11	31
% neither agreeing nor disagreeing	13	15
Base N	(247)	(631)

Table 1.1   Continued

Do you think that civil rights leaders are trying to push too fast, are going too slowly, or are they moving at about the right speed?

	Southern Whites	Northern Whites
% too fast	40	30
% too slow	8	10
% about the right speed	52	60
Base N	(1,322)	(3,641)

Source: American National Election Studies (1980–1990 pooled).

now held by many whites who are not sympathetic to black social and economic equality or to civil rights advances.

Southern whites in particular continue to be rather hostile to black political, economic, and social progress. Using survey data from the 1980s, I show in table 1.1 that southern whites have conservative impulses on racial issues.[12] They are, in fact, much more likely to take conservative positions than white northerners, who are included in the table as a basis for comparison. A majority of southern whites, for instance, accept individualistic explanations for the black condition or at least do not ascribe present-day inequality to the legacy of slavery and discrimination. Equality is a matter of effort, and if blacks worked harder, goes this line of logic, they would achieve equal status in society. Not surprisingly, a large majority thus accept an individualistic solution to the problem. Most believe that the federal government should not work to equalize the races, socially or economically, and that blacks should not expect any preferential treatment from the government. Welfare and policies like it are viewed as such treatment and are disliked and rejected by many. Fully three-quarters of southern whites take a skeptical view of welfare and especially of black welfare recipients. Together, these related conservative beliefs and attitudes inform positions on a variety of racial issues and, most important, are socially acceptable and reinforced throughout the country, above all in the South. Even as the race issue has evolved, the South has continued to be the most racially conservative region in the country, thereby providing some continuity with the past.

The second element of the racial realignment argument is that the Democratic party has changed sides on issues of race. Since Goldwater and since the replacement of the old southern Democrats the *southern* parties have become quite differentiated on questions of government involvement in promoting racial equality and on many other questions of political significance to blacks. One way to illustrate just how differentiated the parties have become on racial issues is to look at the voting behavior of southern Republican and Democratic congressmen. The great change that has taken place in the South since the 1960s is apparent in table 1.2.[13] Southern Democrats and southern Republicans now vote very differently on civil rights issues. On two amendments to the Voting Rights Act Extension (1981), for example, southern Democrats were generally opposed to the easing of "bail out" procedures (procedures offering covered jurisdictions greater consideration in exempting themselves from the act). On one of these votes, more than three-fifths of southern Democrats voted against the amendment, and on the other, three-quarters did so. More than 80 percent of southern Republicans voted in favor of both amendments. More recently, in 1990, 86 percent of southern Democrats and but 8 percent of southern Republicans voted for a civil rights bill reversing some Supreme Court decisions that limited job discrimination lawsuits.

This pattern is also evident in votes on issues of symbolic importance to blacks. In 1986, close to three-quarters of southern Democrats voted to encourage President Reagan to urge reform on South Africa; only two of forty southern Republicans joined in. A bill in 1983 to create a federal holiday in honor of Martin Luther King's birthday garnered 85 percent of southern Democratic votes but only 37 percent of southern Republican votes. There is little doubt that on issues of race, Democrats and Republicans have been distinctively different for some time.

More important, according to those documenting a racial realignment,

Table 1.2 Congressional Votes in the 1980s

Vote Distributions on Discrimination Issues

	Southern Democrats	Southern Republicans
A 1981 Voting Rights Extension		
Vote #1	26–41	32–4
Vote #2	16–50	29–7
B 1984 Civil Rights Act	70–6	24–10
C 1990 Civil Rights Act	62–10	3–35

Vote Distributions on Symbolic Issues

D 1981 South Africa Rugby Team	35–30	0–37
E 1983 Martin Luther King, Jr. Holiday	69–12	13–22
F 1986 Misc. South Africa Demands	52–19	2–38
G 1986 Override Reagan Veto on S. Africa Sanctions	60–4	9–30

The following descriptions come from the *Congressional Quarterly Almanac.*

A Two hostile amendments to the Voting Rights Act Extension: (1) Butler, R-Va., amendment to allow three-judge federal district courts to hear petitions by jurisdictions seeking to bail out from coverage of the Voting Rights Act. (2) Campbell, R-S.C., amendment to allow a state covered by the Voting Rights Act to bail out from coverage if two-thirds of its counties are eligible to bail out.

B Passage of the bill to make clear that the bar to discrimination in Title IX of the 1972 Education Act, Title VI of the Civil Rights Act of 1973, and the Age Discrimination Act of 1975 covers an entire institution if any program or activity within the institution receives federal assistance.

C Passage of the bill to reverse or modify six Supreme Court decisions that narrowed the reach and remedies of job discrimination laws and to authorize monetary damages under Title VII of the 1964 Civil Rights Act.

D Zablocki, D-Wis., motion that the House suspend the rules and adopt the concurrent resolution stating the sense of Congress that the Springbok National Rugby Team of South Africa, on tour in the United States, should not play rugby in the United States.

E Hall, D-Ind., motion to suspend the rules and pass the bill to designate the third Monday of every January as a federal holiday in honor of the late civil rights leader the Rev. Dr. Martin Luther King Jr.

F Wolpe, D-Mich., motion to suspend the rules and adopt the resolution to express the sense of the House that the president should urge the South African government to engage in political negotiations with that country's black majority; grant immediately unconditional freedom to Nelson Mandela and other political prisoners; and recognize the African National Congress as a legitimate representative for the black majority.

G Passage, over President Reagan's Sept. 26 veto, of the bill to impose economic sanctions against South Africa.

this partisan difference has become increasingly obvious to white south-erners. Any ambiguity stemming from past party positions has now dis-appeared, and new party images have evolved. Survey data show that the southern public has become quite clear about the two parties' positions on race. For instance, as to the question of party positions on whether the federal government "should make every effort to improve the social and economic position of blacks and other minority groups" or "should not make any special effort to help minorities because they should help them-selves," more than 60 percent of southerners see the Democratic party as favoring efforts to help blacks and other minorities. Fifty-seven percent view the Republican party as opposed. Fewer than one in five southerners views the Republicans as being on the liberal side of this issue or the Democrats as being on the conservative side.[14]

The parties thus have become markedly different in the eyes of south-ern voters, and Grofman (1990), for one, argues that the Democratic party label "[has lost] its old connotation of 'being for the little guy' and [is] taking on a racial meaning" (9). As the term *liberal* has come to mean "pro-black" and as the Democrats have become known as the party that represents blacks, he writes, there has been an obvious "link between race and 'white flight' from the Democratic party in the South" (1).[15]

The process has been self-reinforcing. As more whites have left the Democratic party, it has become more "black." As blacks have become a larger part of the party's constituency, they have become more involved in party affairs, and the party has become increasingly attentive to their concerns. Minority candidates even have emerged to represent the party. In the eyes of the public, the Democratic party has become more closely identified with blacks, which has led to even further white defections. As Chandler Davidson (1990) writes about the transformation in Texas, "The previously all-white Democratic party was now increasingly the refuge of black and brown voters, as many whites continued to flee that party much as they fled neighborhoods when black and brown home-seekers moved in" (238).

What is more, the motivation of party switchers may not even have been racial. As is well established in the political sociology literature, when all one's friends, family, coworkers, and associates identify as Republican, the compulsion for one to do so as well is powerful (Berelson, Lazarsfeld, and McPhee 1954). In the South, so goes the racial realignment argument, people have been flocking to the white Republican party because it is the socially reinforced thing to do. "Political preferences are not constructed or sustained in a social vacuum," write Huckfeldt and Kohfeld (1989). "Prior to the events of the postwar period, it was difficult for Republican preferences to survive among white southerners. Now, in the late 1980s, it has become difficult for Democratic preferences to survive within many segments of the white electorate. In states like Mississippi, it has undoubtedly become socially unacceptable for many whites to support the Democratic party" (58). The process by which a "politically adrift white population" (40) has found its way to the Republican party thus would seem difficult to reverse.

The second puzzle I address in this study follows from these basic facts of southern politics and society and from the racial realignment scenario. For if racial attitudes continue to have vitality in southern electoral politics, if the parties have differentiated on racial issues, if southern voters recognize these differences, and if race has contributed so much to Republican strength, why did race not propel the party forward across the board? If, as Grofman (1990) writes, the effects of race are "commonsensically obvious to the informed observer" (1), how have the Democrats held on for so long? Why have many whites stayed in the Democratic fold? Are biracial coalitions really possible for the Democrats? How are they constructed and maintained? These questions are interesting because to be answered they require an examination of the assumptions that many carry as to how race and politics mix.

The two puzzles sketched out here are related, and the solutions to them are interrelated. First, conservatism and several popular Republican administrations did not give the Republicans the advantage one might expect in lower-level elections. Second, neither did race appear to be giving Republicans the lower-level advantage one would expect. Just what did the Democratic party do right in these years? Where did the Republican party go wrong? These are the questions that motivate what follows.

In this book, I offer a solution to these puzzles and some answers to these questions. My vehicle for approaching them is a study of southern congressional campaigns, for such a study affords some sense of the choices offered to southern voters and puts to the test some of the grand assumptions people carry about politics in the South.

"History is a relentless master," said John F. Kennedy,. "It has no present, only the past rushing into the future." The problem I have faced in doing this work is that of describing and analyzing a moving target. Politics in the South have undergone substantial change through the 1960s, 1970s, and 1980s and continue to change in the 1990s. In fact, 1994 may be the year that demarcates a partisan system based on one set of dynamics from another. Some years must pass before this is known. Whatever happens, the tale of how Democrats held off full-scale realignment for so long a time, of decades of simultaneous Republican success in presidential elections and Democratic success in lower-level elections, of the surprisingly protracted transition from southern Democracy to southern democracy is worth telling because it adds another chapter to the fascinating political history of the region, a chapter with some important and generalizable political lessons.

What is more, the seeds of change lie within this situation. If the Republicans continue to make gains at the congressional level and at levels on down, they will likely do so because they have studied the lessons of the present and learned from them. Of course, Democratic strategy too will evolve and adjust. What follows, then, is not a prediction. Instead, it is a description and analysis of a baseline from which change can be measured and an attempt to capture a moment when the past rushes into the future.

2 The Case for Context

To understand political choices, we need to understand where the frame of reference for the actors' thinking comes from—how it is evoked. An important component of the frame of reference is the set of alternatives that are given consideration in the choice process. We need to understand not only how people reason about alternatives, but where the alternatives come from in the first place. The process whereby alternatives are generated has been somewhat ignored as an object of research. *Herbert Simon, "Human Nature in Politics"*

IN THIS BOOK, I tell a story of how Democratic and Republican candidates for Congress have campaigned for office in the South. It is a description of the strategies they have pursued, the tactics they have used, and their intentions in using them. It is, in short, an attempt to follow Herbert Simon's directive and analyze "the process whereby alternatives are generated," the Democratic and Republican alternatives posed to the southern voter. Simon's larger point, of course, is that the introduction of such political context can help resolve thorny analytical problems. By describing and analyzing elections as I do here, I aim to address the thorny puzzles of the southern realignment.

The argument I make about context is two-pronged. First, the context in which a congressional election takes place, that is, the racial balance of

the district, leads candidates of the two parties to campaign in certain
ways and with certain messages. The point is that much of what goes on
in southern campaigns has a racial element, even if an explicit racial issue
is not introduced into the contest. The racial composition of the district
sets the parameters within which candidates must work and establishes
the conditions for success. Their grand strategies and their specific maneuvers thus depend, to a great extent, on the size of the black and white
populations in their district.

The theoretical basis of this argument is that group or racial conflict
has a powerful influence on political thinking and possibly even on behavior. That is, as groups come into competition over valued resources—
political power, social goods, or even symbols of group identity or pride—
members of these groups are profoundly affected. Even the potential for
conflict, whether real or perceived, has some bearing on intragroup attitudes and on decisions about political issues or political choices defined
by race.

Substantial evidence exists that white racial-political attitudes are influenced by the racial environment or the potential for racial-political
conflict in one's environment. As I show elsewhere (Glaser 1994), the
more heavily black the southern county, the more racially conservative
white racial-political attitudes tend to be (see also Giles 1977 and Giles
and Evans 1986). This relation is strong and monotonic over a variety of
racial-political measures. What is striking, though, is that negative affect
toward blacks and acceptance of negative stereotypes about blacks appear
to be unrelated to racial environment (Glaser 1994). This strongly suggests that it is group or racial conflict, and not just the legacy of the past,
that influences attitudes that sit at the intersection of race and politics.
Where blacks have more opportunity to exercise political power or to
demand a larger share of societal resources, southern white attitudes
reflect greater hostility to black political aspirations.

What I argue here is that the potential for group conflict shapes incentives that party politicians are very sensitive to. Of course, these incentives change as the racial balance of the district changes. Campaign

behaviors, messages, and strategies—both Democratic and Republican— respond directly to the changes in these incentives.

These behaviors, messages, and strategies, in turn, shape the context of the vote choice. Herein lies the second major prong of my argument. As Simon cautions, before one attempts to analyze the individual decisions of voters, it is worth knowing something about the options they have before them. In this case, the puzzles of the southern realignment become less puzzling when the political alternatives that have been offered to southern voters are fully explored. For when analyzed in context, the political choices made by southern voters appear to make sense.

The predominant understanding of southern voting behavior starts with the observation that the Republicans have long been the more racially conservative party in the region, while Democrats are the racial liberals. As chapter 1 illustrates, this is certainly the case. But this does not take into account the Republican message that has been communicated and how it has been put out or, more important, what the Democrats have done to counter it. Voters do not behave in a vacuum. They respond *to* something: to political stimuli, to candidates, to political campaigns. Their behavior is, in part, the result of the choices that are available to them. The congressional choice posed to the southern voter at the congressional level has rarely been just "racial conservative or racial liberal" or for that matter, "conservative or liberal." It has been much more complicated than this.

Once a more useful and complete picture of the choice offered to southern voters is painted, it becomes clear that in spite of the Republicans' success in presidential elections, Democrats have had a strategic advantage over Republicans in southern congressional elections, and in fact much of that advantage has come from their handling of race. Southern Democrats have been able to keep together a tenuous black—white coalition in a variety of racial environments in the region. They have done so by blunting the edge of racial issues in these campaigns. They also have cultivated some significant offensive issues of their own with which to court white voters and to counter the conservative advantage that

Republicans have had. An analysis of Democratic campaigns shows why and how they have won southern congressional elections in thirty years of prolonged realignment and how they must operate if they are to win congressional elections in an increasingly precarious future.

The perspective that guides this study is that race has continued to influence southern politics, and in profound, if not always expected, ways. Although it is true that a New South has emerged, this characteristic of the old political system has persisted. It is not the legacy of the Old South that has led this to be the case. The region has admirably purged itself of the worst of its past. But while southern blacks have access to the ballot and to political office as never before, in fact, partly because of these developments, political incentives are such as to keep race an important electoral factor in the region.

Racial Variations and Calculations

To investigate the first prong of my argument, that the racial balance of the congressional district is a primary factor in determining the course of a southern campaign, it is worth sketching out the quantitative logic of the congressional campaign.

First, the larger the black population, the bigger the head start Democratic candidates have as they enter a contest. Democratic candidates benefit from the fact that a large majority of blacks identify with their party. But a large black population does not automatically transfer into Democratic votes, and much of the campaign revolves around the fact that blacks must be courted, their support reinforced. Table 2.1 illustrates how different assumptions about comparative turnout and black solidarity can lead to highly divergent strategic situations.

The proportion of blacks to whites in the district does not always translate into the proportion of black to white voters in an election. Much depends on the turnout rates of the two groups. A look at turnout rates that are 10 percentage points apart is illustrative. For example, in a district in which 20 percent of the population is black (about the average in the South), blacks may comprise anywhere from 16 to 25 percent of the *electorate* depending upon the turnout rate differences of the two popula-

Table 2.1   Demographic Considerations of Southern Strategists

Black Percentage of the Electorate Given Various Levels of Black Turnout
(Assumption: Turnout in Special Election is 33 percent)

	10% Black Population	*20% Black Population*	*30% Black Population*	*40% Black Population*
Black Turnout 10% < White Turnout	8%	16%	24%	33%
Black Turnout = White Turnout	10%	20%	30%	40%
Black Turnout 10% > White Turnout	13%	25%	37%	48%

Democratic Headstart Given Various Levels of Black Support
(Assumption: Black Turnout = White Turnout)

	10% Black Population	*20% Black Population*	*30% Black Population*	*40% Black Population*
80% of Black Vote to Democrat	8%	16%	24%	32%
90% of Black Vote to Democrat	9%	18%	27%	36%
95% of Black Vote to Democrat	10%	19%	29%	38%

Percentage of White Vote Needed for Democrat to Win Given Various Levels of
Turnout and Black Support
(Assumption: Turnout in Special Election is 33 percent)

	10% Black Population	*20% Black Population*	*30% Black Population*	*40% Black Population*
80% of Black Vote to Democrat / Black Turnout 10% < White Turnout	47%	44%	42%	35%
90% of Black Vote to Democrat / Black Turnout = White Turnout	46%	40%	33%	23%
95% of Black Vote to Democrat / Black Turnout 10% > White Turnout	43%	35%	24%	9%

tions. The difference is quite meaningful to both Democratic and Republican candidates.[1]

It is certainly true that most southern blacks identify with the Democratic party and vote for Democrats in elections up and down the ticket. Democratic candidates thus have to win a much smaller portion of white votes than would be the case given smaller black populations. The size of their head start does change appreciably, however, if Republicans make inroads into the black vote. In the zero-sum game of electoral politics, the difference (in a district that is 20 percent black) between strong black support for the Democratic candidate (80 percent) and almost unanimous support for the Democrat (95 percent) is a difference of three percentage points in the end result (six points when one considers that every gain is a loss for the opponent). This, of course, can be significant in a close election.

Southern campaigns are fought out on two fronts that vary in relative importance according to the racial balance of the district, turnout rates, and Republican inroads into the black vote. On one front, Republicans and Democrats battle for their share of the white vote. On the other, Democrats try to maximize the black vote as Republicans try to minimize that Democratic advantage. Democrats thus must balance their need to maximize black turnout with their quest to hold on to a significant minority of whites. They also must keep the Republican candidate from cutting into their black support. The Republican goals of maximizing their share of the white vote and depressing black turnout or cutting into the black electoral monolith are not so potentially contradictory. Nonetheless, their task is formidable.

This brief sketch of what it takes for Democratic and Republican candidates to win in the region sets the stage for what is to follow. Four main hypotheses flow from this discussion, hypotheses that both stand on their own and are interrelated.

Hypothesis 1: In majority white districts, Republican strategy should change as racial environments change. The larger the black percentage of a majority white congressional district, the greater the imperative of Republican candidates to win a larger share of the white vote and the more likely whites are to respond to an issue of race. In heavily black majority white districts, then, Republican candidates will be most likely to introduce a racial issue, an issue aimed at uniting white voters, into a political campaign and will be most likely to make it a major part of their campaign.

Hypothesis 2: For Democrats, the incentives also shift with change in the racial environment. In all majority white districts, Democrats will attempt to construct biracial coalitions. However, the larger the black percentage of a majority white district, the more likely Democrats will be to risk white votes to win black votes. At no point will they abandon one goal for the other and racial issues will always be approached in a gingerly way.

Hypothesis 3: In a majority black district, the strategic incentives should reverse. Democrats will seek to maximize the black vote, even at the cost of white votes, and racial approaches should be more likely to be embraced. This is crucial given that lower black turnout rates are more costly to Democratic candidates where blacks comprise a larger proportion of the population (see table 2.1). Republicans, on the other hand, will seek to build biracial coalitions and should handle racial issues with more moderation and more caution.

Hypothesis 4: Democrats should have more of an advantage in majority black districts than Republicans in majority white ones, mostly because the white vote is not as unified as the black vote. Given the limited Democratic goals in majority white districts, campaigns that are even modestly successful in drawing whites will win. This would be the key to Democratic success in the South and the solution to the realignment puzzles.[2]

This book represents an attempt to test these expectations, to hold them up to reality. The results of these tests reveal much about how the southern partisan system has changed and how it has remained the same. In addition, they offer more general lessons on how race and politics have mixed in the post–civil rights era.

Methodology

How politicians behave, what they say on the stump, what their campaign advertisements claim and what they charge of their opponents, whom they choose to speak to and whom they avoid, and what vehicles they use to communicate with the electorate all have some impact on voters' decisions. Yet describing and analyzing elections in this way is expensive and labor intensive. It involves going to the source and observing politics in action. It requires hustling to get people to talk with you (including conservative Republicans suspicious of a Berkeley address), dealing with unexpected circumstances (such as a hurricane threatening off the Gulf Coast), figuring out logistical nightmares (if I ride with the candidate from Alexander City to Montgomery, how will I get back to my car?), and sometimes risking personal safety (riding at seventy miles an hour on winding country roads with an unhappy, distracted campaign manager behind the wheel).[3]

From an analytical standpoint, there is another problem with participant-observer research that discourages political scientists interested in electoral behavior. It involves making generalizations based on a small number of observations and describing something not easily analyzed in a grand or more general way. As a result, many political scientists leave descriptions of elections to journalists, who generally look at each election as a separate entity. They bypass this descriptive process. They look at aggregate data or even survey data and draw conclusions based on the application of certain assumptions to their findings. Although such findings are often of great value, the assumptions are often left untouched.

The descriptions in the following chapters are all of special elections held to fill seats vacated by the death or resignation of a member of Congress. The six elections, all won by Democrats, represent more than half such elections from the 1980s and early 1990s. They took place in Mississippi's Fourth District (in the summer of 1981), in Texas's First District (in the summer of 1985), in Virginia's Fifth District (in spring 1988), in Alabama's Third District (in the spring of 1989), in Mississippi's Fifth District (in the fall of 1989), and in Mississippi's Second District (in the spring of 1993). The shaded areas of the map in figure 2.1 indicate exactly where these districts are located in their various states. Table 2.2 is a summary of the six elections, listing the candidates involved, the margins of victory, and other basic information.

Figure 2.1 Congressional Districts in the Study

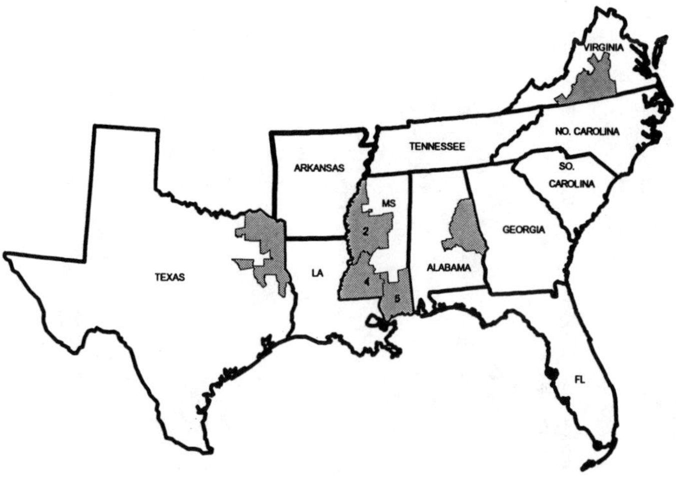

This map represents the districts as they looked through the 1980s. The 1993 congressional race in Mississippi 2 took place in a district that is marginally different from the one shown here.

I observed three of the elections at firsthand. For the elections in Alabama 3, Mississippi 5, and Mississippi 2, I traveled to the district and followed the campaigns around. I attended campaign speeches, press conferences, political rallies, church services, meetings with black ministers, commercial tapings, and candidate debates, I spoke with the candidates, and I met with numerous other actors involved in the drama. I interviewed as many people as would see me—Democrats and Republicans, journalists and candidates, campaign managers and media consultants, black ministers and white union leaders, national and state party representatives, local party hacks and campaign volunteers—thus gathering a variety of not always congruent perspectives on the same set of events. Through my interviews and observations and through local newspaper reports of the campaigns, I have pieced together fairly detailed accounts of these elections. The newspapers were especially useful in my analysis because they showed which of the candidates' messages made it to the public. Although the candidates often complained about their coverage

Table 2.2 Summary of Cases

State / District / Result	Candidates	Incumbent	Date of Election	% Black Population in District	Winner / Margin of Victory	Average Reagan / Bush % in 1980–88	Presidential Approval Rating*
Ms 4	Wayne Dowdy (D) Liles Williams (R)	Jon Hinson (R)	July 1981	42%	Dowdy 51%–49%	58%	59%
Tx 1	Jim Chapman (D) Edd Hargett (R)	Sam Hall (D)	August 1985	19%	Chapman 51%–49%	54%	63%
Va 5	L. F. Payne (D) Linda Arey (R)	Dan Daniel (D)	June 1988	25%	Payne 59%–41%	61%	51%
Al 3	Glen Browder (D) John Rice (R)	Bill Nichols (D)	April 1989	28%	Browder 65%–35%	55%	63%
Ms 5	Gene Taylor (D) Tom Anderson (R)	Larkin Smith (R)	October 1989	19%	Taylor 65%–35%	67%	70%
Ms 2	Bennie Thompson (D) Hayes Dent (R)	Mike Espy (D)	April 1993	59%	Thompson 55%–45%	48%	52%

*Percent approving the president's performance in the Gallup Survey most recently conducted prior to the election.

("The sorry-assed media didn't let me get my message out," said one), the part of the message that made the newspaper was of greater importance to understanding what happened than the part that was ignored.[4]

In all three cases, I spent as much as two weeks in the district during the home stretch of the campaign. This strategy had its advantages and disadvantages. The end of a campaign is a period of great activity. It is also when the media campaigns are waged. I thus had more events to observe and more commercials to view or hear by covering the final frenetic days. The downside of this decision was that the candidates and their campaign staffs were very busy and much less available at this time. Where possible, I reinterviewed people after the election when they were less hurried and more candid.

Working backward, I have reconstructed the events of the three other elections. Much of this was done by scouring local newspapers (such as the *Danville [Virginia] Bee*, the *Dallas Morning News*, and the *Jackson Clarion-Ledger*). I also interviewed candidates, campaign managers, political consultants, and reporters involved in these elections. Even with the campaign so far in the past, most of the people I talked with had clear, detailed recollections of events. In fact, these interviews often benefited from greater hindsight. The interview subjects were more candid because they were less wary of the interviewer and more emotionally divorced from the events of the campaign; and they were not talking to me in a speeding automobile heading for the next campaign event or with a lot of harried campaign workers interrupting.[5]

In conducting this research, I was confronted with some difficult choices, several of which need to be justified before I proceed. Why congressional elections rather than some other type of elections? Why special elections? Why these particular special elections when there were several others to choose from?

Why congressional elections? Most important, the first puzzle that structures this work has to do with mixed electoral results, the disparity between Republican presidential success and the party's weaker performances in congressional elections on down. In solving this puzzle, unlike Earl and Merle Black (1992), I look to the conduct of congressional

Table 2.3   Turnout in Special and Off-year Elections

	Special Election	1986 Election in Same District
Mississippi 4	32%	35%
Texas 1	27%	22%
Virginia 5	27%	23%
Alabama 3	19%	37%
Mississippi 5	37%	27%
Mississippi 2	41%	44%
Average	31%	31%

elections rather than presidential elections. This is because it is the results of these elections that have defied expectations. The more interesting question is not how Republican presidential candidates have won
votes in the South, which is not particularly surprising, but how congressional Democratic candidates have held on.

Congressional elections are preferable to state legislative elections for
very practical reasons. Congressional campaigns command far greater
public attention than elections to the state legislature. They are covered
by the newspapers. The candidates are invited to forums and debates.
Voters are more likely to have some information about these elections and
are more likely to base their decisions on information obtained in the
campaign. They are, simply put, much higher profile elections.

I look at House elections rather than Senate elections because there are
a greater number of them to choose from. Moreover, congressional elections, in most cases, involve more "local" politicians who are familiar with
the district and its inhabitants. Their campaigns are tailored to a smaller
area and are, in this sense, more diverse and more interesting. House
elections are large enough to merit public attention, but small enough to
be considered local. They best fit the requirements of this project. Moreover, Republicans have enjoyed relative success in Senate elections. House
seats are, in some sense, the line of first defense. These elections have
represented the highest level of Democratic dominance in the region.

Special elections are but a small subset of all congressional elections, and they are unique in several ways. They are held independently of other elections. They are often held in isolation, with nothing else on the ballot. They are characterized by lower turnout (Sigelman 1981).[6] Yet "specials" offer some excellent analytic opportunities, and I have tried to take advantage of them. Most important, these elections are all for open seats. In 1988, 99 percent of incumbent congressmen were reelected by an average margin of 38 percentage points.[7] The advantage of incumbency is so great that elections involving an incumbent are more predictable and less interesting. It makes most sense, from my perspective, to look at open seat elections, in which neither candidate enjoys an incumbency advantage. Almost by definition, special elections meet this criterion.

A second reason for looking at special elections is that they are, in fact, isolated from other elections. In the words of one journalist, "They're the only game in town." This is a great advantage for two reasons, one practical, the other analytical. The practical advantage is that special elections often are covered intensively by the media. Because there is usually little else of political interest going on, local and even national reporters have more time and inclination to cover these elections. They also attract journalistic attention because many political observers attach some meaning to special elections. They are "straws in the wind," precursors to upcoming elections and thus indicators of what is to come. Or they are an early electoral measure of how a president is doing. Whatever the case, there is more information available from these elections than from single contests held during the regular election cycle. This has made it possible for me to uncover information in those cases in which I did not witness the campaign. Finally, many of these special elections take place over a short period of time. The compressed nature of the election makes it easier to study, both in terms of following events in person and reconstructing events.

The analytical advantage that specials offer is that one can attribute (cautiously) the final results to the effectiveness of the campaigns, to the circumstances of the particular election. There are no coattails. If there are party levers to pull, they are less important. Most analysts of congressional elections consider local factors to be much more important than national factors in determining results. Still, congressional elections held in conjunction with national elections have another variable that must be considered in understanding the results. This research strategy thus removes a complicating factor from the analysis. Those who go to the polls in these elections are going only to cast a congressional vote and not a presidential (or gubernatorial or senatorial) vote. The campaign that more effectively gets its supporters to the polls is at an advantage, and neither side can count on voters activated by another campaign. This makes it easier to isolate the strategic factors that make the biggest difference. As this is an important objective of this project, investigating special elections makes good sense.

This is not to say that national forces are unimportant in these elections. They frequently do command national attention. Pundits interpret them as referenda on presidential performance or on some important issue facing Congress. National party leaders set them up as measures of party strength. National figures visit the districts and national money flows into the campaigns. And there is some evidence that special election voters, like midterm voters, may be evaluating the presiding administration as they cast their votes, offering support to those who interpret these elections as referenda on how the president is doing.[8] Still, even though the economy and perceptions of the president may have some bearing on voting decisions, the candidates must harness these national forces in getting their supporters to the polls. Gauging the effectiveness of the campaigns in doing this is more easily done when the congressional election is the only game in town.

The understanding of special elections as national referenda does introduce an additional methodological snare into the project. Most of the (limited) literature on the topic suggests that members of the president's party are at a fair disadvantage in midterm and special elections. Kernell (1977) argues persuasively that, in midterm elections, assessments of presidential performance affect congressional voters, particularly those disapproving of the administration. In this light, the inevitable losses to the governing party in American midterm elections and in British by-elections, an even more direct counterpart to special elections, have been understood to be the result of negative voting, of people penalizing the national government in local elections (Mughan 1986; Erikson 1988). As to special elections, Sigelman (1981) shows that three-quarters of all party turnovers in special elections from 1954 to 1978 represented losses by the president's party (there were twenty such turnovers in ninety-four special elections). Although this statistic does not properly illustrate the disadvantage that members of the president's party are at, cursory evidence suggests that special elections follow the pattern set by midterm elections and by-elections.[9]

Here the analysis runs into a potential problem. If part of the purpose of this book is to explain how the Democrats held off low-level realignment at a time the Republicans dominated presidential contests, my interpretation may be colored by the fact that I am studying special elections. Perhaps Democrats won these contests because, through the 1980s, they were the out-party and out-parties have an inherent advantage in these types of elections.

Fortuitously, the six special elections in this study enable me to address this problem—they are temporally proximate to a general election. One other finding from the literature on British by-elections is that the more time that passes after the election, the greater the likelihood the government's support will decay (Studlar and Sigelman 1987).[10] Moreover, the closer the by-election is to the *next* general election, the less likely the government's party is to be penalized by the voters (Studlar and Sigelman 1987). There is no theoretical reason to believe that American special elections are much different. To my advantage, five of the six special elections I study here were held shortly after a general election. In all but the Virginia case, the special was held three to nine months after an inauguration, not much time for hostility to the administration to build. In Virginia, the special election was held in June 1988, just five months before a presidential election.

Moreover, evidence suggests that the Republican presidents were extremely popular in these districts around the time of the elections. In four of the five districts holding elections between 1980 and 1992, Reagan and Bush won more than 60 percent of the district vote in the presidential election most proximate to the special. In the fifth, Mississippi 4, Reagan won a much smaller majority six months prior in the 1980 presidential election. That Mississippi special election, however, was held just a few months after Reagan was shot, a period during which he enjoyed enormous popularity. Indeed, the national presidential approval ratings for Reagan and Bush were very strong at the time of four of the five pre-1993 specials in this study, the exception again being Virginia (see table 2.2). The point, of course, is that a simple presidential penalty interpretation of special elections would not likely explain the Democratic congressional victories in these cases. Democrats won for reasons other than their out-party status.

The final methodological issue to be addressed here is, why these six special elections? This might be called the sampling problem, and it is a problem faced by others who do participant-observation research. As Richard Fenno (1990) writes, this is a problem with no perfectly satisfactory solution: "My answer at the beginning [of my research] was I don't know; my answer today is, I'm not sure. Nothing better characterizes the open-ended, slowly emerging, participant observation research than this admission. If I had been certain about what types of representatives and what types of districts to sample, I would already have had answers to a lot of the questions raised in [my] book" (59). Like Fenno, I found this stage of the process to be very difficult, and the defense of my choices reflects this. The research decisions involving which elections to witness were especially difficult. My original plan was not just to look at Democratic victories. Indeed, in all three of the campaigns I visited, the Republicans either were favored at the beginning or were given a good chance of winning. Limited resources made each choice difficult, and my decision to go to the Mississippi Delta, the Gulf Coast, and central Alabama instead of Houston, Miami, Ft. Worth, Dallas, or north-central Virginia had to be made without any knowledge as to how these elections would play out or who would win. The choices, in hindsight, were good ones as all three were competitive, spirited contests, if not always close in the end.[11]

Choosing the other three cases to include in this set also had to be done carefully. These choices too were made somewhat in the dark, before I knew what the final composition of my cases would be. As the project evolved, it became clear that to approach the puzzles of mixed realignment, to determine what the Democrats' congressional candidates were doing right at the same time that their presidential candidates were losing, I should study situations in which the outcome was genuinely in doubt at the beginning. Situations deemed by the press or party politicians or both to be tests of realignment were most interesting to me.[12] I also sought variation in the districts. Most important was variation in racial composition, which contributed to my ability to test a major line of my argument. Indeed, in the sample as a whole, Mississippi 2 is a majority (58 percent) black district, Mississippi 4 has a very large minority of blacks (42 percent), Alabama 3 and Virginia 5 have moderately large black populations (28 and 25 percent, respectively), and Texas 1 and Mississippi 5 have black populations slightly under 20 percent.[13]

The districts are varied in other ways, as well. There are two districts with sizable urban and suburban areas (Mississippi 4 and Mississippi 5), yet these and the rest of the districts also cover rural areas. Though Old South in character, two districts are in the outer states of the region (Texas 1 and Virginia 5); four, of course, are from the Deep South. Clearly Mississippi is overrepresented, but the districts in Mississippi that I studied are significantly different from each other and are representative of other areas in the South. In two of the elections a Republican was being replaced. The elections also were held under different electoral rules. In some, partisan primaries were held with the winners meeting in a general election; in others, nonpartisan elections were followed by an election between the top two vote-getters (if no candidate achieved a majority in the first round); in yet another (Virginia), candidates chosen in party conventions faced off in a general election. Even in the nonpartisan elections, the runoff was always between a Republican and a Democrat.

Parts of the South are not represented in this sample. There are no elections from Atlanta, New Orleans, Miami, Houston, or Dallas-Ft. Worth, or from their suburbs. These cities are so overwhelmingly Democratic, however, and their suburbs so Republican that these parts of the South have come to look like urban and suburban parts of the North, and there is not all that much to explain. The historically Republican parts of the South (eastern Tennessee and western North Carolina) are also not studied here, nor are the parts of the region most northern in character and population (northern Virginia and southern Florida). There has been no realignment in Appalachia to explain. South Florida and northern Virginia (and South and West Texas, for that matter) are interesting but rather unique parts of the region.

The six cases thus represent a large part of the Old South, that rural part of the region (though dotted with small cities) most steeped in southern values and tradition. It is now very politically competitive territory, and territory that many have been expecting the Republicans to win for years. It is the battlefield on which realignment has taken place over the past thirty years and will be taking place in the future.

3 Racial Issues in the Congressional Campaign

RACE IS ALWAYS A FACTOR in southern congressional campaigns. As I argue throughout this book, the racial composition of a congressional district determines which strategies will be most effective, what tactics are to be used, how a candidate's time will be spent, what media are to be employed, what issues will be highlighted. Race is never far from the minds of southern campaign managers. It cannot be.

This does not mean that an explicitly racial issue arises in every southern campaign. Most campaigns, in fact, are not fought over issues that one might associate with racial politics—voting rights, affirmative action, symbolic gestures to the black community. Where such an issue does arise, though, it often becomes the focus of the campaign. The candidates keep reaching for it. The commercials and literature highlight it. The media cover it in almost every report. What follows are descriptions of two campaigns in which this happened, one in southwest Mississippi, the other in eastern Alabama. Not every southern campaign looks like these two, but they are worth studying because they illustrate dramatically how Republicans have sought white votes and Democrats have sought black votes through racial issues.

Mississippi 4— "It's scurrilous, dirty politics"

In McComb, Mississippi, a small city in the southern part of the Fourth District, the downtown is almost a ghost town. Most of the storefronts are empty and boarded up. The tenants who have stayed are suffering. No pedestrians are to be seen. Twenty-five years ago, this is where one would have found the whites-only lunch counter. No one, white or black, eats here now. About two miles toward the interstate is the mall, busy and thriving. Young couples with strollers browse the stores, and children, black and white, crowd the arcade. Inside, it looks and feels like any mall in the United States except that the fast food restaurant serves catfish and red beans with rice.

Mississippi's Fourth District is a mix of the old and the new; it is a district of contrasts. It has eleven rural counties, which are heavily black and economically depressed. It also contains Jackson, the state's largest metropolitan area, and its suburbs. Although part of the city is predominantly black and poor, the northern section of town and its suburbs are mostly white, white collar, middle class, and Republican. The district is split in a variety of ways; it is 42 percent black, 49 percent urban and suburban, and about half Republican.[1]

In this district Republicans achieved some of their first breakthroughs in Mississippi. It was here, in 1972, that Thad Cochran became one of the state's first two Republican congressmen to serve more than one term since Reconstruction (Trent Lott also was elected in 1972 in the neighboring Fifth District).[2] In 1978, Cochran became the state's first Republican senator since Reconstruction. His congressional seat was filled by another Republican, Jon Hinson, his administrative assistant in Washington.

At first, Hinson looked as if he, like Cochran, would be electorally secure and that the district would stay in Republican hands for years to come. The son of a prominent Tylertown political family, Hinson convincingly defeated John Stennis, Jr., the son and namesake of Mississippi's legendary senior senator, in 1978 and appeared to be invulnerable. Upon arriving in Washington, he was described in the *Almanac of American Politics* as likely to "vote—and to win votes—as Cochran did" (Barone, Ujifusa, and Matthews 1979, 485). In 1980, however, Hinson ran into trouble. In the course of that campaign, he was forced to acknowledge that he had been arrested for an obscene act at the U.S. Marine Corps Monument in Arlington Cemetery. He also admitted to being a survivor of a devastating fire at a gay theater in Washington. Though he denied being a homosexual, claimed to have undergone a religious experience, and offered his new wife as evidence, he clearly had a problem in the very conservative Mississippi district. Yet he was able to weather these storms. Said one supporter, "Some folks would rather have a queer conservative than a macho liberal and they may be right" (Harris 1981).

One year later, though, Hinson again found himself in difficulty after being arrested with another man for attempted sodomy in a public restroom in a congressional office building. This incident could not be ignored: Hinson's partner was black. "[That] added insult to injury here in Mississippi," said a black community leader several months after the incident. "There are still a zillion jokes about it" (Harris 1981). Under pressure from national and state Republican leaders, Hinson resigned his office, setting the stage for a special election in June 1981.

Cochran and Hinson had won the previous five elections for two major reasons. First, whites from the Jackson area had become overwhelmingly Republican. Cochran, who was from Jackson, was the first to benefit from this constituency, which has provided the base for every Republican candidacy since. Second, Cochran and Hinson were helped enormously by independent black candidates on the ballot. In 1972, Cochran won the open seat election with less than half (48 percent) the vote. His Democratic opponent fell four points short as the independent Eddie McBride siphoned off 8 percent of the vote.[3] In Hinson's first run, in 1978, a black independent took 20 percent of the vote. This actually mattered less than it had earlier because the Republican won an outright majority (53 percent) of the vote. But two years later, Hinson won reelection with just 37 percent of the vote. The black independent outpolled even the Democrat in this race, 33 to 30 percent, which was the major reason that Hinson was able to survive his first scandal. Part of Hinson's success also can be attributed to the fact that he hailed from a rural county in the southern part of the district. This helped him win enough rural white votes to add to his Republican base in Jackson.

The special election in 1981 to replace Hinson posed a problem for the Republicans. Because of the rules governing special elections, they would not be able to count on an independent black candidate in this race. The election, like many other special elections, was to be held in two stages. The first, an open, nonpartisan contest, would narrow the field to two candidates (if no one candidate won at least 50 percent of the vote). The second election would be between the top two vote-getters. Should it come to a runoff, the Democrats would not be split along racial lines.

Anticipating that several Democrats were certain to throw their hats into the ring, the Republicans calculated that their best chance for retaining the seat was in winning a majority in the first election. With this in mind, the Republicans held a caucus and settled on one candidate several months before the first election. Prior to the event, all of the major hopefuls agreed to abide by the decision of the caucus, thus allowing a Republican the opportunity to win the election while the Democrats were still divided. The caucus, after a day of intense politicking, settled on Jackson businessman Liles Williams, himself a former activist in the state Democratic party. Williams, a leader of the Religious Roundtable and a successful businessman, faced several prominent Democrats in the first round.

Republicans, in the second special election of Ronald Reagan's tenure, pumped a great deal of money and effort into the first primary. It was an especially good time to defend their seat. The primary was held just twelve weeks after Reagan was shot, and that event had built up a reservoir of support for the president. The Republicans mailed out eighty-five thousand letters under Reagan's signature to voters in the district and spent more money in that primary than in any previous congressional campaign in Mississippi history (*Jackson Clarion-Ledger* 1981). Williams did quite well, winning 45 percent of the vote in the primary, but fell short of the majority needed to avoid a runoff. Ironically, he likely was hurt by the presence on his right of two Ku Klux Klan candidates ("Vote Right, Vote White, Vote Wheems" was one electoral battle cry).[4] Even if he had won these votes, however, he would have fallen a few points short of victory.

The man Williams expected to face, if a runoff election was necessary, was Mike Singletary, who had run against Hinson in 1980. Singletary banked his campaign on making an issue of Hinson, arguing that the same "power brokers" who had backed Hinson and thus "embarrassed the district" had selected Williams (Walsh 1981). It was a message designed to appeal to conservative rural whites. Strategically, though, it was a miscalculation because another Democrat, by activating a less-competed-for black vote, made it to the runoff. That Democrat was Wayne Dowdy, the part-time mayor of McComb.

At the time of the election, legislation to extend the Voting Rights Act for five years was pending in Congress. Testimony was being heard on the legislation in Washington, and even the president was mulling over his position on the issue. Whereas Williams, Singletary, and the other candidates in the race approved of modifying the act or rejecting it altogether, Dowdy came out unambiguously in support of the extension, the only major candidate to do so (there were no black candidates in the field). Part of the reason that Dowdy's second-place finish was so surprising was that the other candidates believed that in supporting the extension Dowdy had "completely alienated his white base" (Walsh 1981).[5] Yet Dowdy pulled in enough black voters to collect 25 percent of the overall vote in the primary, considerably more than Singletary's 14 percent, third-place finish.

The extension of the Voting Rights Act also became the most important issue of the second phase of the campaign. Williams took a strong stand against extending the act in an attempt to woo white voters. His argument was basically that it was unfair that the South, which had shown so much progress in voting rights, was still being singled out. A *Jackson Daily News and Clarion-Ledger* editorial endorsing Williams summed up his position on this issue: "Progress in Mississippi must not go ignored by those who would continue to punish the South for the past and at the same time ignore that voting rights problems continue to exist in other regions of the nation" (*Jackson Daily News and Clarion-Ledger* 1981). Williams raised the issue often, and the media, both local and national, wrote about it in almost every report and editorial. It dominated coverage of his campaign.

As noted, Dowdy supported extension of the act as it was. "It was the right thing to do," he said. "I thought it had brought Mississippi far and that there were only minor hindrances associated with it, which is what I said in the campaign." While it is true that when pressed, in debates for example, Dowdy did speak of his support of the legislation, he did so in rather terse statements. His support for the legislation was not brought up in any of his campaign television commercials. And Dowdy even declined to get involved in a controversy over the order of the candidates' names on the ballot in several counties. When Republican clerks in a number of heavily black counties put Williams above Dowdy on the ballot (as opposed to listing the names alphabetically as they were elsewhere), some Democrats charged that this would confuse illiterate black voters and was thus in violation of the Voting Rights Act. The state attorney general ruled on the issue, declaring that alphabetical order had to be used. Nonetheless, Dowdy purposely chose not to pursue the matter. Although he did not dodge the issue of extension, he was not going to do anything to make it more salient than it was already. "A lawsuit would only serve to confuse the voters," he told a *New York Times* reporter (Clymer 1981a).

The message Dowdy directed toward black voters, however, was quite different. On the circuit of black churches, in front of black audiences, and on black media, Dowdy highlighted his support of the Voting Rights legislation. If his stand in public was subdued, his targeted message to blacks was loud and clear. "Martin Luther King and Medgar Evers gave their lives so you could vote," said Medgar Evers's niece in a Dowdy advertisement played on black radio stations. "Now Ronald Reagan and Liles Williams are trying to take your right to vote away. . . . Wayne Dowdy has the courage to publicly say that Wayne Dowdy would vote for the extension of the Voting Rights Act" (Treyens 1981a). The Republican state chairman, not surprisingly, was unhappy about these advertisements, calling Dowdy "one of the greatest race baiters elected to office in Mississippi in the last 20 to 30 years. It's scurrilous, dirty politics" (Treyens 1981a). But his complaints and the reporting of the radio advertisement in the Jackson newspaper had little impact on the outcome because the controversy broke after the election. The advertisement was run only on the last day or two of the campaign.

The major issue in Williams's campaign, other than the Voting Rights Act Extension, was his support of President Reagan and Reagan's support of him. Williams's polls showed the president with a 74 percent approval rating in the district (Broder 1981b), and the campaign did all it could to link their man to the president. Reagan's endorsement of Williams was included in the Republican's campaign literature and in his half-page advertisements in the *Jackson Clarion-Ledger*. As noted above, letters under Reagan's signature were sent to eighty-five thousand of the district's Republicans. At one point, the president even made a phone call to Williams that was piped over a loudspeaker to a rally. "We're waiting for you up here and need your help," declared Reagan to the candidate and his enthusiastic crowd.

Williams made support for Reagan's budget cuts a major tenet of his campaign. The dramatic cuts were being debated in Congress, and Williams sought to capitalize on the issue. He did make sure to distance himself from the cuts in Social Security proposed by the administration. Nonetheless, the *Washington Post* reported that "Williams has portrayed himself as a textbook disciple of Reaganomics preaching federal parsimony and tax cuts" (Harris 1981).

Dowdy's campaign, on the other hand, emphasized local issues, and his appeals for rural white votes had populist overtones. Dowdy railed against foreign aid. He criticized the administration's plans to send $3 billion to Pakistan, arguing that southwest Mississippi's problems should be addressed before Pakistan's. "We must balance the budget," he announced to a rally in McComb, "but while people here at home are making cuts and sacrifices, other countries are receiving our money" (Mullen 1981). On the stump, Dowdy also attacked the Federal Reserve Bank for high interest rates, Washington lobbyists, and both political parties. At one point in the campaign he even declared, "I'm running against the President of the United States, the U.S. Chamber of Commerce and every oil company in the world." (Putnam 1981a). Dowdy's style fit his populist message. He was the wealthiest candidate in the entire field of original candidates (*Jackson Daily News and Clarion-Ledger*, 1981), but his country background, his folksy manner, and his relaxed "person-to-person homestyle" (see Fenno 1978) made him a good fit for the rural half of the district.

Although he took an anti-Washington, populist message to the electorate, the Democrat was cautious when talking about Ronald Reagan. Dowdy's reference to the president was that Reagan was running against him, not that he was necessarily running against Reagan. This theme was evident in Dowdy's advertisements, one of which led with, "Last year we elected a president and we have a very fine man. Our election now is for congressman and Ronald Reagan is not a candidate." Wayne Dowdy's negative message was not about the president but rather his policies and, most important, how they would affect Mississippi. Williams, so completely aligned with the president, would "rubber stamp" Reagan's program, argued the Democrat, and would not oppose cuts that would have an adverse effect on the district (Clymer 1981a).

In the end, Dowdy's strategy worked. Outspent by Williams ($372,000 to $277,000 [Ehrenhalt 1983, 843]), disadvantaged by his opponent's ties to the popular president, running in a district that had elected Republicans to Congress in the previous five elections, Dowdy won nevertheless. His margin of victory was quite small, indeed, about eleven hundred votes, leading him to joke at his victory party, "On our budget, we cannot afford a landslide" (*Washington Post* 1981a). The advertisements on black radio, the speeches in black churches, and, most important, Dowdy's message to the black community bolstered black turnout, and this, more than anything else, led to his victory.

One measure of the effectiveness of Dowdy's effort to get blacks to the polls is the increase in turnout from the first to the second election in largely black counties. As might be expected, turnout went up from the primary to the runoff in the district as a whole, a difference of three points (to 32 percent). In predominantly (75 percent) black Claiborne County, however, turnout rose nine points (to 29 percent) from the first election to the second; in 82 percent black Jefferson County, turnout rose from 25 to 35 percent. Though aggregate data make it impossible to tell for sure, the vote in these counties was almost certainly along racial lines, and Dowdy appears to have won nearly all the rural black vote. In Jefferson County, Dowdy took 77 percent of the vote and in Claiborne County, 74 percent. Dowdy overwhelmed Williams in the black neighborhoods of Jackson as well. In one Jackson precinct, for instance, Dowdy beat Williams 814 to 4. Totals from other black precincts were almost as lopsided (Treyens 1981b). In an election decided by such a narrow margin, the larger-than-expected black turnout was crucial. A black organizer who was involved in the campaign said, "I'd never seen such enthusiasm in a campaign before and haven't since. When you go after the Voting Rights Act, well, that's sacred." The state's Republican chairman also attributed Dowdy's victory to his candidate's emphasis on the Voting Rights Act, which "helped motivate the black turnout" (Clymer 1981b). Even Dowdy accepted this analysis of the election. "There are lots of folks we've [the Democrats] lost," he said pointing to the white, middle-class neighborhood outside his office window. "In an election like that one, we had to get black votes. When the Republicans went public and strong on this [the Voting Rights Act], it really energized the blacks."

Dowdy needed to do more than motivate black voters. His candidacy was premised upon an ability to win rural white votes as well. He won only 45 percent of the vote in Hinds County (Jackson), where about half the votes in the district were cast. He also lost counties holding the district's smaller cities. Williams carried Warren County (which holds

Vicksburg) with 57 percent of the vote and Lincoln County (which holds Brookhaven) with 51 percent. But Dowdy won by large margins in the rural parts of the district. In almost every county, including those he lost, Dowdy's percentage of the vote was greater than the percentage of blacks in the county. In Copiah County, a 48 percent black county, Dowdy won 61 percent of the vote. In 30 percent black Lincoln County, the Democrat took 49 percent of the vote.[6] The exceptions, interestingly, were the three most heavily black districts. Again, although aggregate data allow only a good guess as to voting patterns of particular groups, it appears that Dowdy did in fact put together an effective coalition of blacks and rural whites.

In Washington, where small pieces of electoral information become invested with great meaning, Dowdy's victory became quite significant. It was variously interpreted as a referendum on the president, a warning for conservative Democrats, and a message on the Voting Rights extension. Democrats gleefully pointed to Dowdy's victory as an illustration of public discontent with Reagan's program. "They voted their pocketbooks," said Tip O'Neill in the election's national postmortem (Clymer 1981b). Congressman Tony Coelho, chairman of the Democratic Congressional Campaign Committee, added that the victory was a repudiation of "the idea of a Solid South for Ronald Reagan" (*Washington Post* 1981a). Republicans rejected these interpretations of the election, arguing that Williams was damaged by his partisan association with Hinson. Nonetheless, the Democrats savored a moment of success after an otherwise dreary electoral season.

Insofar as Dowdy's victory was interpreted as at least a partial repudiation of Reagan in a staunchly conservative place, it became a vehicle for liberal Democrats to penalize conservatives in the party who had supported the president over the party. The chairman of the national party, Charles Manatt, and some liberals in the House used Dowdy's victory to call for the disciplining of the boll weevil Phil Gramm and others of his ilk. Manatt charged that Gramm had participated in Democratic strategy sessions on the budget and then actively worked with the administration to sabotage his own party's position (Broder 1981a). The Connecticut congressman Toby Moffett introduced a resolution to the House Democratic Caucus to discipline Gramm, and though Gramm was not punished at that time, he was soon thereafter.

Finally, Dowdy's victory sent a message to Washington on the Voting Rights Act. Whereas the other two interpretations of the Democratic victory were fiercely contested, this one was not; the Voting Rights Act should be extended. As the *Washington Post* editorialized the week following the election, the "message from Mississippi" was that renewal of the act was politically acceptable and the right thing to do (*Washington Post* 1981b). Dowdy's victory was by the slightest of margins, but it carried with it symbolic value to Democrats in Washington eager to make a point.

Dowdy had a little bit of time before having to prepare for the next election cycle. He faced Williams in a rematch in 1982. The situation was even more favorable for Williams in this race because several heavily black counties were taken out of the district in an effort to create a majority black district to the north. Enjoying name recognition and running as an incumbent, though, Dowdy held back Williams's challenge. He went on to win successive elections by progressively larger margins, until in 1988 he vacated his seat to run for the Senate (unsuccessfully, it turned out). He was replaced by another rural Democrat, Mike Parker. Like Dowdy, Parker faced a Jackson Republican and did not encounter an independent black candidate in the general election. Under these circumstances, he effectively reconstructed Dowdy's winning coalition of blacks and rural voters.

Alabama 3— "It's not a race issue. It's a heritage issue"

In 1964, Barry Goldwater went "hunting where the ducks were," that is, set out to capture the South with a racially conservative message. His candidacy that year may have been a failure on a national scale, but it had an impact in the South. Goldwater won several states in the region and had some coattails, carrying seven southern Republicans to victory in the House elections of 1964. One of these seven turnovers came in Alabama's Third District (at that time the Fourth). Two years later, in elections otherwise favorable to Republicans, the Democrats won four of these seats back, including that in the Third District. As a George Wallace floor leader in the Alabama state legislature, Bill Nichols was able to defeat the Republican rather easily.

For the next twenty years, Nichols represented the district, which covers the east-central portion of Alabama. A prototypical Deep South district, it is mostly rural and has a sizable black population (28 percent). Its largest town, Anniston, has a population of just thirty thousand, but the district takes in some of the suburban areas around Birmingham, Montgomery, and Columbus, Georgia. The district's economy is based on agriculture, textiles, timber, and the military. The Anniston Army Depot, where almost all of the U.S. Army's transport vehicles and tanks are repaired, is the district's largest employer (Ehrenhalt 1987, 21). Also in the district are Auburn University, a large state university, Jacksonville State University, and Tuskegee Institute, one of the nation's first black universities, founded by Booker T. Washington more than a century ago.

Bill Nichols saw to it that the district, with its large universities and its dependence on the military, got its share of federal pork. From his senior position on the Armed Services Committee, the congressman brought millions of military dollars into the area. A solid conservative, he was renowned in the district for the service he provided and went virtually unchallenged by the Republicans throughout his tenure. When he suffered a fatal heart attack at his Capitol desk in December 1988, it set off a flurry of activity among prospective candidates, Democrats and Republicans alike. Just three hours after Nichols died, a Washington-based media consultant said that he was called by a prospective candidate. "The body wasn't even cold," he said. Such early jockeying often occurs when a seat opens up after a long congressional career.

A special election was scheduled for the following spring. Prior to the general election, each party scheduled separate primaries, which were to be held in two rounds. Unless a candidate drew more than half the votes, the top two candidates from the first primary would compete in a runoff, the winner advancing to the general election.[7] The Republican candidate was chosen in the first round. No Democrat, however, emerged from the first primary with a majority, and the top two candidates squared off.

The winner of the Republican primary was State Senator John Rice. Only months before, the thirty-seven-year-old Rice had been a Democrat but had switched parties after several battles with the Democratic leadership of the state senate. With the Republican governor, Guy Hunt, and Jack Kemp by his side, Rice publicly and proudly announced his defection. In a district in which 60 percent had voted for George Bush the previous November and 58 percent had voted for Hunt in 1986 (National Republican Congressional Committee 1988), such a move had great political possibilities. Giving some indication that Republican chances appeared to be good, party money flowed into Rice's campaign. With two weeks left before the general election, Rice had received $54,000 in cash or in-kind services from Republican congressmen and the state and national Republican parties. His Democratic opponent had only $40,000 from such party sources at that time (Smith 1989d).[8]

The two top vote-getters in the Democratic primary were the Alabama secretary of state, Glen Browder, and the black mayor of Tuskegee, Johnny Ford. The Democratic primary runoff was an interesting race, as it posed both problems and possibilities for both candidates. Ford was a strong, capable candidate, but his race (and the fact that he was married to a white woman) worked against him in this conservative district. A Browder campaign consultant, impressed with the politically savvy mayor, remarked, "If he were white, he'd be going to Congress." Several others, Democratic and Republican, echoed this sentiment. Recognizing that the black vote would not be enough to give him the Democratic nomination and that he would need white votes, Ford devised a two-pronged campaign plan. The first element of his strategy was to emphasize his conservative views and conservative background. Ford put forth conservative positions on gun control, abortion, and other social issues, positions, he contended, that were shared by the black voters of the district as well as the white. But his advocacy of such positions was aimed more at whites than blacks. Through the years, Ford had developed a reputation for being a conservative and an accommodationist. He even endorsed Richard Nixon in 1972 and George Wallace for governor in 1974 (Barone, Ujifusa, and Matthews 1979, 8). If any black candidate could make inroads into the conservative white vote in the Third District, it was Johnny Ford.

The second element of Ford's strategy was to downplay race. He avoided racial issues in the campaign and spoke often of how he thought that whites in the district could support him. This is not to say that he was blind to reality: "It would have been naive to think that it [race] wasn't in folks' minds," he said. "But you just have to smile and work on, to ignore it and move on. You have to do something constructive because white people have to be comfortable with you." This attitude permeated his campaign.

If Ford had any chance of winning, it was by energizing black voters while not stirring up resentment among white voters. In the end, these goals may not have been compatible. Bringing Jesse Jackson into the district to speak at some black rallies shortly before the Democratic runoff represented a decision by the Ford forces that turning out his black base was more important than not alienating potential white voters. Jackson drew large, enthusiastic crowds, but his visit was covered by the media and may have cost Ford some white votes, if indeed he had any to begin with.

Browder, a former professor of political science at Jacksonville State University, had specialized in the study of public opinion and voting behavior. He recognized that he too had important tactical decisions to make vis-à-vis Ford. He had to beat Ford in the runoff, but he needed Ford's help to mobilize black voters in the general election. He also had to worry about being tied too closely to Ford by the Rice campaign lest this lead to white backlash. "The one thing we worried about and were very glad and frankly surprised they [the Rice campaign] didn't do," said a Democratic media consultant, "was to run a commercial putting Browder's face next to Ford's face, trying to link the two of them together. 'Two peas in a pod' or something like that."

Given this situation, Browder completely downplayed race in his primary campaign and went to great lengths to show Ford great respect. As a front-runner, Browder had little to gain by participating in a debate that would only help to publicize his opponent. Yet he acceded to Ford's request for a televised meeting. Although confident of victory in the runoff, he treated the mayor as a serious opponent, showing Ford that he respected him as an adversary. This attitude was reflected in the debate. Browder's debate strategy, according to his campaign manager, was to draw distinctions between the two candidates while taking great pains to avoid being negative. The debate, in fact, was described as a love fest by one of the Democratic campaign consultants.

By taking Ford seriously while showing restraint in his campaign against him, Browder hoped to earn Ford's help in the general election. The strategy worked. On the night of Browder's primary victory, Ford threw his support completely behind Browder. He became a major force in turning out the black community for the Democratic nominee in the general election, campaigning quite a bit for Browder and taking him around on the black church circuit, a campaign environment, an advisor noted, that Browder was not completely comfortable in.[9] Browder's campaign manager estimated that, in the end, Ford delivered about 75 percent of his primary vote to Browder. "Johnny Ford really stepped up to the plate," the manager said appreciatively some months after the election.

Ford also had something to gain in the Democratic runoff: name recognition and public exposure in anticipation of the creation of a majority black congressional district following redistricting in 1990. Hoping that Browder's home county and the surrounding counties in the northern part of the district would be moved into another district ("Those counties don't belong in this district. They're too different from down here," he complained), Ford hoped to emerge from the election as the major black candidate of the future. Moreover, Ford saw an opportunity to cultivate important contacts through Browder. Browder received large contributions from labor (about 60 percent of his PAC contributions and one-third of his total campaign funds came from unions [Smith 1989d]), and Ford expressed interest in being introduced to some of Browder's friends in the AFL-CIO. As expected, Browder handily beat Ford, 63 percent to 37 percent, but Ford came out of the election well situated for his next campaign.[10]

From the beginning, the Browder-Rice contest attracted national interest. The election was one of two special elections taking place five months after the November presidential election. These two elections were the first tests of the partisan strength of the Bush administration. They offered some indication, at least among insiders, of how the president was doing, and in this case, how the new head of the Republican National Committee, Lee Atwater, was doing. The Alabama race became particularly important after the Democrats won a surprising and symbolically important victory in the first contest, an election to fill Vice President Dan Quayle's old congressional seat (vacated by Dan Coats, who took over Quayle's Senate term). The Republicans were quite unhappy with this development, and Atwater even expressed embarrassment over the Indiana loss (McNeil 1989). The Alabama race thus became even more important for the national Republican party.

The race quickly became acrimonious. In addition to calling Browder a "Michael Dukakis liberal" and "a national Democrat," Rice labeled him "a powderpuff" and "a wimp." At one point, a Rice press release even charged that "while our boys were dying in the rice patties (*sic*) in Viet Nam, my opponent, Professor Browder, long hair and all, was in the classroom giving lectures on the immorality of America's involvement in Viet Nam" (March 15, 1989). The charge was based on the recollection of a Rice campaign aide who happened to be one of Browder's students in the early 1970s. "He was a McGovern person," said the aide. "We discussed everything from Vietnam to welfare." Browder responded that he had held "pro-and-con discussions about Vietnam" in his classroom and that the former student had misremembered Browder's position. To support this, Browder called in another former student of his, Democratic Lieutenant Governor Jim Folsom, Jr., who recalled that his professor did not "preach against Vietnam" and that he had short hair (Burger 1989b). Browder's campaign aide later announced that Browder had absolutely supported the war at that time (Yardley 1989b).

Rice excoriated Browder further for being beholden to big labor. Given the endorsements and campaign contributions that Browder had received from various labor unions, he was an easy mark. Governor Hunt, who campaigned with Rice on several occasions, criticized Browder's labor contributions as being from "liberals . . . from Brooklyn, New York and Washington, D.C." (Yardley 1989c). Another surrogate for Rice, the vanquished Democratic primary opponent Jim Preuitt, claimed that Browder had "sold his soul to national labor unions" (Smith 1989b). Rice himself brought notice to Browder's "friends" in a debate. "There's a labor influence in this race," he said. "I believe Glen needs to answer it" (Yardley 1989d). To further highlight Browder's debt to organized labor and their own independence from "special interests," the Republicans also publicly returned almost $3,000 in contributions from "people we don't like" (Smith 1989e). Given the financial circumstances the campaign later found itself in, this was a rather bold public relations maneuver.

Browder took to the offensive as well, though it took some prodding from his campaign advisors. Browder accused Rice of holding an "off-the-wall, radical philosophy" (Burger 1989a), and he ran an extremely negative television advertisement throughout the campaign calling the Republican candidate Hand Grenade Rice, his nickname in the state legislature. Rice had a reputation in the legislature for being hotheaded and unpredictable. He even characterized himself as such. "I enjoy the lightning," said the candidate. "I like to fight. I'm not a sedentary person [or] a couch potato, and I refuse to accept defeat." But the advertisement did more than bring up his personality; it connected it to some of his more dogmatic proposals. The commercial featured a grenade ticking beneath a picture of Rice, "looking like he has a bad hangover." The grenade blows up after Rice's dangerous record and philosophy are discussed. It was a wickedly negative commercial, one that stunned the aggressive Rice. "I got my butt kicked on TV [in a commercial] that was about as low as human morals can stoop," said Rice. "It's damaged me probably for the rest of my life. It hurt my family, my mother, my business. It's sick that politics is like that." The commercial was all the more effective as Rice's campaign funds dried up in the final weeks of the campaign, making defensive or even retaliatory television advertisements impossible.

On the positive side, Browder and Rice both had well-defined strategies. Browder's campaign was devoid of controversial issues. He seemed practiced at responding to questions about issues in brief, vague remarks. On a summary of the candidates' positions given to senior citizens before a debate sponsored by the American Association of Retired Persons (AARP), Browder's answers were often just one sentence long. And his responses in the debate were not any more detailed or enlightening. In some cases, they were evasive. He supported raising the minimum wage but refused to say where it should be set, a point of contention between President Bush and Congress at that time. On his backing of Bush's "no new taxes" pledge—Browder did not sign such a pledge himself—he refused to name any specific cuts he would make to reduce the deficit. When asked about his position on abortion, Browder responded that he was personally opposed to it but that the issue was before the Supreme Court (in *Webster v Reproductive Health Services*) and that he would wait until the opinion came down (well after the election) before coming to any conclusions.

Browder's positions on controversial and ideological issues were intentionally vague because he saw little electoral advantage to be gained by taking hard-line positions. On abortion, for instance, he told a newspaper reporter, "I see no sense in me getting involved in an issue that's a highly emotional issue that might override what I consider some very substantial issues and my ability to provide my representation to this district. It is not the thing that's the most important factor or even one of the biggest factors in the issues that are important on people's lives such as defense jobs, textile jobs, senior citizens and Social Security" (Yardley 1989f). Browder's desire to avoid controversial issues annoyed some ("At least [Mr. Rice] has an answer, gives an answer," said a black minister from Anniston [Yardley 1989h]), but surprisingly neither his opponent nor the local press scored him over it.

When he did express a position, it was most often a conservative one, deflecting Rice's charge of liberalism. "We're not going to let them make this a fight about a liberal against a conservative," Browder told a *New*

York Times reporter. "I'm a moderate conservative and he's so radical that he's completely off the table" (Apple 1989). Browder's more public positions on aid to the Nicaraguan contras, taxes, and gun control indicate that the moderate conservative label was appropriate. Yet, again, his positions on many of the issues were hard to discern.

The most important element of the strategy was to stake his claim as Bill Nichols's natural successor as the district's watchdog in Washington. As illustrated in the above statement, Browder did not want his positions on issues to interfere with this impression. Nichols's reputation in the district was extraordinary. In his twenty years of service, he had brought large amounts of federal money into the district. Browder and Rice both attempted to claim his legacy, but Browder made a better case for himself. Rice held that he and Nichols had an ideological kinship, and Rice's mentor, Governor Hunt, argued that Nichols "would have felt very comfortable in the Republican Party" (Yardley 1989c). Browder's reference to the late congressman was more practical. For one thing, the Anniston newspaper reported that Howell Heflin, one of the state's two Democratic senators, and other members of the state's Democratic delegation would work to open a spot on the Armed Services Committee for Browder (Yardley 1989g). Although there is some question as to how much influence Heflin had over committee assignments in the House, Rice did not challenge the Democrats on it.[11] Heflin's declaration was important not only because it came from a popular and respected state politician, but also because this committee assignment had enabled Nichols to do so much for the district.[12]

Browder also touted his efforts to reform education in the state. In 1985, he had spearheaded legislation to institute a merit-pay program for teachers, a program supported by the Alabama Education Association (AEA), the teachers' union. The key to their support was that Paul Hubbert, executive secretary of the organization, would be able to appoint a large number of members to the board that set criteria for the evaluation of teachers. The legislation passed, though one year later, when the AEA withdrew its support of the program, it died. Nonetheless, Browder pointed to it as evidence of his practical solution for educational problems in Alabama and even used an apple on his campaign signs to make a symbolic connection with the voters.[13]

Throughout the campaign, Browder was content to let Rice talk about national issues, so long as he was able to identify himself with local issues that involved pragmatic activity and service to the district. A national Democratic campaign consultant said, "The Republicans essentially wanted to play the presidential campaign over again. Let Rice talk about national issues. We want to talk about roads and bridges and military bases." And, he could have added, education. In a nutshell, Browder's strategy was to portray himself as reasonably conservative, to talk little about divisive issues, to paint Rice as extreme and unpredictable, and to portray himself as Bill Nichols's heir apparent.

John Rice's strategy was guided by his philosophical fervor, which was both a strength and a weakness in the campaign. Rice did stake a claim to being the only "true conservative" in the race. Browder, he argued, was a genuine believer in the liberal cause. In reality, the differences between the two candidates were not all that great, as evidenced by a survey of their voting records in the House.[14] But Rice did his best to make the most of these differences and, in his rhetoric, was unquestionably the more conservative candidate.

In making this comparison, he especially criticized Browder's education bill, arguing that it showed how the Democrat was "a creature of labor interests" and tied to liberal special interests like the teachers' union. At a press conference, with a sign mocking Browder's signature apple as "Teacher's Pet Brand," Rice charged that Browder's bill had cost Alabama taxpayers $1.4 billion (Smith 1989a). It was not clear where that figure came from, and later in the campaign, he modified this estimate and charged that Browder's "liberal boondoggle" had cost taxpayers $18 million (Smith 1989b).

Not all of Rice's conservative appeal was based on building a comparison with Browder. He articulated his conservative philosophy at every campaign appearance. Zealously attacking the federal government ("In

Washington, they create chaos and call it government"), labor unions, and national Democrats, Rice spent a lot of time pledging against raising taxes and talking about reducing the size and scope of the federal government. He often highlighted his zeal for the conservative cause by taking unbudging positions on the issues. On the minimum wage, Rice was not only averse to raising it, but philosophically opposed to the very concept of a federally imposed standard. He parted company with President Bush on gun control, rejecting a ban on foreign-made, semiautomatic assault weapons (Smith 1989e). And to illustrate his opposition to taxes, he publicly signed a Taxpayer Protection Pledge sponsored by Americans for Tax Reform. When the press asked if this meant that he would not vote for a tax hike even if it was supported by President Bush or was earmarked for reducing the national deficit, Rice responded, "No, period." There was some give-and-take between the candidates on the tax issue, as Rice had voted to raise taxes while in the state legislature. The Republican argued that he had cast these votes only to keep nursing homes open (Smith 1989c), but the questions of who voted to raise state taxes, how many such votes were cast, and how much money was brought in as a result of these votes dominated much of the campaign dialogue. "Neither one of [the candidates] should be proud of their record," said the head of an independent Alabama antitax group (Smith 1989b). Rice attempted to take an uncompromising position against taxes anyway.

In his desire to express his federalist vision, Rice said early in the campaign that he would like to see the federal budget cut by 50 percent and argued that the federal government should not be funding city and county projects. In part Rice simply had a strong preference for local decision making and in part he believed that too much of the money that flows to Washington does not flow back (Smith 1989b). Rice backpeddled on some of these stands and in fact denied calling for the 50 percent cut after Browder began attacking the idea while highlighting his own pork barrel potential (and noting that for every dollar Alabama sent to Washington, $1.38 came back). Still, Rice's comment was so well publicized that Browder was able to keep Rice tied to it. "If you didn't say it then I suggest you form a posse and find [the other] John Rice out there who thinks the federal government should be cut by 50 percent," said Browder at a candidate forum.

Another part of Rice's assault on the federal government was his advocacy of local control of schools. Federal aid to education, he said on more than one occasion, came "with too many strings attached." Local governments should take on more financial responsibility, even if it means higher local taxes, because of the burdens placed on the schools by the federal government. Because he never really identified the specific burdens placed upon local school districts by the federal government, his remarks were open to interpretation. The federal government's role in the desegregation of Alabama's schools was at least intimated in these remarks. When asked to be more specific about his position on busing to achieve desegregation, the Republican told a reporter, "I just don't agree that we need to spend so much time and effort trying to reach that" (Smith 1989e).

If Rice's conservative appeals were not overtly racial in the early stages of the campaign, this changed when his campaign started losing ground in polls and in fund-raising. At this point, the candidate introduced the Confederate flag into the campaign. The issue revolved around a controversy that went back to 1985, when both Rice and Browder were in the state legislature. When some black state legislators objected to a Confederate flag being present on the House floor, Rice voted to keep the flag up and Browder did not cast a vote. Rice charged that Browder "walked out the back door and refused to vote" (Yardley 1989e). To dramatize the issue, John Rice pulled a small Confederate flag from his pocket and waved it during his final statement in a televised debate. The issue, he said, was courage, the courage to take a stand. He repeated this claim in a mass mailing, one of three to go out near the end of the campaign.[15]

When editorialists and black leaders objected to this message, Rice's campaign officials denied that the flag was a racist issue. In a most telling exchange earlier in the campaign, a Rice official said that racial issues would not be a part of the campaign. Later in the same conversation, he said that the campaign was contemplating bringing up the flag issue.

When asked if this was a racial issue, he responded, "No. It's not a race issue. It's a heritage issue. It's only a racial issue to the blacks." Despite his interpretation, the issue was laden with racial overtones and, from the perspective of many people interested in the election, was patently an attempt to stimulate white backlash.

The televised debate marked a new stage in the election. Rice's campaign manager had calculated that the Republicans would need only 15 percent of the black vote to be the majority party in the district. Near the end of the campaign, Rice, way down in the polls, running out of campaign funds, and believing that the Republican party had forsaken him, apparently abandoned even that goal in his quest for white votes. In the Anniston newspaper, a Rice official spoke of "writing off" the black vote or at least the 85 percent of the black vote that "[walked] lockstep with Joe Reed [the executive director of the Alabama Democratic Conference, the major black political organization in the state]." The reason, he said, was that "[Reed] pays them to vote" (Smith 1989g). This inflammatory statement left little doubt as to Republican intentions. Political campaigns would not write off a large bloc of votes so publicly unless there was something to be gained from it. In this case, the vote-buying charge and the flag incident were part of a desperate last-minute effort to stimulate a white backlash against Browder.

Browder's response to the Confederate flag issue and the vote-buying charges was essentially not to respond. He did not answer Rice's taunt in the debate. And he did not make any comments about it to the press. He left that to others. His campaign manager made a statement to the press that the candidate was ill the day of the vote and had an excused absence (which was, in fact, the case). In the postdebate analysis, the executive director of the Alabama Democratic Party compared Rice to the recently elected former Klansman David Duke.

Browder's public silence was purposeful. As the congressman now recalls, "I was not going to let him engage me personally [on that issue]." Nonetheless, the Confederate flag issue was highlighted in his appeals to blacks, which were made through the black churches in the district, on black radio, and in direct mail that infiltrated the black community. In one leaflet, sent out at the very end of the campaign, the Democrats used a photograph of Rice holding the Confederate flag. That piece, blasting Rice for his position, contributed to a much stronger black turnout, according to the campaign's black turnout consultant. Rice's campaign essentially handed Browder a message to take into the black community.

The week before the election, Browder met a campaign supporter who predicted his victory. "I believe the Lord is going to see you through this," said the woman. "I hope so," answered Browder, "But ya'll help the Lord out." On election day, there was concern as to how much the Lord was on Browder's side for there was a remarkable discrepancy in the weather in different parts of the district. While a series of tornadoes touched down in the northern part (Browder's home base), the southern counties (Rice's—and Ford's—turf) were in sunshine. With electric power out in some parts of Browder's home of Calhoun County, the largest county in the district, and people warned to stay indoors, the Democrats started looking into filing a lawsuit nullifying the election. It was unnecessary as Browder won and won big.

In the end, Browder took 65 percent of the vote, winning the black vote overwhelmingly and, if a pre-election poll is any indication, winning the white vote as well. In the last poll of the election, Browder had a 46 to 38 percent advantage among white voters with 16 percent undecided (Rilling 1989). Moreover, black turnout equaled white turnout in this election, according to the national party consultant. This turned a Browder victory into a "rollover." The election, which at one time appeared to be promising for the Republicans, instead was the second embarrassment for the party in a week.

Browder's victory was a model for Democratic victory in the region. Just months after George Bush's great electoral success in Alabama, Browder's strategy and, perhaps more important, his counterstrategy led him to a major victory. The result was not lost on the Democratic presidential candidate Michael Dukakis, who called Browder with his congratulations shortly after the election. Browder recalls the conversation ending with Dukakis saying, "If I had used your playbook, I'd be calling you from a different location."

Republicans and Racially Conservative Messages

At some point in all of the cases studied in this book, a racial issue arose. These two cases best illustrate the dynamics of a campaign in which a racial issue became a major issue in the campaign and serve as ideal types in this analysis. Why did Republicans in these cases bring up these issues (and it was almost always the Republican candidate who did so) and how did they generally fashion their racial message? How did Democrats respond to these issues and blunt their effectiveness?

The temptation for Republicans to raise a racial issue is always there. This is particularly true in heavily black areas, places with histories of white backlash to the civil rights movement and places where blacks now wield electoral power. Mississippi's Fourth District, 42 percent black, Alabama's Third District, 29 percent black, and Virginia's 25 percent black Fifth District, the other case in which a racial issue was prominent in the campaign, all have long histories of racial strife and racial politics. Racially conservative messages are often designed to appeal to disaffected white Democrats because Republicans and their staffs believe that there is political mileage in them. They believe that by adding white backlash votes to their loyal Republican core of voters, they can win a majority in the district.

The Republican candidates in these two cases introduced explicit racial issues into the campaigns after assessing the racial composition of the district and adding up their supporters. Liles Williams's district in Mississippi, as noted, was 42 percent black. Assuming that Dowdy would win almost all of the black vote in the runoff, and even assuming that whites would turn out in greater numbers than blacks, Williams would have to win the great preponderance (about three-quarters) of the white vote. The Voting Rights Act Extension issue had already been introduced into the campaign in the preliminary round. All the candidates except Dowdy opposed extension of the act and together polled 75 percent of the vote. Given the arithmetic of the situation, it made great sense for Williams to highlight the voting rights issue in his general election campaign.

The major play given the issue by the Jackson papers seemed to reinforce this strategy. In its editorial endorsing Williams, the Sunday edition (produced by both the morning and afternoon papers) went on at great length about the issue (*Jackson Daily News and Clarion-Ledger* 1981). In fact, more than half the editorial was devoted to an endorsement of Williams's position on the issue. Williams's campaign put out other messages, to be sure, but his opposition to the Voting Rights Act Extension was highlighted in all of his appearances and in many of his campaign advertisements. "The Voting Rights Act was the main issue of the campaign," said Wayne Dowdy. "At least, of [Williams's] campaign."

John Rice did not bring the Confederate flag issue into his campaign until the last two weeks of the campaign, though his managers were holding it in reserve in the weeks prior to the election. The issue came out near the end for several reasons. Rice's campaign started to suffer financially toward the middle of the campaign. It was unable to advertise on television during the final two weeks. With every slip in the polls, the Republican's money dried up more, and Rice lost even some national party help.[16] Rice's campaign manager had calculated that his candidate needed to win more than 65 percent of the white vote and planned his strategy accordingly. The problems faced by the campaign near the end, however, necessitated a dramatic move. The campaign needed exposure, and it was apparent that Rice's themes were not working. When the last poll of the election showed Browder to be well ahead, even among whites, Rice made some outlandish charges. He charged Browder with being a draft dodger (the Democrat was rejected by the military because of a congenital back condition) and, worse, with "teaching against the Vietnam War" in his classes. Neither charge received much attention, at least in the newspapers. At this point, Rice began waving the Confederate flag issue. Browder's campaign manager said, "He talked about it everywhere, had a very nasty piece of literature on it, just was banging away at it." The televised debate allowed him to make the point to an even larger audience. And by waiting until the closing statement, he also kept Browder from responding, should the Democrat have been so inclined. In the newspaper reports of the debate, the Rice campaign added that the Democrats were buying black votes. The racial issues injected into the campaign were more than attempts to lure white voters: they were last-ditch efforts to save the foundering campaign. The Rice campaign had planned to use these issues in the mail (which they did), but the course of the campaign required them to use it on television and in the papers.

The Republicans used racial issues because they saw them as a way of appealing to voters across ideological and party lines. When Rice's campaign manager called the flag issue a heritage issue instead of a race issue, his reasoning was that the heritage issue was one that appealed to people of many different political perspectives. Pride in the South, a sense of southernness, he claimed, were not liberal or conservative sentiments: "People are proud of the flag around here. They put 'em up in their offices. You see 'em all over the place. Even Dukakis' campaign manager had one up in his office. He's our Calhoun County director now. Man, he's constantly complaining about some of Rice's right-wing stands. But he's with us on this one." From the perspective of Rice's campaign manager, the issue had the potential to supersede other issues. Moreover, it would do so with a group of voters that both sides vie for in Deep South elections. Rural votes, in the view of many of the participants, are normally Democratic but can be lured over to the Republicans with racial issues. The Democrats agreed. "They [the Rice campaign] thought they were going to ride the [flag] issue," said a Browder campaign official. "And they could have. No doubt about it, the issue does have relevance down here, but it's mainly to the white, rural male in the district."

If Republicans have been trying to appeal to white voters like the southern Democrats of old, their message, in fact, has been quite different. How Republicans have characterized their campaign message is of great interest because it illustrates what has changed and what has stayed the same in southern politics. For the most part, southern Republicans have recognized that outright racist appeals are no longer socially acceptable. Republican campaign managers vigorously deny that they are trying to appeal to racist attitudes with their campaign tactics, and candidates take great offense when they or their tactics are labeled by others as racist. Their messages are tailored to white audiences, to be sure, but they are substantially different from the campaign messages of the old-time southern Democratic demagogues. Their message on race, they claim, is conservative, not racist.

Political observers argue that the Republican message on race is relatively new. Carmines and Stimson (1989) discuss the evolution of racial issues in the period immediately preceding the civil rights movement and the years since. Racial conservatism, they argue, is not equivalent to racism. Rather, it is "a new species, originating as a minor adaptation . . . from generalized conservatism" (190).[17] If a racist issue is one characterized by antipathy toward blacks (or black antipathy toward whites), a racially conservative issue is one based upon conservatism. A racially conservative issue may have political appeal because of widespread antipathy toward blacks, but this does not have to be the case. Whatever the intent, southern Republicans have articulated their positions on these issues in terms of individualism or distrust of the federal government or some other conservative principle.

In the elections described in this book, Republican candidates consistently raised racially conservative issues, that is, racial issues expressed in conservative terms. Most often, the Republican racial issue paralleled other campaign appeals to "get the government off our backs." In the Virginia election described below (see chapter 4), the Republican Linda Arey campaigned against a civil rights bill, calling it "an unprecedented intrusion on our private lives." Her campaign commercials highlighted her opposition to "Grove City, the *Civil Rights Restoration Act*" (emphasis added), while her opponent "favored more federal interference in our lives" (Baker 1988). Her rhetoric is interesting, first, because she used the issue to attack the federal government, a long-standing tradition in southern Virginia and one upon which many political careers have been based. Second, though she could just as easily have avoided calling the Grove City bill by its formal name, Civil Rights Restoration, she chose to use it. This allowed her to raise the racial issue in people's minds without talking about what the bill would do or how it would affect blacks and whites, indeed without even uttering the words *black* and *white*. As she shaped the issue in a thirty-second campaign spot, the choice was avoiding federal interference "in our private lives" or restoring civil rights, not much of a choice in southern Virginia.

John Rice's complaint that federal money for education came with too many strings attached also had racial connotations. Rice was playing upon sentiment against the federal government on the issue of school desegregation (and also school prayer). "We don't need the federal government telling us how to run our local affairs," said Rice at a debate. "We need to run our own affairs to support our schools financially and with our prayers." Rice's comment had two elements to it. He was attacking federal intrusion into local affairs—decisions he felt were best made at the local level. And he was making a none-too-subtle reference to one of the earliest and most volatile racial issues of the civil rights era. The issue of school desegregation is still quite touchy. In both Alabama and Mississippi, I often was told by Republican campaign workers that school integration had ruined the educational system for whites. Desegregation had brought violence, racial disharmony, and lower standards to the schools. Rice's "too many strings attached" message addressed these sentiments.

Rice also spoke of abuses in federal housing programs, another attempt to link federal government activity and race. Federal housing programs were good when they were taken advantage of "by little old ladies who kept nice gardens," said Rice at a candidate forum. They now have become "a real tragedy" and are fraught with abuses. In making these comments, the candidate was not explicitly talking about blacks and was explicitly attacking the federal government. But it was not the federal programs that were the problem, it was the people they were directed toward. In this case, such people include an inordinate number of blacks. What is different about present-day southern politics is that Rice did not say this.

In addition to these racially conservative appeals, Republicans made racial appeals in the name of fairness—fairness to whites, fairness to southerners, fairness to Republicans. Behind Rice's Confederate flag waving was the contention that whites are having to give something up to support black civil rights gains. Whether that be their heritage or the quality of their educational system, this is the sentiment that Rice attempted to tap.[18] One Rice campaign aide, a former Democratic county chairman and a college-educated mother, tried to articulate this position: "Nothing against the black folks from around here. They're a genteel people on the whole. But when you bring some folks up, when you try to equalize them, you've got to bring other folks down. And we're tired of being brought down." She was not necessarily talking about helping blacks economically, though that was part of it. Rather, she was expressing an ill-defined resentment of blacks, a belief that black economic, social, and political gains are made at the expense of whites. The Republicans believe (and may well be right) that this sentiment is widespread in the South, and they attempt to take advantage of it.

Liles Williams's opposition (and the opposition of the *Jackson Clarion-Ledger*) to extending the Voting Rights Act was framed as an issue of fairness—the fairness of singling out the South in dealing with these voting rights issues. Stating that the South had made so much progress in the area of voting rights and noting that other areas of the country also had severe problems, Williams argued that to extend the act was to *punish* the South for its past misdeeds—misdeeds that had been acknowledged and addressed. He was not arguing to take away black voting rights or to "turn back the clock," but his position was certainly unsympathetic to blacks for it called for the abolition of an important vehicle for black political progress. Although not advocating the reversal of civil rights gains for blacks, his stance was clearly an appeal to conservative whites in the district who had this in mind.

Republicans have complained about fairness in the electoral process too. Their complaints have often taken the form of charges that the Democrats are paying blacks to vote or that other illegal activities are taking place. When John Rice's campaign manager was quoted in the newspapers to the effect that the campaign was writing off the black vote because the Alabama Democratic Conference paid blacks to vote, it was part of a two-part strategy to generate a white backlash (the other part being the Confederate flag issue).

Republicans have been slowly adjusting to competitive politics in the South. Not only are they starting to field better, more qualified candidates, but they are testing various political strategies and continuing to refashion their message. Looking at the arithmetic of winning a congressional campaign in the South, Republicans have continued to rely heavily on racial issues. Not every Republican campaign is as racial as the ones described above, but some racial appeals seem to arise in nearly every election. This at least was the case in all of the elections studied here. There are problems with raising these issues, however. If they have solidified some white votes, they also have helped Democratic candidates win black votes.

How Racial Issues Help Democratic Candidates

Contrary to what one might expect, Republican candidates have often helped their Democratic opponents by raising racial issues. Democrats have been able to turn the issue to their advantage. Given how these issues play out in the campaign and given how Democrats communicate with black constituents, it is not surprising that this has been the case.

Democrats recognize how important the black vote is to their electoral prospects. But they have the difficult task as well of keeping white voters in the fold. As a result of these sometimes contradictory goals, Democrats generally do not respond with much vigor or volume to racial issues raised by their Republican opponents. They state their position, which is the racially liberal position, but they do so cautiously and softly, and they do not elaborate much. Wayne Dowdy's public response to the Voting Rights Act Extension issue, for instance, was clear but subdued. He announced his support for the measure but said little else, at least publicly or in the media. Sometimes it is not even worth it for Democrats to counter Republican charges. Glen Browder, in the Alabama race, never responded to John Rice's Confederate flag waving. "He didn't want to touch that one," said his campaign manager.

With regard to racial issues, Democratic candidates have walked a tightrope, but they seem to be good at it. If they choose to talk about racial issues in public, they do so in measured tones and in few words. They have little to gain by articulating racially liberal positions in the press or in a debate. They have much to lose. And they are willing to test white support only so far. Most Democrats figure that they benefit when the salience of a racial issue is not raised further. A restrained, brief statement of their position on the issue is all that is necessary and need not antagonize white voters sympathetic to Democrats. None of the white Democratic candidates discussed in this book would be mistaken for a champion of black issues by their public support of such issues. This is mostly because of *how* they have made their stand. Some white voters may support the Republican on the basis of the Democratic position on racial issues, but as the Democratic candidate has not vociferously and self-righteously asserted these positions, there is less of a danger that white voters will identify the Democrat as the so-called candidate of the blacks.

Emphatic public statements on racial issues are not necessary to court black votes in the South. Democrats have fared well by comparison to their Republican opponents *and* to their Democratic predecessors. At least from the perspective of the candidates, black expectations of white Democrats have not been very high and have been easily met. The Virginia Democrat L. F. Payne, for example, believed that it would take very little to generate black support in his district. Payne benefited from being compared not only to his opponent, but also to his predecessor, characterized by one Democratic activist as a "Byrd Democrat of massive resistance and a racist" (Bland 1988a). The result, according to Payne, was that blacks made no demands upon him to come out stronger on the issues raised by Linda Arey. Payne and his Democratic colleagues appeared sympathetic to blacks in sheer contrast to those who had come before and to what the alternative would be.

Black Democratic leaders appear to understand the constraints that white Democrats work under. They do not require white Democrats to take bold stands on racial issues to win their support so long as their overall record on issues of interest to minorities is good. In the context of a discussion about the Confederate flag, the field director of the Alabama Democratic Conference told me that he did not care that Browder did not respond strongly to Rice: "We would not make that issue the litmus test for our support. It's a political issue that most [white Democrats], even liberals and moderates, couldn't touch."

In spite of Democratic reluctance to champion racial issues in debates and in the press, Democrats do make strong pitches for the black vote. The Democratic position is perhaps best summed up by a black turnout specialist of the Democratic Congressional Campaign Committee, who said, "You've got to approach the black vote surgically, because the white vote in many of these places is so volatile. So you don't talk much about it [racial issues] in front of white audiences and you really drive it home in front of black audiences." Much to the advantage of Democrats, blacks can be approached "surgically." Although the South has desegregated, patterns of association there, as in the North, are still separate. Because of these patterns of association, a politician seeking to communicate with black voters can do so easily. Most important, he can reach black voters without having white voters hear his message.

The major channel to the black community has been through black opinion leaders who give the white Democrat credibility with blacks. White candidates generally have not had deep ties to the black community. The blacks they have known are those with whom they have worked in the state legislature or in party politics prior to their candidacy. These politicians provide the candidate with access to black voters. They serve as liaisons to the community and line up ministers, businessmen, shop stewards, and other black opinion leaders who, in turn, carry the Democrat's message to the black masses. Johnny Ford gave Glen Browder access to and legitimacy with black voters. A black member on the staff of the Virginia Democrat L. F. Payne escorted him to black churches and black functions. And a black state legislator from Gulfport served as a facilitator for Gene Taylor, the Democratic candidate from Mississippi's Fifth District, becoming, as another black leader put it, "Taylor's man."

With the help of these black elites, white candidates can reach black voters through a number of sources. The black pulpit has been used for several decades to reach black voters. Ministers carry great prestige in most southern black communities. When black ministers from around the district speak on a candidate's behalf, introduce him or her to their congregations, and remind their flock two days before the election to go to the polls, that candidate has a powerful advantage. When black ministers charge their parishioners, as one Jackson preacher did in 1981, with the "Christian duty" of voting for the Democratic candidate because "segregationists and racists are planning to turn back the clock" (Clymer 1981b), the message is all the more convincing. What is more, blacks who attend church are much more likely to vote than those who do not, particularly in the South. In presidential elections in the 1980s, 60 percent of southern blacks who attended church every week voted (n=97). Of those who did not attend church or who attended infrequently, only 17 percent voted (n=70).[19] Working through the black churches is all the more effective because it has allowed southern Democrats not only to reach blacks, but to reach those blacks most likely to go to the polls.

Blacks also can be reached via black media. Black newspapers offer opportunities to advertise, but an even more important channel is "narrowcasting" on black radio. Black radio is an effective medium for Democrats as it is much less expensive than television and reaches a well-defined group of people.[20] Moreover, said a Virginia media consultant, "You can hit a lot harder on radio because the other side has more difficulty keeping track of what you are saying."

Black radio was used in every one of the Democratic campaigns examined here. And, as noted above, the Republican's conservative stand on a racial issue often supplied the material used in the commercials. White Democrats were able to use the Republican's position and, in the words of a Washington political consultant, "incite people." Democratic campaign managers described their typical radio message in highly graphic terms. Said one, "[The Republican candidate] thinks niggers should be out in the field picking cotton. They don't want you to go to the polls." And another, "If you don't vote, the Republicans will think you're dumb. Don't let them take your right to vote away." These are paraphrases (by the managers themselves) of previous Democratic advertisements on black radio and illustrate how strong the message can be.

By appealing to blacks through these channels—black leaders, the black church, black media, and of course, direct mail—white Democratic candidates have appealed to blacks surgically. Whites do not attend black churches. They do not listen to or read black media. Residential segregation makes direct mail into black precincts viable. Whites simply do not hear the Democratic message directed toward blacks.

What is more, two other important sets of actors in the campaign—the media and the Republicans—do not pick up the message. The nature of campaign coverage in the general media (radio, television, and newspapers reaching a general public) has allowed Democratic candidates to run these segregated campaigns. The way congressional campaigns, even special election campaigns, are covered, the Democratic candidate has frequently been able to pursue a two-pronged strategy, one aimed toward whites (see chapter 4), the other toward blacks. First, newspapers in small cities like Greenwood and Biloxi, Mississippi, and Anniston, Alabama, generally are staffed by young, inexperienced reporters. Some are not reporters by training and are not interested in making journalism a career. Although they are intelligent and enthusiastic recent college graduates, their understanding of politics and campaigns is often limited. Few of them have much background in politics. As one reporter told me, the campaign was "a lot of fun after working on the court beat for the past year. But I don't really know very much about politics." His questions at a press conference confirmed this admission. It is difficult even for the best reporters to cover much more than the surface of any story, and those without much understanding of the topic generally do not.

Second, reporters (experienced as well as inexperienced) cover the big events of the campaign—the press conferences, the debates, the speeches, the visits by state and national dignitaries. Their coverage of candidates in the day-to-day campaign is limited. For one thing, little of the handshaking and baby kissing is newsworthy. Reporters do not have the time to cover these events, and their column inches already are filled with coverage of lively debates and press conferences. For another, even if reporters wanted to cover these types of events, they must depend upon campaign managers to tell them where the candidate will be on a certain day at a certain time. And campaign managers, even when they know where the candidate is scheduled to be (which is not always the case), do not necessarily wish for reporters to know. Thus while many important events and issue positions and controversies are recorded in local newspapers, reporters cover only a portion of the campaign.[21] Part of what does not get reported is a Democratic candidate's visit to a black church or other campaign activity in the black community.

If Democrats can count on the media not to cover their forays into the black community, they are less sure that Republicans will not catch wind of what they are saying in the black community. If Republicans do hear of Democratic charges, as in the Jackson, Mississippi, race, they respond angrily. Even in that case, however, when Williams's campaign manager accused Wayne Dowdy of being "one of the greatest race baiters elected to office in Mississippi in the last 20 or 30 years" (Treyens 1981a), it was too late. It was only after the election that Republicans became aware of inflammatory Democratic radio advertisements. As a precaution against Republican exploitation of these appeals and because limited funds almost always necessitate the saving of their media campaigns for the closing week of the campaign, Democrats (and Republicans too for that matter) save their most hard-hitting charges for the end of the campaign. Opponents thus have a limited time to respond to such advertisements, even if they do find out about them, which is not guaranteed. The last frenzied days of the campaign leave little time for monitoring radio stations in the district and coming up with a response. Keeping track of the logistics of one's own candidate is difficult enough. Keeping track of one's opponent's activities is beyond the capability of most campaign organizations. This has made Democratic tactics with regard to the black community all the more effective.[22]

In the final analysis, Republican attempts to win white votes with racial issues—a message that no doubt works with some voters—can be costly. Democrats can easily turn the issue against them in the black community, thereby bolstering black turnout. What is more, they can do so *without whites hearing their message.* "Race baiting is a classic error," said one Texas Democratic consultant. "If the Republicans can appeal to prejudice without being called a bigot, then it works. But it's so easy to create a backlash."

Republican racial issues have given Democratic candidates a platform in the black community. White Democrats do not often have much experience approaching black voters. Although they have alliances with black leaders, state legislators, and other politicians they have dealt with in their careers, white Democratic candidates and their campaign staffs often do not have informal connections to the black community. They are unlikely to have spent much time prior to the campaign in black neighborhoods, black churches, or black stores. They are not likely to socialize with blacks. On several occasions, I was told that a white candidate was not comfortable in front of all-black audiences. A racial issue introduced into the campaign gives the white Democratic candidate a reason to be in front of blacks appealing for their votes and makes the situation much more comfortable.

White Democratic candidates have needed something to generate enthusiasm among blacks. Southern blacks are neither necessarily quick to warm to white Democrats, nor do they appear to connect deeply with white candidates. Black Democratic leadership may support a white Democrat, even with good reason, but such backing does not automatically translate into an enthusiastic response from rank-and-file black voters. In the Alabama race, for instance, Glen Browder's support of black voter registration activity when he was secretary of state generated some good will among the top guard of the Alabama Democratic Conference. They wholeheartedly supported him in his congressional campaign once Johnny Ford had been eliminated. But Browder still required something to enable him to connect with the average black voter in the district. John Rice's Confederate flag gave Browder something to advertise in the black community.

It is difficult to assess exactly how many votes are won and lost through racial issues. No doubt the number varies from election to election. That all the cases here illustrate Democratic success is some indication that such issues work to the advantage of Democrats. Southern Democrats win by constructing a tricky biracial coalition, a coalition that is still possible in much of the region when they successfully finesse racial issues.

4 Courting White Voters

THE STORY UP TO THIS POINT has been about how southern Republican congressional candidates try to attract large shares of the white vote, how Democrats try to maximize the black vote, and how these two strategies are related. The margin of victory, however, comes from neither the black vote nor the white Republican vote. The difference between winning and losing turns on white votes, traditionally Democratic whites who could go either way and more often than not have gone the Republican way in presidential elections.

If Democrats are to win white votes in the South, they must do more than simply downplay their positions on racial issues. And they cannot simply hope that white Democrats will automatically vote their party label. They must give whites a reason to vote for them. Democrats do not need to win a majority of the white vote to win elections in the South (see chapter 2), but they must be able to attract a significant minority of the white vote to succeed.

The three cases to follow, one in East Texas, one in southern Virginia, and one in southern Mississippi, illustrate some prototypical southern campaigns, both Democratic and Republican. On the Republican side, the candidates have Washington connections and try to make the most of them. They put forth extremely conservative positions and charge their opponents with being liberals or with associating with liberals, which is almost as bad. On the Democratic side are three candidates who deemphasize ideology and party ties and highlight what they can do for the people of the district. The result is a campaign that pits "national Republicans" against "local Democrats." And in each case, it is the local Democrat who wins.

Texas 1— "Tora! Tora! Tora!"

In the South, a yellow dog Democrat is one who would vote for a yellow dog before voting for a Republican. That the term is used as a compliment tells much about the power of an old attachment in the face of new and powerful political forces. It is an attachment that has allowed the Democratic party to control places like East Texas since Reconstruction. From 1870 to 1985, the year of the special election studied here, Democrats represented Texas's First District.[1] From 1928 to 1985, in fact, only two congressmen served the district: the populist Wright Patman held the seat for nearly fifty years, and the conservative Sam Hall for almost ten.

But many believed that the time had come for a Republican to represent what the columnists Rowland Evans and Robert Novak (1985) called a "congenitally Democratic" district. By the mid-1980s, Republicans were winning large majorities of district votes in presidential, senatorial, and gubernatorial elections. The district went overwhelmingly for the southerner Jimmy Carter in 1976, but Ronald Reagan beat Carter by about one thousand votes in 1980 and trounced Walter Mondale in 1984. Phil Gramm dominated the district in his Senate election in 1984, and Bill Clements won there in the gubernatorial election of 1986 (calculated from Scammon and McGillivray 1986).

At the time of the election in 1985, however, Republicans had yet to win any low-level positions in the district. Democrats controlled every single courthouse in the district's twenty counties (Attlesey 1985g), and every local officeholder with a partisan identification was a Democrat (King 1985a). It is difficult to know just how large the Democratic advantage in the district actually was because the state does not register voters by party and because it is difficult to get public opinion data in an area with no major media outlets. One guess comes from a Republican pollster familiar with the area who estimated that Democrats had a ten-point advantage (Attlesey 1985d). Whatever the exact figure, self-identified Democrats outnumbered Republicans in East Texas in the mid-1980s.

Given its demographics, it is not surprising that politics in the First look so much like politics in other parts of the South. The First is actually more like neighboring Louisiana and Arkansas in character and population than it is like the rest of Texas. It is one of the poorest districts in the state and has a large population of blacks (20 percent) and few Hispanics. It has several small cities of about thirty thousand (Texarkana, Paris, and Marshall) but is mostly small town and rural. More than one-third of its voters are over the age of sixty-five (King 1985c), making it the district with the oldest population in the state.

These features have led many to identify it as a prototypical southern rural district. That and its reputation as a tenacious Democratic stronghold led confident Republicans to attempt to invest this election with a lot of meaning. Though only one seat in the House, if won it would be, they claimed, a highly symbolic bite out of the once Solid South. If this district were to fall, few others in the region could be considered safely Democratic. Yet the election meant even more. The Republicans argued that the contest would be a demonstration, that it would initiate an eastward domino effect, in which other southern districts would finally fall out of Democratic control. They, of course, were hoping that such an interpretation would bring others—voters, donors, prospective candidates—to the same conclusion, fulfilling their prophecy. "If the Republicans can win in that district," said the chairman of the state Republican party, "it is Armageddon for the Democrats in Texas" (Attlesey 1985e). National Republicans too saw this as a wonderful opportunity and put out a similar message.[2]

The opportunity was created by the Republicans in the first place. Senator Phil Gramm, himself a former Democrat, engineered the circumstances that led to the vacating of the seat when he recommended the incumbent congressman, Sam Hall, for an open federal judgeship in Texas.[3] After Hall accepted the offer, Gramm set out to recruit a Republican candidate to replace him. His first choice, Ed Howard, a popular Democratic state senator from Texarkana, could not be persuaded to switch parties and turned him down (King 1985a). Gramm then approached Edd Hargett, a rancher and a former star quarterback with Texas A&M, the Houston Oilers, and the New Orleans Saints. Hargett, having positive name recognition in the district and a ready-made network of Texas A&M alumni, was a potentially attractive candidate.[4] And though he had not held public office before, indeed because of his lack of experience he had few if any negatives going into the campaign. Hargett took up the offer.

In addition to recruiting a quality candidate, Phil Gramm encouraged other Republicans to stay out of the race. This gave Hargett a shot at winning a majority of the vote in the nonpartisan primary, thus avoiding a runoff between the top two vote-getters. In a low turnout election with a divided Democratic field, this was considered well within the realm of the possible. Gramm assured Hargett a steady supply of funding. By the time of the primary, Hargett—and Gramm—had raised almost half a million dollars (King 1985a) and spent three-quarters of a million dollars (Attlesey 1985b). By the general election, Hargett had spent one and a half million dollars (King 1985d), three times more than his opponent (Nelson 1985), and certainly more than one would expect of a first-time candidate running in a cheap media market.[5] In fact, the flow of money into Hargett's campaign compelled Democrats to charge that the Republicans were trying to buy the election. House Speaker Jim Wright decried the "outsider-funded, Madison Avenue advertising campaign" and said it was "lamentable [that Republicans] think you can buy a congressional seat just like you buy a seat on the New York Stock Exchange" (Attlesey 1985a). Finally, Gramm hired major Republican strategists—the political consultant Lee Atwater, the pollster Lance Tarrance, and the media consultant Roger Ailes—to run the campaign. In short, he was putting a fair amount of prestige and political capital at stake. A Republican victory in the First District, according to one newspaper account, "[became] a personal crusade [for Gramm], an effort to establish himself as a GOP kingmaker and unquestioned leader of the state's Republican Party" (Attlesey 1985h).

Gramm's machinations notwithstanding, Hargett did not win the majority necessary to avoid a runoff. In winning 42 percent of the vote, however, he was far ahead of his nearest competitor, the Democrat Jim Chapman, a former district attorney from one of the western counties in the district. Chapman was the only candidate from this part of the district, which likely helped him win 30 percent of the primary vote (Attlesey 1985c). A member of an old political family in the area (going back five generations), Chapman was fairly well known to East Texans. Moreover, he had used his tenure as district attorney to establish some fine conservative credentials. In that position, Chapman claimed a 99 percent conviction rate in more than two thousand felony cases (Attlesey 1985i). With characteristic Texas bravado, he boasted that he made Dallas District Attorney Henry Wade, famous for his twelve-hundred-year sentences, "look like a sissy" (Barone 1985). If Chapman had any liability going into the congressional contest, it was that he had angered some important Democrats in an unsuccessful challenge to a popular state senator, the same Ed Howard whom Phil Gramm had tried to coax into joining the race.[6] Nevertheless, Chapman appeared to be a strong candidate, at least in part of the district, going into the runoff.

Both candidates were cautious in talking about their parties. Hargett tied himself to President Reagan as much as possible, and the president made two commercials for the campaign. The candidate also brought to the district several big-name national Republicans, including Vice President Bush, Congressman Jack Kemp, and Treasury Secretary James

Baker. But Hargett's campaign literature and commercials *never* mentioned his Republican affiliation, and he rarely brought it up in campaign appearances (Attlesey 1985g). In fact, many of his campaign appearances ended in a Texas A&M "yell practice," prompting the Democratic governor, Mark White, to comment that "[Hargett is] running as an Aggie and I don't blame him. That's far more popular than being a Republican" (Hillman 1985).[7] When party label was brought up by the Republicans (in a party-sponsored commercial featuring the former Democratic congressman Kent Hance), it was to urge Democrats to "bite the bullet" and support Hargett because "the national Democratic Party is not the one we grew up with" (Attlesey 1985f). Hargett himself acknowledged that his party label was somewhat of a problem. He qualified his remarks by saying that he had encountered little hostility while out campaigning ("Except for one time when I was thrown out of a factory because I was a Republican. And that fellow may just have been mad about the economy"). Yet, as he recalled it, "There were a lot of people who were friends of mine, not bosom buddies or anything, but friends, who wouldn't vote for me because I was a Republican."

Chapman, too, was careful in talking about his Democratic affiliation. He thus took great pains to distance himself from the national party leaders. "I'm a conservative," Chapman would say. "I'm not tied to any one party" (Attlesey 1985e). In a debate with Hargett, he declined even to say how he had voted for president in 1984 (Evans and Novak 1985). Given the Democratic advantage in partisan affiliation in the district, however, Chapman was careful not to totally reject his affiliation. In striking a balance, Chapman referred to himself as a "conservative Democrat," not a "national Democrat."

Hargett's central campaign strategy was to tie Chapman to the national Democrats, to label him as a liberal, and to establish himself as the conservative standard-bearer. He first claimed that Chapman, as a Democrat, could be expected to support liberals and liberal positions on such issues as gun control and affirmative action for homosexuals. In raising the homosexual issue, Hargett was taking a page from the campaigns of several other Texas Republicans who had effectively used homosexuals as a rhetorical target.[8] In his Senate race the year before, for instance, Phil Gramm took his opponent to task for accepting a campaign donation that was collected at a gay male strip joint (Barone and Ujifusa 1987, 1133).

Chapman also was beholden to big labor and eastern bosses, argued Hargett, the hard evidence being pro-Chapman "Dear Brothers and Sisters" letters from local AFL-CIO Central Labor Councils and the United Auto Workers. When Chapman denied that he was too close to labor and claimed that he had informed the unions that he did not want their endorsements (though he had no objection to donations), Hargett attacked him again. A Roger Ailes commercial in the last week of the campaign excoriated Chapman for not acknowledging his relation to big labor (Evans and Novak 1985).[9]

Hargett worked hard to distinguish himself from Chapman, which was difficult because the Democrat was so vocally conservative. He basically attempted to paint himself as the more doctrinaire conservative and as the candidate who would not be obligated to Tip O'Neill. Such standard conservative issues as gun control and family values and standard conservative rhetoric were central to his campaign. And he aimed to damage Chapman's conservative credentials.

Indeed, Chapman's first goal was to deflect Hargett's liberal charges. He made bold declarations against gun control and abortion. He spoke in favor of a balanced budget amendment. He advocated prayer in schools. Yet Chapman was on the defensive when discussing conservative issues and sought to steer the campaign toward other issues. "We had to bash Tip. We had to come out right away on a constitutional amendment on prayer in school," said a Democratic consultant. "Then we could get on with it."

As they did. In spite of Hargett's financial advantage, the Chapman forces controlled the agenda. The Democrat's initial strategy appeared to be to capitalize upon Hargett's lack of experience. Hargett, according to a Democratic radio ad, was hand selected by Republican power brokers at "a secret meeting" and then sent to "charm school" to learn his lines: "Presto, an instant Congressman" (King 1985c). It was more than just the process that was being referred to here. The theme developed as Chapman's campaign team noticed that at Republican events, Senator Gramm would often take the microphone to answer questions directed at Hargett. In the words of Chapman, it all played into the notion that "the Republicans are trying to wow you with glitz and poor ol' Edd doesn't know what he's doing."

It was not just Hargett's inexperience that was the issue. The nature of his candidacy, argued the Democrats, compromised his independence. Anticipating this line of attack, Hargett responded to the inexperience charge by arguing that there were too many lawyers in Washington as it was. As for his independence, Hargett argued that he would not be "a rubber stamp for anyone. . . . I'll vote for President Reagan when he's right for East Texas and I'll vote against him when he is wrong for East Texas" (King 1985c).

Hargett was not as prepared to counter Chapman's two other campaign issues. The most widely discussed issues in the campaign and in press reports about the campaign were Social Security and foreign trade, both initiated by the Democrat. Given the large number of senior citizens in East Texas, Chapman, as early as the primary campaign, tried to capitalize on the Social Security issue and campaigned aggressively against a proposal to freeze Social Security cost-of-living adjustments that had passed the Republican-controlled Senate with the blessing of the Reagan administration. After the primary on June 29 and throughout the general campaign, Chapman continued arguing that the Republicans posed a threat to senior citizens, this despite the fact that the administration and Senate Republicans, under pressure from House Democrats, abandoned the freeze by mid-July, two weeks before the general election. Rep. Claude Pepper, the elderly representative wholly associated and identified with the issue, campaigned with Chapman in the district, and senior citizens were sent a letter from Pepper endorsing Chapman as the man "[who would] help us protect Social Security from the Republican onslaught" (King 1985c). A victory by Hargett would be a "terrible blow" to Social Security, warned Pepper. The message had two purposes. First, it linked

Hargett to the wrong side of the Social Security issue. Second, it linked him to the Republican party, an association that might be offensive to older Democrats.

Hargett's campaign responded to the Social Security issue in a television advertisement, a variation of an advertisement that Republicans frequently have used to defuse the issue. In this advertisement, an elderly woman shucking peas turns to the camera and chastises Chapman for trying to scare old voters with false information. "Shame on you, Jim Chapman," she scolds, all the while waving a pea pod at the camera. In another commercial, Hargett charges Chapman with distributing a campaign pamphlet on the Social Security issue that looked like an official government document. The countercharge that Chapman was not playing fair on the issue was clever, but it was a defensive response, an indication that the campaign was being waged on Chapman's turf.

The major issue in the Chapman campaign, however, was trade policy. With the oil and gas economy in shambles and a district steel plant in trouble, Chapman wanted to talk about jobs. What was most clever about his discussion was the scapegoat he found for the unemployment problem. Noting the recent layoffs at the steel plant, Chapman campaigned vigorously against the unfair trade policies of the Japanese on steel, as well as the unfair policies of other countries. "Korean steel, Canadian lumber, Argentinean dairy imports, Saudi oil and gas, Italian textiles. Right down the list, you name the industry, you name the country, we're getting our lunch eaten by subsidized foreign imports," said Chapman on the campaign trail as he called on the "greatest country in the free world" to reverse its "unilateral disarmament" on trade (Taylor 1985c). And he made the effective connection to the district. "[When American markets are] flooded with foreign goods that aren't made by Americans, it costs Americans their jobs," Chapman said, pointing out that the district's unemployment rate had increased 31 percent in the previous year (Attlesey 1985e).

This Democratic message got a big boost when a Texarkana newspaper quoted Hargett as saying, "I don't know what trade policies have to do with bringing jobs to East Texas" (King 1985c). Chapman chided

Hargett for this comment throughout the remainder of the contest and featured it in television and radio advertising that ran frequently in the closing weeks of the campaign.[10] Hargett, a self-described free trader, tried to control the damage by declaring that he knew how bad the steel plant closing was because his brothers had lost their jobs there. But again he was on the defensive. The newspapers were covering these exchanges instead of those initiated by Hargett. When Chapman gleefully pointed out that Hargett's campaign hats were made in Taiwan, the Republican's problem on the issue only got worse. There was little Hargett could do to counter this revelation. Chapman's campaign managers felt that this was the turning point of the campaign, which one called a " 'Tora! Tora! Tora!' campaign" against "Japanese imperialism."[11]

Of all the races described in this book, racial issues played the least important role in this one. Chapman's campaign aggressively pursued the black vote, bringing in numerous black campaign operatives from Austin to canvass black precincts and working the black churches. It advertised extensively on black radio stations. Chapman's advertisements attempted to portray Hargett as a stiff opponent of civil rights, but the charges had little effect because Hargett had so few racial themes in his campaign. The Hargett campaign did complain that the Democrats had a "task force of 25 hired, professional black operatives" in the district (Attlesey 1985f), a claim the Chapman campaign falsely denied. But there was little else in the Republican rhetoric on racial issues. This is, in part, because the black population in the district is not as large as it is in some of the other districts examined in these chapters. It is also likely a reflection of Edd Hargett's discomfort with these issues. Some attributed this to Hargett's football career, in which he played with and befriended many black players. Whatever the source, his reticence on racial issues surprised Democratic campaign officials, who claimed that Hargett's Republican handlers were expert in running racial campaigns.

A racial controversy did come up, however, during the campaign. The Thursday before the primary election, Assistant Attorney General for Civil Rights William Bradford Reynolds wrote to Gov. Mark White charging that the preclearance provision in the Voting Rights Act had been violated in the setting of the date for the election. Reynolds, citing the notification provision of the act (intended to keep officials from setting election dates that might discriminate against minorities), threatened White with unspecified legal action. By Monday, White had agreed to have the state formally notify the Justice Department. The primary was held as scheduled, though several media outlets reported on the confusion about the election (Taylor 1985b). In mid-July, the issue arose again, this time with the Justice Department raising the matter in federal court. A Texas election official argued that other such vacancies had been filled at least forty times since the enactment of the Voting Rights Act without the state having to preclear the date (King 1985b). Governor White, as before, argued that the demand was unreasonable, citing a 1983 federal appeals panel ruling that the setting of dates for special elections did not require preclearance. Ironically, that suit, not filed by the Justice Department, was brought in the special election of 1983 won by Phil Gramm (Sanders-Castro 1985, 7). In the Chapman/Hargett election, although the Justice Department did not allege discrimination in the setting of the date, the three-judge panel ruled against Texas, requiring the state to submit preclearance papers by August 9 (actually several days after the election) or have the election declared void.

The state ultimately did comply with the order, but Texas Democratic officials argued throughout the controversy that it was part of a Republican plan to dampen political participation. Low turnout in either the primary or the general was considered to work to Hargett's advantage, so their argument went, and Atwater was using his ties to the administration to "chill" turnout, particularly black turnout, by creating confusion about the elections. Governor White called it a politically inspired trick by the Reagan administration (King 1985b), and Rep. Don Edwards, the chair of the House Judiciary Subcommittee charged with overseeing the Civil Rights Division of the Justice Department, referred to the incident as an attempt to intimidate minority voters. "Only in the final two weeks of a hotly contested campaign, with the Republican candidate in trouble, does the Justice Department push forward to force the state to submit their plan for approval," said Edwards (Kurtz 1985). Justice Department officials responded to the charge, touting their tough enforcement of the law and denying that their decision to pursue the matter was motivated by a desire to assist the Republican candidate. "This whole matter has been worked up by career attorneys and Brad [Reynolds] just approved what they did," said a spokesman for the assistant attorney general (Kurtz 1985).[12] Looking back at it, one Democratic pollster believed the incident ended up helping Jim Chapman. He believed that the Republicans ended up raising the salience of the election for blacks with the lawsuits. If indeed this was the case, it was a tactical error.

In the end, Chapman pulled out a narrow victory, winning 51 to 49 percent by fewer than two thousand votes. National Democrats rejoiced over the victory, claiming that the Republicans had failed their own test. The notion that the South was realigning, said one campaign strategist, "was clearly not feasible," and Paul Kirk, the chairman of the Democratic National Committee, argued that "the talk about realignment is still only a Republican dream" (King 1985d). Republicans tried to paint the defeat as favorably as they could. Trying to put a positive spin on a disaster, Rep. Guy Vander Jagt, chairman of the National Republican Congressional Committee, called the loss "a smashing victory. To even be competitive in that district is indeed a historic realignment" (*New York Times* 1985). Still, it was a bitterly disappointing loss. Jim Chapman recalled meeting Lee Atwater some time after the election. "He told me that my election was the only one that ever gave him the dry heaves for three days," crowed the Democrat.

Atwater's distress was heightened because the election failed to provide his party with the demonstration they needed to initiate a broader low-level realignment in the region as a whole. He and his colleagues vowed to continue the effort. Phil Gramm, for one, issued a bold warning as the campaign drew to a close: "Win or lose this race, this is only my first involvement. We're going to keep on building the party until we're hunting Democrats with dogs" (Attlesey 1985h). His efforts continue, and several years later, this election was still on the minds of Republican strategists. "It was a phenomenal opportunity," said a Washington Republican consultant looking back "It could have been a turning point."

Virginia 5—"I'll take the district any day of the week"

Virginia is usually thought of as one of the more racially liberal states of the South. The election of a black governor there in 1989 enhanced this reputation. But parts of the state are still very conservative on racial matters. The area of the state known as Southside has been and continues to be the racially conservative bastion of the state. It was here that the most stubborn resistance to civil rights changes was met. It was here that schools closed for five years rather than desegregate. It was here, in the town of Danville, that police attacks "worse than Bull Connor's" sent almost fifty blacks to the hospital for demonstrating against downtown segregation (Branch 1988, 822). And it was here that George Wallace won 37 percent of the presidential vote in 1968,[13] one of only two Virginia districts he carried.

Most of Southside Virginia is encompassed by the Fifth District, which is heavily rural and comprises one-quarter of the territory of the state but only one-tenth of its population. Although the cities of Roanoke and Richmond sit on its border, the only sizable town in the district is Danville. Lynchburg, Jerry Falwell's hometown and what many would consider the capital of the Christian Right movement, is partially in the district. The area is mostly agricultural (the major crops raised in the area are soybeans and tobacco), but the region's soil is not overly fertile and the area is relatively poor. It has a large black population, blacks making up one-quarter of its residents. This and the other demographic characteristics of the district's population make the Fifth a district more like North Carolina than north Virginia.

The district's long-time congressman W. C. "Dan" Daniel was one of the last old-time southern Democrats. A proud boll weevil and a remnant of the Byrd machine, Daniel was one of the most conservative congressmen—Democratic or Republican—in the House of Representatives, averaging a 4 rating on the Americans for Democratic Action scale and an 87 on the American Conservative Union scale between 1980 and 1988 (Ehrenhalt 1987). According to these scales, he and Sonny Montgomery of Mississippi were the two most conservative Democrats in the House, and the old congressman was quite proud of this. Indeed, he often would boast that he voted with President Reagan more often than 77 percent of his colleagues did. Daniel was particularly conservative on racial issues, voting consistently against such measures as the extension of the Voting Rights Act, the Martin Luther King national holiday, and other issues of interest to blacks, symbolic and substantive. Nonetheless, the congressman was very partisan. He joked that he voted with Tip O'Neill only two times per session (once to vote for O'Neill as Speaker and once to close the session), but, as one Democratic official told me, he was devoted to the Democratic party and often advised the party on Democratic opportunities in the state. Despite Ronald Reagan's popularity in the district (in 1980, he won 55 percent of the vote; in 1984, 65 percent), Daniel was unchallenged throughout the Reagan years. In fact, after Daniel's death in 1988, the Republican district chairman could not recall the last candidate fielded against Daniel (Elving 1988).[14] Daniel was willing and able to hold office until his final days and died just four days after he resigned. During his final few terms, he often hinted at retirement, thereby holding off challengers, who recognized that waiting for an open seat was preferable to running against an institution.

When the open seat finally did materialize, it offered an outstanding possibility for Republicans. Political pundits saw this as a symbolic election, one in which Republicans had an excellent chance. A *Congressional Quarterly* headline declared, "G.O.P Sees New Day in Southside Virginia." They were not the only ones who saw this as a Republican opportunity. Strategic politicians did as well. Democrats were not sanguine about their prospects. Several Democratic legislators declined to join the race, and the party ended up nominating L. F. Payne at the state convention. A successful businessman from the northern part of the district, Payne had never before held public office and was a virtual unknown. The major political struggle was on the Republican side, with State Senator W. Onico Barker and Reagan White House aide Linda Arey vying for the chance to face Payne. Both candidates were attractive. Both had experience in government and a base from which to raise money. Arey had worked several jobs with the popular administration. Barker had name recognition in the district and a constituency in the city of Danville. Such quality candidates emerge when their chances are best. That a fierce nomination battle arose among Republicans is testimony to how good Republican prospects were thought to be.

The two Republicans waged a fierce battle for the nomination. Arey, who entered the race first and spent months doing the difficult "retail" work necessary to cultivate a network of delegates, had a distinct advantage over Barker, who decided to enter the race much later. Arey also had the support of the Reverend Jerry Falwell, who found her administration credentials attractive. Furthermore, Falwell was angry with Barker for having led a campaign against a tax exemption that would have benefited his church empire. Barker had some advantages, however. Most important, he had the support of Republican party officials in the district and the state who perceived that a woman might have difficulty winning a congressional race in this part of Virginia. In the end, Arey's superior organization and more ideological followers led her to victory, but it was not without cost. Barker and many of his followers left the convention bitterly disappointed.

With high expectations pinned to her, Arey's most immediate concern coming out of the convention was to attempt to bring the party together and soothe tensions with Barker. Her best efforts failed. Barker and his staff had resented Arey from the start as an outsider. The nomination battle and above all Arey's alliance with Falwell added to the ill feelings between the two camps (Elving 1988, 1009). Following the convention, several of Barker's aides came out publicly for Payne. And although Barker himself never formally endorsed Arey's opponent, he made it clear whom he was supporting. Arey described taking a seat next to Barker at a debate only to see him move to a seat next to Payne. She told of Barker snubbing a campaign rally featuring George Bush that took place one block from his house. When the Roanoke newspaper reported the state senator drinking beer from an L. F. Payne for Congress cup at the Pittsylvania County Rib Festival (Eure 1988b), the act was seen as being tantamount to an endorsement.

If the first goal of Arey's campaign was to bring the Republicans back together, the second element of her general campaign strategy was to claim the legacy of Dan Daniel. Daniel had called her "his ideological soulmate" in a Richmond paper shortly before he died, and Arey considered this to be an implicit endorsement. She talked of this endorsement often on the campaign trail and said that she would continue in his conservative tradition. Her positions on issues distinctly aligned her with "the beloved conservative congressman," and she spoke often and fondly of her personal ties to Daniel.

Along these same lines, Arey sought to strike the appropriate comparison, to characterize herself as the bona fide conservative and to tag Payne as a liberal. In her first press conference following the Republican convention, she said, "The issues will break down very clearly along liberal and conservative lines. L. F. Payne is a liberal Democrat in the Jim Wright tradition and I'm a conservative Republican in the Dan Daniel tradition" (Elving 1988).[15] If elected to Congress, Arey vowed to "fight the liberal leadership [of Congress]" (Bland 1988h). Payne, on the other hand, would have to cater to it.

Most important, Arey tried to establish the fact that she was a conservative and L. F. Payne a liberal on a highly publicized racial issue. At her first press conference, in her first response to a question as to how she and Payne differed on the issues, she brought up the Civil Rights Restoration Act. This bill, introduced in response to the Supreme Court's *Grove City* decision, required that an organization receiving federal funds in any of its parts must comply with fair hiring practices throughout the whole organization. President Reagan vetoed the bill, and Arey said that she would have voted to sustain his veto, whereas Payne would have voted to override it.[16] In a radio commercial entitled "The Clear Difference," her campaign sought to make the contrast as stark as possible. Arey's ad claimed that she "opposes Grove City, the Civil Rights Restoration Act, while he [Payne] favors more federal interference in our lives" (Baker 1988). For good measure, it added that whereas she backed George Bush in the presidential primaries in 1988, Payne "supported [either] Michael Dukakis *or Jesse Jackson*" (Baker 1988, emphasis added). The either/or construction made it a true but inflammatory statement. If Payne were to respond to the ad, he would put himself in a difficult position with either his black or his white supporters. He chose to ignore it.

Arey's attempts to establish herself as the truly conservative candidate extended to other issues as well, most notably drugs, taxes, and abortion. On drugs, Arey took a hard line, calling for the death penalty for anyone convicted twice of selling drugs to anyone under the age of nineteen (Bland 1988h). Payne's position on this was tough, though not this extreme. Arey criticized the American response to drugs coming from Central America. "In the old days before the liberals took control of the CIA and made it an impotent agency, the CIA would have taken care of Noriega," said Arey, calling for a quite aggressive approach to the problem of supply (Bland 1988h).

Trying to exploit a potential link between Payne and "tax-and-spend Democrats," Arey pounced upon Payne's refusal to sign a "No new taxes" pledge sponsored by a conservative taxpayers' organization. Payne waved the pledge off with the comment, "She's always shoving something in front of me to sign" (Baker 1988), but clearly here Arey had an edge over the Democrat in establishing herself as the real conservative.

A Roman Catholic in "the buckle of the Bible Belt," Arey took a position on the abortion issue that she believed ingratiated her with right-wing Protestants who might otherwise have been opposed to her candidacy. In one debate, in fact, she called for a "human life amendment to the Constitution" (Bland 1988d). Though it was not entirely clear what this meant, it was clear that it represented a more uncompromising position on the issue. Once again, her hard-line stance stood in contrast to Payne's position, which was that an abortion should be up to a woman, in consultation with her family and her minister.

A third major element of Arey's strategy was to take advantage of her Washington connections. Arey brought in national figures like Vice President Bush and her former boss at the Department of Transportation, Elizabeth Dole, to campaign for her. Bush, in fact, spent an entire day stumping for Arey. Each visit brought with it some front-page stories in the district's newspapers and allowed Arey to publicize her ties to the popular Reagan administration (Reagan even cut a radio commercial for her). The value of these visits for Arey was more than just being seen with political celebrities. They played into a campaign theme that the staff worked hard to develop. Part of their message, as highlighted in Elizabeth Dole's testimonial speech to a Pittsylvania County rally, was that Arey had the "intelligence, integrity, and aggressiveness" and the knowledge of Washington that would make her effective from the start. This message was inevitably reported with mention that Payne had no experience in Washington (Bland 1988i). Bringing in Bush and Dole also allowed Arey to demonstrate the clout she had with the administration and how well she could serve the district. Arey's campaign manager said, "[Bush's visit] shows what she can do for the district. Getting the vice president to the district on his 64th birthday is not exactly the easiest task" (Bland 1988k).[17]

There were nevertheless some serious problems with the conception and the implementation of Arey's campaign strategy. First, there was controversy over Dan Daniel's supposed endorsement, coming as it did from the Democratic incumbent. Arey herself told of being encouraged to run by Daniel, who, she said, wanted a conservative to take his seat. She spoke of old ties between their families (Arey's father, a country doctor, had cared for Daniel's parents in their "dotage"). She described Daniel's brother approaching her at the funeral home and reiterating the congressman's endorsement of her. She tried to muddy up the partisan difference by saying, "Labels don't matter" (Bland 1988h). One surrogate, Rep. Stan Parris, supported this by arguing that Daniel was "kind of a Republican" and noted that Daniel had told him that Arey was "a really nice lady" who was capable of replacing him (Bland 1988f). Arey's Democratic detractors, though, argued that she had filed for the Republican nomination before he had resigned and that she obviously had intended to challenge him. Daniel's son was among those who publicly objected to her attempts to claim his father's endorsement (Bland 1988g), which certainly undercut one of her strongest appeals.

Second, even though Arey was the more conservative of the two candidates, she had difficulty, as a woman candidate, in the culturally conservative district. She faced, for instance, a dilemma about whether she should use her husband's name or her maiden name. The first was the more acceptable practice in the conservative district, but her husband's name (Skladany) was foreign-sounding and ethnic (Czech), potentially problematic in the Fifth. Arey decided that her maiden name was better known in the district but felt that she was "damned either way."

The abortion issue too posed a problem for the Republican that she certainly would not have faced had she been a man. Early in the campaign, Arey was asked by a Lynchburg reporter if she had ever had an abortion. Shocked and dismayed at the question (she believed it was planted by a disgruntled Republican opponent), Arey chose not to dignify it with a response. Because she did not answer the question with an unequivocal no, however, it came up again, and her "private business" was discussed extensively in several of the district's newspapers, again undercutting an issue that should have worked to her favor.

The biggest problem Arey had as a woman candidate simply may have been that she had strong opinions and a forceful personality. These are qualities admired in political candidates, especially ideologically pure candidates, but they are not qualities appreciated in rural Virginia women.[18] The zeal with which she pursued conservative issues undoubtedly appealed to some, but her style likely worked against her in the conservative district, particularly when she was compared to L. F. Payne. One voter was quoted in the Roanoke newspaper as saying, "I think he's more a listener and she's more a talker" (Eure 1988b). To Arey's supporters, she was high energy and principled. To her detractors, she was shrill, aggressive, and hyperactive. Unfortunately for Arey, the negative impression may have won out. Said Payne in hindsight, "This was an election where issues didn't matter as much as impressions. At first Linda came across well, but I think she may have wore on people. In comparison, I came across as stable and sensible." Arey spoke along the same lines, though from a slightly different angle. She argued that her candidacy was threatening to men and women her own age and that even her best performances on the campaign trail may have contributed to this problem. "Now L.F. I like a lot," she started. "And he's a bright guy. But he's a businessman. I had just been in the public liaison office at the White

House making speeches all over. I know I did extremely well in several of the debates. Yet every time I bested my opponent, [University of Virginia political scientist] Larry Sabato would tell me that men—and women— were rushing to support L.F."[19]

Third, Arey's quest for white votes via the Grove City issue may have been undercut by another campaign appearance she made. Arey marched in the Martin Luther King Day parade in Danville, which she believed may have cost her the votes of some white Danvillians. Her appearance in the parade did not help her with blacks. Neither, as she had hoped, did her family's reputation for racial progressivism (her father crusaded to open the public library during massive resistance, her sister went to the first integrated school in the area). "I got enough black votes to fill five phone booths," said the candidate. "I can only look back and feel I was naive."

Finally, although the national visits and visits by Republican congressmen from northern Virginia were important to the campaign, they did not compensate for the lack of enthusiasm from local and state Republican elites. Arey's problems with the Virginia Republican party may have been related to her caucus victory over Onico Barker. It may have been because her return from Washington bred some resentment. Whatever the cause, Arey complained that local and state Republican officials did not help her campaign very much: "I had good support from outside the district, but no one from inside the district ever put their arm around me and said 'She's one of us.' Not one member of the Virginia state legislature from the district ever introduced me to another person. None of them ever took me up and down Main Street and introduced me to the banker, the pharmacist, or the barber." In retrospect, Arey was most disappointed by the lack of support she got from the Virginia Republican party and felt that "the hemorrhage in my own party," the lack of support from her opponent in the Republican convention and his followers, was her biggest problem in the general election.[20]

L. F. Payne was a self-made man who had developed the Wintergreen ski resort in central Virginia. Wintergreen was successful and, though a relatively new enterprise, well known in the district. Moreover the resort brought hundreds of new jobs to the area and provided Nelson County with about half of its tax base. Though Payne was a political novice, his business experience was, according to his campaign strategist, a great selling point for Virginia voters. Payne, he argued, was instantly respected in the district and had great credibility as a fiscal conservative. In fact, Virginia Democrats had had some previous success with businessman-candidates, and Payne was recruited into politics by Norman Sisisky, a Pepsi-distributor-turned-congressman from Virginia's Fourth District.

As a successful businessman, Payne had the resources to run a viable campaign. This was doubly important as he was an unknown from the sparsely populated northern part of the district. Payne loaned himself about $275,000, which gave him a fairly large financial advantage over his opponent. Arey spent $359,000 on her campaign, Payne $563,000 (*Danville Register* 1988). The large campaign chest enabled Payne to saturate the heavily populated southern tier of counties with advertising. All the television stations that serve the district are located outside of it (in Roanoke-Lynchburg, Richmond, Raleigh-Durham, and Greensboro-Winston-Salem-High Point), so that reaching district voters involves reaching many people outside the district as well. Political advertising in the Fifth is thus a fairly expensive proposition.

Of course, Payne's self-financed campaign, which was clearly an advantage, could well have turned into a liability if the Republicans had effectively put the right populist twist on it. Anticipating that the Republicans might try to use Payne's wealth against him, the Democrat's campaign consultants sought to create an image of Payne as "a regular guy." The Republicans did indeed attempt to make an issue of Payne's campaign spending. Shortly after the Democratic caucus, which was held two weeks before the Republican caucus, the state GOP chairman called Payne "a BMW liberal trying to sell himself to Chevy conservatives" (Bland 1988a). Later, a national Republican consultant charged him with being more interested in "selling five dollar hot dogs and writing checks on his mountain" than in meeting the people (Bland 1988j). The antidote to these charges was to paint a common picture of the Democrat. Payne often would talk of his humble origins, which qualified him as a self-made man as well as a regular guy. His staff, in a story in the Danville paper, portrayed him as a tobacco chewing, cowboy boot wearing, hiking and fishing enthusiast who wore jeans and open shirts and played on the Wintergreen employee basketball team (Bland 1988j). Payne's mild demeanor contributed to the image his staff was trying to cultivate. Of course, the irony of the situation was that it was personal wealth that made it possible for Payne to advertise his modest image.

Payne's campaign manager put high priority on "inoculating" the public against the inevitable charges that Payne was a liberal. Given the two-week head start granted the Democrats, they were able to refute the charge even before it was made, as it was, again and again. As with the money issue, part of the Democratic response was to highlight Payne's history, his business and engineering background, his military service, and his education at the Virginia Military Institute (VMI). "How many liberals do you know from V.M.I.?" asked his campaign manager. Campaign commercials were cut showing Payne in a hard hat at Wintergreen and emphasizing his business background. At rallies, other politicians, notably Gov. Gerald Baliles, hailed Payne's private sector success and argued that he would bring "a no-nonsense business approach to government" (Bland 1988e).

In television advertisements as well as in his appearances in the district Payne highlighted his conservative positions, especially on fiscal and military issues. He argued for the balanced budget amendment to the Constitution, adherence to the Gramm-Rudman-Hollings spending targets, and a line-item veto for the president. These positions were consistent with the conservative businessman theme his campaign was trying to develop and were highly visible in his campaign. The candidate also stressed his support for Star Wars research, aid to the Nicaraguan contras, and school prayer. He was unmistakably to the right of center on many issues of importance to Southside Virginia.

Payne, however, did not claim to be a conservative clone of Dan Daniel. His support of the Equal Rights Amendment and of choice on the abortion issue as well as his positions on a number of other issues would have been anathema to the ultraconservative Daniel. He intimated, in response to a reporter's question, that he could be expected to support the Democratic party more than Daniel had. When asked if he would vote along party lines more frequently than Daniel, he skillfully hedged the question: "I think I would vote in a manner that well represented the district, and I would vote however I felt my constituents wanted. My views and those of constituents are the same, we have the same views and values, and I could do a good job representing the district" (Bland 1988b). Nonetheless, it was quite apparent that he would offer something different from Dan Daniel.

Payne, like Arey, brought in politicians to campaign for him. But whereas Arey brought in national Republicans, Payne brought in Democrats from around the state, most notably Governor Baliles and Sen. (and former governor) Charles Robb. "With these guys and some old Byrd Democrats behind me," Payne said, "people couldn't believe that I was Teddy Kennedy." Bringing in Democrats from around the state did more than simply solidify Payne's claims to being a conservative. It helped develop a second campaign theme: Southside Virginia versus big city Washington. The Payne campaign aggressively sought to turn Arey's connections to the Reagan administration against her. The Democratic campaign claimed that Arey was "out of town and out of touch," a carpet-bagger who had moved back to the district to run for Congress. They emphasized an insider-outsider theme at every campaign stop. As Baliles said to a local crowd, "We can choose to send Virginia values to Washington or we can choose to bring Washington values to Virginia." He left little doubt as to which was the preferable option. The Democrats predicted even that Arey would put her house up for sale the day after she lost the race (and so she did).[21] They tried to make her Washington resume a "negative," and in this way, said Payne's campaign manager, "The more Washington showed up, the more it played into our hands."

The Payne forces likewise highlighted district issues in their campaign, emphasizing jobs and fair trade practices instead of ideology and the president. The seven hundred jobs that Payne had created in the district complemented the theme of "jobs . . . being stolen from Virginia by unfair foreign trade." In touting his support for a trade bill that had recently passed in Congress, Payne claimed that he would "be a watchdog over unfair foreign practices involving district products" (*Danville [Virginia] Bee* 1988). Arey, on the other hand, opposed the trade bill because of a provision requiring businesses to notify workers of a plant closing at least sixty days prior to the closing. Though she said that the rest of the bill was acceptable, she reiterated her opposition to trade quotas of all kinds. The answer, she asserted, was for "the President [to] work diligently to find timely and effective remedies to correct the problem [of unfair trading practices]" (*Danville Bee* 1988). These responses illustrate Payne's more activist approach to the problem. Payne's campaign manager, who also advised the Texas race described above, claimed to be the first to use the unfair trade message effectively and repeated it in many of the southern campaigns he advised. He especially emphasized how the issue tied into the local theme the campaign tried to develop. "She emphasized Washington and we emphasized the district," he said. "I'll take the district any day of the week."

As to Arey's position on the Grove City legislation, Payne's response was subdued. He stated his support for the legislation but did not make it a centerpiece of his campaign. He did, however, use Arey's position and the *Richmond Times Dispatch* editorial excoriating Payne for his stand on the issue in appealing for black votes. A black turnout expert from the Democratic Congressional Campaign Committee (who also worked the Alabama and Mississippi 5 races) noted that Arey's stand on the issue "was played to the hilt" in every piece of Democratic literature sent to the black community.

Payne himself felt that black support would be easy to court, not only because he compared favorably with Arey on this issue, but because he compared favorably with Dan Daniel. Payne said, "[Daniel] was so conservative, I was a breath of fresh air [for blacks]." For these reasons, Payne did not feel that blacks "made unrealistic demands on me." He did not have to appear as a champion of black issues to win their support. But he did do those things necessary to win black votes. He advertised on black radio. He lined up black opinion leaders. And, accompanied by a black assistant campaign manager, he visited dozens of black churches in the district.[22] His attempt to reach out to the black community and his moderate positions generated a lot of support, said a black community organizer: "He was a refreshing change. He came in to listen and didn't make promises we all knew he couldn't keep. We said to him, listen, we know you can't change the world, but at least you know we're here."

In the end, Payne defeated Arey rather convincingly, 59 percent to 41 percent. He ran against another conservative Republican six months later in a closer race. His opponent in that contest was a state senator who had not introduced a bill in his entire eight-year tenure ("Lots of people around here kind of liked that," said Payne), but the Democrat turned back this challenge. In 1990, the Republicans did not even field a candidate against him. Being assigned to the Public Works and Transportation Committee and the Veterans' Affairs Committee, Payne was well positioned to deliver on the local promises he had made in his first campaign and to do what was necessary to defend his seat over time.

Mississippi 5— "Gene Taylor and Friends Welcome George Bush"

On weekends, the beautiful white sand beaches of southern Mississippi are filled with sun worshipers and volleyball nets. The focal point of the coast is the town of Biloxi. Biloxi ends at the beach in seafood shacks, a boardwalk, and gift shops advertising souvenirs from hurricane Camille, which devastated the region in 1969. This town caters to tourists. Indeed, the Gulf Coast is known as the Redneck Riviera, and the area makes the Fifth District unlike any other in the state.

The Fifth is different from the rest of Mississippi in other ways as well. Demographically, it is quite distinctive. The three counties on the coast, which contain the cities of Biloxi and Gulfport and more than half the district's population, are urbanized and, compared to the rest of Mississippi, fairly white collar and affluent. Even Hattiesburg, the only city in the eight and one-half inland counties of the district, has a large white-collar population, as it is home to a large state university. The rural area in the district is unlike the rest of the state. Its land is not as rich as the land along the Mississippi River, and the economy is based more on timber than agriculture. The coastal area is distinctive in that it is home to many Roman Catholics, many of them migrants from the New Orleans area, and has a smaller black population than the rest of the state. Blacks comprise only 19 percent of the district while Mississippi as a whole is 31 percent black.

Economically, the district is also rather unique. In addition to the tourism and timber industries, the seafood industry is important to the coast. Although it is not unusual for a southern economy to be dependent upon the military, this district is especially so. It is home to numerous military bases, the Stennis NASA Center, a major shipbuilding industry, other industry dependent on military contracts, and two Veterans Administration hospitals. Up and down the coast these military installations provide jobs and feed service industries, which are especially important when the tourist season ends. As one local put it, "We'd starve to death without military money around here."

The demographics and economics of the district have made it hospitable to Republicans for a number of years. This dominance has been overwhelming in presidential elections since the early 1970s. Indeed, in 1972, this was the most Republican district in the country in a most Republican year; Nixon won 87 percent of the vote in the Fifth. At the congressional level, the district also has been very supportive of the GOP. The district was represented for sixteen years by former House Minority Whip Trent Lott. Lott, an aide to the longtime boll weevil congressman William Colmer, changed parties for the 1972 election and was the first Republican to represent the district since Reconstruction. He enjoyed huge support throughout his tenure, and when he decided to leave the House in 1988 for a run at the Senate seat being vacated by John Stennis—a position he won—the Republicans kept the district in the fold.

Larkin Smith, formerly the Republican sheriff of Harrison County (which includes Gulfport and Biloxi), succeeded Lott by defeating a popular Democratic state senator from the coast, Gene Taylor. Smith designed his campaign's theme around his resume. His experience as sheriff and his role in bringing a federally funded drug-interdiction organization to Gulfport gave a certain credibility to his law-and-order and antidrug message and made him a heavily favored candidate in the conservative district. He also held a great advantage over Taylor in funding (he outspent

Taylor by more than three to one), and, more important, he had a huge advantage at the top of the ticket. Indeed, in 1988, George Bush's 69 percent in the district was bettered in only a dozen districts in the entire country. Although Smith's ten-point margin of victory was somewhat smaller than many in the media and in politics expected, it was assumed that he would hold the seat for many years.

Larkin Smith did not have much time to make his mark on Washington. He had been in office only six months when he was killed in a plane crash near Hattiesburg. His death set into motion special election procedures. Because Mississippi law dictates that the seat be filled within one hundred days of the vacancy in a nonpartisan election, the campaign was to be short and frenetic. This was especially the case because the runoff was scheduled by the governor to follow only two weeks after the primary (if no candidate won a majority in the primary). Three candidates—one Republican and two Democrats—emerged in the weeks following Smith's death to make the race.

The Republican in the contest was Tom Anderson, Trent Lott's administrative assistant in Washington. Anderson had served Lott for sixteen of the prior eighteen years, taking two years off to serve as the Reagan administration's ambassador to six island nations in the Eastern Caribbean. Republican leaders approached the election with confidence. One national Republican consultant told me as he headed down to Mississippi to advise the campaign that a runoff would be unnecessary. This, after all, was a district very partial to Republicans. Even though Anderson was relatively unknown and even though party labels would not appear on the ballot, he was sure to have the resources to saturate the district with his name and to fully advertise his GOP connection.

Anderson also had a major advantage in that he was the only Republican in the race. To maximize his chances, other Republican candidates were forced out of the race even before it started. Because there was only one Republican in the race, it was hoped a runoff could be avoided. At the very least, Anderson was absolutely certain to make the runoff. With this in mind, his boss Trent Lott engineered the best of circumstances for his employee.

Lott's task was tricky. The plane crash had essentially martyred Larkin Smith. Following his death, many Republicans had urged his widow, Sheila Smith, to run for the seat, and she did unofficially declare that she would announce her candidacy with the support of Republican dignitaries, including Senator Lott. Although Lott, Anderson, and Smith all denied it, it was widely believed and was reported in the local press that Lott forced Mrs. Smith out of the race before she officially got in. Other declared Republican candidates bowed out of the race as well, the papers reporting that the senator watched from the doorway as two Republican state legislators announced their change in plans at a news conference (Cassreino 1989).

The Democratic candidate whom the Republicans were most concerned about was Mike Moore, Mississippi's attorney general. The young, aggressive Democrat had taken fully 87 percent of the vote on the Gulf Coast in his campaign for attorney general in January 1988. He had the backing of several prominent national Democrats and was the leading Democrat and "the man to watch" according to Democratic insiders. Enjoying strong support from blacks and labor and a promising reputation among national Democrats, Moore looked like a formidable opponent. Also in the race was Gene Taylor, the young state senator from the coast who had won 45 percent of the vote against Larkin Smith in 1988. The low-key Taylor had name recognition and the basis for a campaign organization already in place. Nonetheless he was considered the lesser of the two Democrats and was underestimated by both of his opponents.

The three candidates were close on most major issues. All three were antiabortion, tough on drugs, budget-balancing, pro–school prayer, anti–gun control conservatives. The major issues in this part of the campaign thus became the candidates themselves. The two favorites, in particular, had some immediate problems to face.

Ironically, the effort to create favorable circumstances for Anderson (and the public knowledge of this effort) created unanticipated problems for the candidate. Despite the fact that Lott was enormously popular in the district ("You've got God and Trent on a popularity index and I'm not sure who comes first," said one Democratic campaign official), his role in the campaign became an issue. Foremost, Lott's involvement created an image problem for Anderson, who, previously unknown in the district, now had to make the case that "he was his own man." The press started to pick up on this, asking Anderson in debates whether he was an independent thinker. And, of course, the two Democrats also worked on this theme. Moore said, "I'm really incensed about one of our leaders picking someone out for everybody else to vote for. If Trent wants to run for Congress, he ought to" (*Gulfport Sun-Herald* 1989a). Taylor said, "The people of South Mississippi, not Washington, should pick the next congressman" (Cassreino 1989). Interestingly, it was Lott, not Anderson, who responded to the charges in the newspaper. To Moore, he said, "I tell you what he'd better do: Instead of talking about me, he needs to be looking after his own knitting. The fellow asked to be attorney general. I say, 'let's let him be attorney general'" (*Sun-Herald* 1989b). To Taylor, Lott responded, "Gene Taylor better tend to his own knitting. He's got to deal with Mike Moore" (Cassreino 1989). These responses, of course, made it appear that Lott was looking after Anderson's knitting.

As the campaign progressed, the problem refused to go away. Democratic and Republican elites continued to speculate whether Sheila Smith had been blackmailed or enticed out of the race by Lott. There was discussion about whether or not Mrs. Smith would have been a strong candidate, a sympathetic favorite who might have scared the strong Democrats out of the race. Mike Moore's campaign manager, in fact, said that his candidate probably would not have run had Mrs. Smith stayed in. The press ran several stories containing denials from the parties involved. And there was some concern that Mrs. Smith would not fully back the Republican ticket. Even after she cut a television commercial for Anderson (dressed in black in a poorly lit funeral home setting), some local Republican party leaders fretted that her endorsement appeared halfhearted.

Anderson also had to deal with Democratic charges of impropriety. Following a Jackson newspaper report that Anderson had received free air travel but had not reported the gift on financial disclosure forms, the Democratic Congressional Campaign Committee called him a "walking scandal." The committee even added to the charge, claiming that he was reimbursed for automobile travel on the same day he received free air travel (Peterson 1989b).[23] Anderson first responded that he had reported the air travel. When the newspaper obtained the reports that showed he had not, Anderson's press secretary claimed it was simply an oversight, that the candidate did not have his own records available, and that the reports would be corrected (*Sun-Herald* 1989b; Peterson 1989b).[24] On top of this, Anderson had to contend with reports that he had improperly impeded a federal investigation of a Louisiana toxic waste firm (Peterson 1989b). The firm, which was fined $6 million for pollution violations, had enlisted the assistance of Lott and Anderson and also had contributed to Lott's Senate campaign and Anderson's congressional campaign. Anderson responded in a debate that he had called the Justice Department simply to get status reports on the case and that he wanted to be sure that the company got a fair hearing. As might be expected, he excoriated the Democrats for their desperate "smear tactics" (Peterson 1989b).

On the positive side, Anderson had a large campaign fund to address these problems and to counter the negative publicity. He attempted to close the name recognition gap with massive direct mailings, one from President Bush, and a television advertising blitz. Whether it was because he was unable to shake his own negatives or because he failed to build up enough name recognition or both, Anderson did not win the first-round majority that the Republicans had hoped for. In fact, he did not win a plurality. Anderson aggressively pursued the Republican northern area of the district in this first campaign and won all of the northern counties, but came in second overall (with 37 percent of the vote) because he did not fare very well on the more populous coast.

Mike Moore followed standard southern Democratic strategy in the campaign, defining himself as a conservative while pursuing some important constituencies, specifically blacks and labor. He actively pursued the black vote, hiring the same Congressional Campaign Committee get-out-the-vote expert who had worked in the Alabama and Virginia races described above. Based on his statewide run for office, he and his staff felt that they had a clear idea of how to pursue the black vote while at the same time retaining white voters. Though he was not considered "a champion of black issues," said one black leader, "he was a friend of ours," and black opinion leaders generally lined up behind him. Moore also had the backing of the labor unions in the district. Though the area is notoriously hostile to unions, an AFL-CIO endorsement enabled him to generate some money with which to run a credible campaign.

Moore originally used that money to advertise his record as attorney general. In his quest for white votes, however, Moore, like Anderson, had an unexpected strategic problem: public opinion polls showed his positive was also a negative. These polls showed that people objected to his running for another office so soon after becoming attorney general. Being perceived as tenacious and aggressive had served him well in his campaigns for district attorney and attorney general. But "aggressive" translated into "overly ambitious" in this contest, and Moore's handlers had difficulty addressing this public perception. "In playing up Moore's record as attorney general, we were playing right into our negative," said his media consultant. "Frankly we tried a lot of things to deal with this problem and none of them worked." Moore ended up coming in third, winning but 21 percent of the vote, a great deal of it from the black community.

Unlike Anderson and Moore, Gene Taylor did not have an albatross around his neck as he entered the first campaign. He had, in fact, some underrated strengths. Although he had lost to Larkin Smith just six months before, he had done better than expected. That race and his tenure as a state legislator gave him an organizational base and some name recognition in the district. As the most underrated candidate, he was spared the attacks of the other two candidates, who built each other's negatives up further. At the same time, Taylor, mostly staying out of the fray, was able to enhance his well-crafted image as Clean Gene. He called even for the state party to remove its commercial attacking Anderson for the airplane and toxic waste matters, self-righteously insisting that he did not want to be associated with negative advertising. When a popular radio disc jockey took to calling him Opie Taylor, after the young do-gooder on the old Andy Griffith show, and his opponents Trent Anderson and Geraldo Moore, it was illustrative of the public images the three candidates had created for themselves.

Conceding the black vote to Moore and the hard-core Republican vote to Anderson, Taylor tried to stake out the middle (a decidedly right-wing middle), calling himself the "bipartisan conservative candidate." It was an appeal that worked well. In spite of the fact that Taylor's opponents were much better financed (Taylor spent only $34,000, while Moore spent $83,000 and Anderson $220,000—Souther 1989b), Taylor actually beat them both with 42 percent of the vote. His moralistic, middle-ground strategy worked so well in the primary that he continued talking about the same things in the runoff. The question was whether this appeal would work with only two candidates in the field rather than three.

The runoff thus featured a race between a very conservative Gene Taylor and an ultraconservative Tom Anderson. The contest was interesting because there was so little philosophical difference between the two candidates. Yet both candidates tried to highlight the differences that did exist, at least as they saw them.

Anderson's grand campaign strategy for the runoff had three major components. First, he attempted to get across the fact that he was the *more* conservative candidate. Because Taylor made a convincing case that he was truly conservative, Anderson did this by taking memorably extreme positions on various issues. The drug issue was one that Anderson emphasized, particularly given Larkin Smith's success with it in 1988 and given the candidate's record in the Caribbean. During one debate, Anderson appeared to advocate assassinating the Panamanian dictator Manuel Noriega (Souther 1989c). In the same discussion, he called for the dispatch of U.S. troops anywhere in the world to fight drugs at their source, and he urged that convicted "drug lords" be subject to the death penalty. His extreme positions were not confined to the drug issue. Anderson said in one debate, "I want to see that we restore prayer in school, not just in classrooms but at football games and sporting events. That's something we need to work very hard at" (Souther 1989d). On taxes, he signed an ironclad pledge to refuse to raise taxes, hoping to force Taylor into an uncomfortable spot. As Anderson happily anticipated, Taylor refused to sign the pledge. The Democrat's reasoning was clever though. He certainly was opposed to raising taxes but would vote to do so if it meant saving an industry or a military base in the district.

Anderson tried to distinguish himself from Taylor in other ways. He called Taylor a "backbencher," made a commercial that questioned Taylor's effectiveness by showing the number of his bills passed in the Mississippi Senate, tried to tie Taylor to "big labor" and "eastern bosses," and argued that Taylor would not be able to get things done in the liberal Democratic party. Republican campaign literature highlighted Taylor's passage rate, his support of a gasoline tax increase, and, rather deceivingly, his "liberal" stands on issues. Taylor pretty effectively responded to these charges. In a story written by a reporter who was to become Taylor's press secretary in Washington, it was noted that Taylor's passage rate was higher than Trent Lott's most recent eight years. It was also reported that the gasoline tax proposal was introduced by a Republican and approved unanimously by the state senate (Souther 1989f). As to a campaign flyer that quoted Taylor as saying, "I think it's crazy that we continue to spend money in law enforcement," the Gulfport newspaper reported that the statement was taken out of context. In making the statement, Taylor, in fact, was calling for more prisons and tougher sentencing: "I think it's crazy that we continue to spend money in law enforcement, and those in law enforcement catch the same people" (Peterson 1989a).

The second part of Anderson's strategy was to activate all those people who had made the Fifth District the Republican stronghold of Mississippi. Part of this attempt can be seen in the allocation of Anderson's time, above all in the primary. He campaigned a lot in the heavily Republican, heavily black northern part of the district in the primary and considered this to be his base even though he came from the coast. But it was obvious from the primary results that the less populated northern counties could not provide him with enough of the vote and that for the runoff, something else was needed. Those voters, Democratic and Republican, who had supported the Republican ticket in the past had to make the connection between Reagan and Bush and Tom Anderson. The answer was to bring in the president himself.

His influence in the district put to the test, particularly after Anderson's disappointing second-place finish in the primary, Senator Lott arranged a one-hour presidential visit to Gulfport. Bush's speech, attended by thousands, televised live, and covered extensively by the newspapers, included an announcement that the president would be attending a drug summit in South America (which fit well into one of Anderson's campaign themes). The president also gave a warm and personal endorsement of Tom Anderson. It was the type of event and media coverage that most candidates can only dream of. Anderson hoped the wonderful publicity would bring wayward Republicans back to his side.

The third prong of Anderson's strategy involved the black vote. Anderson's strategy vis-à-vis blacks was to encourage them to "sleep in," to stay at home on election day. There was little hope that he would win much of the black vote, especially as Mike Moore, who had the preponderance of this support in the primary, had endorsed Taylor in the runoff. But because the black leadership in the district was lukewarm toward Taylor, Anderson's strategy was to attack Taylor in the black community. While in the state legislature, Taylor had voted to close a hospital that served a black community elsewhere in the state. He also voted with the governor to close two historically black colleges, Mississippi Valley State University and Alcorn State University.[25] Many blacks were unhappy about losing schools and hospitals that had served the black community for so long and that were a source of jobs, and Anderson hoped to capitalize on this discontent in his negative campaign.

The point man for this campaign was C. F. Appleberry, a black minister from Meridian, a town outside the district. Under his name, a crude, xeroxed handbill was distributed throughout black neighborhoods in Gulfport and Ocean Springs. Denouncing Taylor for voting to close the colleges and the hospitals, as well as for a vote against allowing "small businesses and minority owned firms to have a guaranteed portion of all State Contracts (*sic*)," the handbill announced, "It is time for us to

WAKE-UP!" and "Mr. Taylor IS NOT OUR FRIEND." There were also several references to black votes being taken for granted by Democratic politicians:

Join me the Reverend C. F. Appleberry in sending Mr. Taylor a message. No longer will we be fooled by electing somebody that says one thing, while he is running for the job, but forgets us after he has been elected!
SEND A MESSAGE—No longer can our votes be taken for granted, just because a candidate has the Democratic Mark beside his name.
SEND A MESSAGE—This Tuesday, October 17, 1989 let Mr. Gene Taylor and other democrates (*sic*) know there are other chices (*sic*) for our votes.

The tag line "VOTE FOR TOM ANDERSON FOR CONGRESS. HE HAS YET TO VOTE AGAINST US" hardly inspired confidence that Anderson would serve blacks effectively, but it was the best reason Anderson's campaign could come up with for staying home.[26] A slightly less inflammatory commercial on black radio stations also featured the Reverend Mr. Appleberry. While gospel singers sang "Amen" in the background, Appleberry declared that "Taylor is not a friend to minorities, to poor people, or to small businesses" and "What is going to happen to your Social Security, Medicare, and Medicaid if Taylor is elected?" The radio ad repeated the flyer's closing line.

Black leaders in the district heaped scorn on Appleberry, one Taylor supporter calling him "a prostitute." Another black leader, not a strong supporter of Taylor, discounted the effectiveness of the Appleberry campaign: "He's from out of town. No one around here knows him and no one's going to listen to him." Nonetheless, the Democrats did not take any chances and responded immediately. They got an injunction against further distribution of the flyer for not being properly attributed to the Anderson campaign. The Democrats were able to move quickly, a state party official said, "because we were expecting something like this," and that may have diminished the effectiveness of the attack flyer.[27] However effective the attack was, it was more an attempt to depress black turnout than to generate support for Anderson.

Anderson's runoff strategy of outflanking the conservative Taylor, reaching out to perennial Republicans, and depressing the black vote had the potential to succeed. Yet, there were several problems—some old, some new—in the execution of the strategy. What was supposed to be the pinnacle of the campaign, Bush's appearance in Gulfport, may actually have worked against Anderson. Once again, there was much speculation that Lott's involvement in the race may have backfired, in part because of the media's reaction. The fact that Bush and Lott were so prominent in his campaign raised anew questions as to what Tom Anderson could do on his own. Editorial cartoonists began to lampoon him as a "lap dog" and as a talking doll whose string was pulled by Trent Lott. Debate moderators continued to ask him how he differed from Lott and Bush and what he had accomplished independently. From the perspective of many different people—journalists, Republicans, and Democrats—Anderson never really came up with a satisfactory answer.

Other difficulties plagued the Republican campaign. It is not clear how much Anderson's problems with his travel reporting or his involvement with the Louisiana toxic waste company hurt him in the end. Taylor refrained from bringing up these issues, confident that the media would publicize them (as they did). But Taylor did bring up Anderson's military record. Like Dan Quayle, Anderson was a National Guardsman during the Vietnam War. In a debate in which the candidates were allowed to quiz each other, Taylor questioned how Anderson could advocate sending American troops abroad to fight drugs: "Do you value those people's lives less than your own? Are you willing to make a commitment with them that you would not make on your own?" Anderson, like Quayle, argued that he was proud of his stint in the National Guard ("right here in Mississippi"), that he could have been called "anytime, anywhere," and that "it would be a delight to serve my country and do anything necessary to protect the freedoms of this country" (Souther 1989c). Though this was a politically sensible response, it did reveal another of

Anderson's weaknesses. It was one thing to say "I served my country and I'm proud of it"; it was quite another to say that it would be a "delight" to do so. It is perhaps unfair to evaluate one word spoken in the heat of a debate, without a script, but Anderson's choice of words is illustrative of a larger problem. He came across as effete and "arrogant" (Barone and Ujifusa 1990, 696) and "above people," particularly in comparison with the "down-home" Taylor (Barone and Ujifusa 1989, 696). Other factors played into this perception as well. Next to the handsome Taylor, Anderson, wearing thick, horn-rimmed glasses, looked bookish.[28] As one Democrat asked me, "Who's gonna vote for some guy with pink glasses?" His $2 million net worth also made the newspapers. Both Anderson and Taylor refused to publicly release their income tax returns, but Taylor was able to cloak himself in the image of the humble, corrugated box salesman. Anderson was unable to portray himself as a man of the people.

Gene Taylor's campaign was either very well designed or very lucky or both. His campaign themes played into Anderson's weaknesses (and Moore's, for that matter), and he did not have to face the major problems that Anderson did. He had some name recognition in the district, he had an easily resurrected campaign infrastructure (though he was still in debt from his previous run for Congress), and, as one advisor said, "He had the stamina to shake five hundred to two thousand hands a day. Add to that all the hands he shook last time and you've got quite a base to start with."

As noted, Taylor's main campaign theme was that he was the "bipartisan conservative candidate for Congress." This involved distancing himself from liberals (like Ted Kennedy) and identifying himself with conservatives, even Republican conservatives. When President Bush came to Gulfport, signs along the highway read, "Gene Taylor and Friends Welcome George Bush." In a televised debate shortly thereafter, he said that he was "closer to George Bush than people realize. I like him. . . . I'm glad he was here" (Souther 1989e). Of course, Taylor did not attend the rally. When asked by a television reporter why he had missed it, Taylor gave the ironic response, "I'm not a party crasher. If I'd been invited, I'd have been there." Though Taylor adroitly handled questions like these, projecting the right public relation to Bush was complicated and posed the campaign some challenges. At a press conference at a military facility, for example, Taylor found a photograph of the commander-in-chief hanging behind him. Before the television camera went on, and after some discussion about what to do, the picture was taken down.

In addition to the attempts to blur party lines, Taylor staked out very conservative issue positions. He "respected all life, including that of the unborn," advocated family values, and favored school prayer. He touted his authorship of one of the country's toughest drug laws (giving mandatory lifetime sentences to anyone convicted of selling more than ten pounds of marijuana or two ounces of cocaine). He promoted himself as a friend of the taxpayer and abhorred wasteful spending. He desired "a nation not afraid to say 'In God we Trust.'" He was, in short, boldly conservative on the campaign trail. In a humorous moment at a Taylor press conference with the conservative Mississippi Democratic congressman G. V. "Sonny" Montgomery, a journalist noted that Taylor was sitting to Montgomery's right. "That's where I'm going to keep him," quipped Montgomery. Taylor laughed and nodded his head in agreement.

One problem with Taylor's attempt to position himself so far to the right was that Anderson, members of the media, and even some callers to a television phone-in show asked how he would get along with his party's leadership.[29] Taylor's response was that there were plenty of conservative southern Democrats in Congress, for example, fellow Mississippians Sonny Montgomery and Jamie Whitten, who were effective and powerful. He claimed that with the help of the Democratic Mississippi delegation, he would have immediate influence. To bring home the point, he spent a day touring military installations and campaigning with Montgomery, a powerful member of the Armed Services Committee and chairman of the Veterans' Affairs Committee. At some press conferences, Montgomery announced that he had secured a spot on Armed Services for Taylor.[30] Having additional letters from House Speaker Tom Foley and the chair of the Armed Services Committee to pass on to the press, Taylor was assured a spot on the committee. In a district where the military is so important to the economy, this was a real boon to his campaign. And Taylor had a specific battle to join. His first priority once in Washington was to keep the Mississippi Army Ammunition Plant open and operating.[31] Taylor also was appointed to the Merchant Marine and Fisheries Committee, another committee overseeing business important to the coastal district.

Besides promising to work for a continued military presence in the district, Taylor spoke of local issues to a much greater extent than Anderson did. He talked incessantly about dredging the Gulfport port channel so that larger commercial ships could pass through. In an area where the seafood industry is important, Taylor talked tough on Turtle Excluder Devices (TEDs). Shrimpers are required by federal law to use these devices to avoid catching the endangered Kemp's Ridley turtle. Taylor was the only candidate to promise legislation to make the TED voluntary (Souther 1989a). As one shrimper was quoted in the newspaper, in support of Gene Taylor, "This is the only country in the world where it's legal to kill a baby, but it's illegal to kill a turtle" (Dockins and Peterson 1989).

Taylor's emphasis on local concerns fit well into his campaign rhetoric, which had a decidedly local flavor. As "South Mississippi's Choice," Taylor made much of the fact that he was from the area. Although Anderson was born and raised on the coast, he had lived in Washington for the past eighteen years, and Taylor labeled him an outsider.[32] Taylor spoke of how his campaign contributions came from local people. Whereas Anderson received a great deal of money from the national party, Taylor in the preliminary election did not receive any, in part because there was more than one Democrat in the field. Taylor claimed that 97 percent of his campaign funds came from local people, a figure from the primary that went down considerably as he received money from Washington during the two-week runoff campaign. He argued, as he had in his campaign against Larkin Smith in 1988, that the lack of support from Washington was evidence that he had not passed a liberal litmus test. National Democrats simply were not much invested in him, argued Taylor, because he was too conservative. With this rhetoric, Taylor catered to the idea expressed by a Hattiesburg television journalist that "Mississippi is an island." Anderson did not.

Taylor emphasized that he was an "average joe," a corrugated box salesman, a middle-class family man with the same problems and aspirations as his constituents. His campaign, he assured people, was run on a shoestring, and his staff did everything possible to make this point. His campaign signs, which were everywhere, were corrugated cardboard with "Gene Taylor for Congress" spray-painted across a crude stencil. His opponents' signs were slick and professional. The Democrat's television advertising also had less elaborate production values, though, interestingly, he had the resources to buy expensive commercial time during the World Series. When the Gulfport newspaper ran a front-page story featuring photographs of a goat wearing a Gene Taylor for Congress sandwich board and a rural tin-roof headquarters advertising new and used tires and Gene Taylor, Taylor's staff rejoiced. The accompanying story reported that because they were "short of funds for voter research, Taylor supporters are calling everyone in the phone book—inviting them to come by the headquarters for a cup of coffee and reminding them that Taylor will be speaking at the George County Fair on Friday" (Peterson 1989c), and it too was well received. This was just the homely image they were projecting. Noting that the pictures and story ran the same day as President Bush's visit, Taylor said some time after the election, "I'm convinced that goat got me more votes than Bush's visit. I heard it so often in the coffeeshops that it had to be true."

Perhaps the most interesting thing about Taylor's attempts to portray himself as humble and his campaign as low-budget was the Republican response to it. Taylor's claims of poverty were met with great derision by Republican officials, who knew better. At Anderson headquarters, visitors were handed editorial columns not about Taylor's wrongheaded positions or his terrible record, but rather a column from the Jackson paper headlined, "Some people tired of Taylor getting fat on 'humble pie.'" The columnist wrote, "But Lord, his beholdin'-to-nobody (*sic*) bit is beginning to wear every bit as thin as the sack-cloth he would have us believe his suits are made of" (McKenzie 1989).

Taylor's campaign was somewhat different from some of the other Democratic campaigns described here in that Taylor did not aggressively pursue the black vote. Perhaps because the payoff is smaller in this 19 percent black district, perhaps because he did not want to change his strategy from the primary (when Moore pulled in most of the black vote) to the runoff, Taylor did not court blacks very actively. One local black leader said, "I'm going to vote for him but that's about it. He didn't reach out enough so I'm not going to try to reach back." As noted, some of Taylor's Senate votes were quite unpopular in the black community, and he did little to indicate that he would be much interested in black issues in Congress.

Taylor's campaign did advertise extensively on black radio, a common practice in southern Democratic campaigns, but did not target the audience. The advertisements were the same as those played on country-western, Top 40, and evangelical Christian stations. These advertisements dealt with jobs, drugs, and the death penalty and did not discuss Anderson's positions on racial issues. As for the black church circuit, Taylor did meet with black ministers the weekend before the election, but he did not appear at the one black church on his Sunday schedule. And the pastor at that church did little more than remind his congregation to vote. Though he mentioned Gene Taylor, it was not a bold endorsement. It was apparent that neither the black community nor Taylor had all that much enthusiasm for the relation.

Though Taylor did not energetically appeal to blacks, his campaign did work hard to turn out blacks on election day. Mike Moore's black turnout expert came over to the Taylor campaign and attempted to establish a network in the black community. Taylor posters went up in barber shops and diners in black neighborhoods, and teams of blacks were recruited to work for Taylor. Taylor's basic strategy vis-à-vis blacks was to line up a few black leaders who had networks in the community and could deliver a bloc of votes. For this to work, he did not need to make a connection with black voters so much as with black leaders. "I have found that in the black community they truly have opinion leaders," said Taylor. "There was a time when it was more prevalent in the white community too. But that's not the case anymore and it sure makes a difference in how you reach for black votes."

In the end, Gene Taylor scored a 65 percent to 35 percent victory. Not his association with Trent Lott, not even a visit from President Bush kept Tom Anderson from losing by an embarrassing margin. In fact, Anderson's percentage of the vote actually went down from the first election, when he won 37 percent of the vote. Taylor's effective campaign strategy and his mastery of what Richard Fenno would call a "person-to-person homestyle" (Fenno 1978) led not only to a victory but to a rout for the Democrats. One year later, in the 1990 election, Taylor solidified his position in the district: Sheila Smith finally got her opportunity to run and was trounced as Gene Taylor took 81 percent of the vote.

Resentment Issues

Democratic candidates must do more to win in the South than just appeal to black voters. They must appeal to whites, and, given the dearth of southern white liberals in the electorate, they must find some issues that endear them to moderate and even conservative whites. I argue that southern Democrats have adapted well to this new environment, to a situation in which they have had to put together a coalition of blacks and whites.

One set of issues that southern Democrats (and to a lesser extent, Republicans) have used to appeal to whites are what I call resentment issues. Resentment issues define an in-group and an out-group. They allow a politician to assess blame and responsibility for the problems of the in-group on an out-group. And they introduce situations that are interpreted as being threatening to the interests of the in-group. That is, they bring group conflict into focus.

Racial issues are resentment issues, but they are a subset of all such issues. Southern politicians, particularly southern Democrats, have latched on to another subset of these issues. Like racial issues, they involve an easily distinguishable out-group. Like racial issues, they feed upon the natural inclinations people have to view the world from an "us against them" perspective. I contend that these issues have been used much like racial issues in political campaigns and have been an important part of continued Democratic success after the Voting Rights Act.

The foreign trade issue, so much a part of Jim Chapman's campaign and also prominent in the campaigns of the Democrats Taylor in Mississippi, Browder in Alabama, and Payne in Virginia, is an excellent example of such an issue. Foreign trade was raised in these campaigns not so much because these politicians expected people to understand the intricacies of tariff policy or international economics. Rather, it spoke to the concerns people had about the suffering U.S. economy and provided an easily accessible answer to the problem. The Japanese were not responsible for the oil bust that devastated East Texas, but when a steel plant closed down in the district, Chapman blamed unfair foreign competition, and the Japanese were an easily identifiable villain that he could point to. When his Republican opponent said that he did not know what trade policies had to do with bringing jobs to East Texas, Chapman's campaign gained further momentum. Hargett spent the rest of the campaign on the defensive, trying to explain his statement. The issue played further to Chapman's advantage when Hargett's campaign hats were found to have been made in Taiwan. The Democrat gleefully pulled the hat out of his pocket during the only televised debate of the campaign in what he described as "the defining moment of the campaign." In the end, it was widely believed that Jim Chapman rode the issue to Congress. The issue was effective, said a Democratic analyst, because "it [seemed] to cut with everyone—farmers, workers, seniors, small businessmen" (Taylor 1985c).

Although Chapman won by a small margin, the Texas election served as a demonstration to other southern politicians, and not the demonstration that the Republicans had hoped for. The power of the issue was apparent to Democratic officials even before the election was over. "The good news out of the Texas race, win, draw, or lose, is that we have an issue we know we can use next year," said the executive director of the Democratic Congressional Campaign Committee (Taylor 1985c). Indeed, a Democratic campaign consultant argued that because of the Chapman campaign, the trade issue had become a standard piece of the southern Democratic repertoire.

The way these Democrats and Republicans talked about drugs also illustrates how an issue can be shaped to generate resentment. Many of the arguments sounded here against drugs were supply-side arguments. It is not surprising that in these campaigns there were many Republican and Democratic calls for the death penalty for drug kingpins (with expansive definitions of the term). Neither is it surprising that little was said about drug treatment centers or education programs, which, of course, are more liberal approaches to the problem. What is surprising is how much of the drug dialogue centered on assassinating the Panamanian leader Manuel Noriega and the effective interdiction of foreign drug runners. Tom Anderson even called for military action against drug cartels in Central America. Voiced in a part of the country where the drug problem is comparatively less severe, these seemed to be rather dramatic proposals.

The foreign aid issue that came up in the Dowdy campaign is a third issue that fits into the resentment category. In highlighting this issue, Dowdy was not only blaming "our problems" on "them," he was making the case that what was rightfully ours was going to them. When he attacked President Reagan's $3-billion package of foreign aid to Pakistan, he argued that while Americans—and Mississippians—were sacrificing under Reagan's plan, "other countries [were] receiving our money." Reagan's budget cuts did not spare Amtrak, farm programs, and veterans' programs, he argued, why should they spare foreign aid? Dowdy's campaign strategy with regard to this issue was masterful. His message had two strands, two elements of a zero-sum game. He talked about who was losing and who was sacrificing as a result of Republican budget cuts and who was benefiting from Republican policies. Taking advantage of his position in the out-party, Dowdy found a comparative advantage where Williams was vulnerable, where the Republican's hands were tied by his public endorsement of the administration.

What do these three issues have in common? For one thing, in each case people of a different race or nationality or both are benefiting at the expense of Americans. These issues are not explicitly racial in content. They nonetheless derive some of their political appeal from the fact that the target of political rhetoric is some racial or foreign out-group, at least in the minds of political strategists seeking any advantage they can.[33] They are often issues with a racial twist, a twist that broadens their appeal. And it is not just that the Japanese, the Latin Americans, and the Pakistanis are easy targets because they are not white. The advantage of resentment issues is that there are so few representatives of these out-groups in the district that the strategy has little electoral cost. There is no one to challenge the legitimacy of these issues, to cry "foul," and politicians are unfettered and unchallenged in making their inflammatory remarks.

The references by campaign managers to Tora! Tora! Tora! and "Japa-nese bashing" also indicate that it is the adversarial aspect of these issues that they feel is most important. A Democratic campaign consultant said that it was not necessarily the trade issue, per se, that was important to the campaign, but "how it played into the big patriotism thing." In his mind, such rhetoric worked and was employed in his election because it not only highlighted a problem, it created an adversary. And Chapman himself believed that it was not that people understood the issue, but they "sensed it. They had this nagging fear that foreigners were buying up our industry, that no VCRs were being made in America." The dual goal of these resentment messages is thus to create a threat and, in the words of a Democratic consultant, "[to] get at some of those pro-American chords that Reagan sounds so well" (Taylor 1985c). In other words, these issues allow Democrats to redefine "us" as well as to blame "them."

Both Republicans and Democrats have used resentment issues in their campaigns on occasion, but Democrats have used them with greater frequency and with more effect than Republicans. The Republicans al-ready have racial issues in their arsenals and, as will be discussed, other campaign themes to play. Democrats have had to do something specifi-cally to "keep whites home," as one Democratic politician put it. Racial issues have not been available to them for obvious reasons. Out of sheer necessity, other ways to appeal to whites have had to be devised.

The trade issue has been especially good for Democrats as Republican efforts to portray themselves as pure conservatives (and even their con-servative convictions) have gotten in the way of taking a protectionist stand. For instance, the Virginia Republican Linda Arey, extraordinarily consistent in the application of her ideological principles, took a strong free trade position in her campaign against L. F. Payne. In this, Arey was not much different from other southern Republicans. For example, in the House, southern Republicans almost unanimously opposed the protectionist Gephardt Amendment to a 1987 Omnibus Trade Bill (only one of thirty-nine congressmen voted for it), while over three-quarters of southern Democrats (sixty of seventy-seven) accepted the amendment.[34] Other votes on trade issues generated similar results. The point, of course, is that Democrats had come upon an issue that distinguished them from Republicans, one that they perceived to be electorally profitable. Said a pollster from the Chapman campaign, "I think the Democrats can win in the South if they take these symbolic tools away from Charlie Black [a national Republican advisor], if they capture the symbols of the campaign from the beginning." Trade has been one such symbol for the Democrats. Resentment issues offer others as well.

A second element of the Democratic resentment strategy to keep white voters in the fold has been to pepper their campaigns with populist appeals in the best of the southern tradition. In these cases, Democrats made class-based appeals of us versus them and attacked large banks, corporations, insurance companies, and other large institutions in their rhetoric. As conservative as the southern electorate is, these southern Democrats believed such appeals to be effective and relied on them to activate and capture the rural white vote and the working-class white vote. As Jim Chapman put it, "People in my district are suspicious of anything big and institutionalized. You can even be a progressive Democrat in my conservative district if you understand this."

These efforts involved more than just selecting the right enemy. They involved capturing an image, forging a connection with the common man. The Democrats spoke at length of their humble roots and the difficult times in their lives and linked their own stories to the issues they were highlighting in their campaigns. Glen Browder's mother, widowed at twenty years of age with three children, was testimony to the need for Social Security. Mississippi Democrat Gene Taylor's advertisements told of how he and his siblings had to move from southern Mississippi to find jobs. Even Virginia's L. F. Payne, a millionaire developer, had modest beginnings and often talked of his father, a retired state trooper, and his mother, a teacher, and their service to the state.

While identifying themselves as common men, these southern Democrats labeled their opponents pawns of the rich and powerful. "Edd Hargett," declared a Jim Chapman radio commercial, "is a *Republican* backed by the *rich*" (Attlesey 1985b), not a popular combination in East Texas. On a television call-in show, Gene Taylor spoke of his supporters as "humble folks" who sent in five-dollar donations to the campaign while Anderson's supporters were rich "fat cats" from far away. Wayne Dowdy borrowed a page from Huey Long, who once observed that corporations (particularly oil companies) "are the finest political enemies in the world" (Williams 1969, 416). Dowdy's television advertisements portrayed his opponent as a stooge of the oil industry (Clymer 1981a), and he declared at campaign rallies, "I'm running against the President of the United States, the U.S. Chamber of Commerce, and every oil company in the world" (Putnam 1981a). When an airplane towing a Williams streamer flew over one rally, Dowdy added that his opponent had "the backing of the big oil companies and now has a hot air balloon and an airplane as well" (Mullen 1981). As this illustrates, populist issues and themes afforded another vehicle by which southern Democrats could appeal to white voters, above all, rural white voters.

The Republicans in these races also had populist chords to ring. Their attacks on big institutions were directed at "big labor," "big eastern labor unions," "big eastern labor bosses," or some other such bugbear. These charges usually came about when Democrats had taken money from labor, sometimes a considerable percentage of their overall campaign fund. It was more difficult to link them to the big forces of eastern liberalism, though, as these were not usually credible charges. Nonetheless, the AFL-CIO and the National Education Association made excellent rhetorical enemies, and the Democrats were guilty by association.

If there has been a problem with an antiunion populist attack, however, it is that some members of labor unions may be offended by the rhetoric.

Republicans have tried, as John Rice tried in Alabama, to create a fine distinction when they make the case that "organized labor and the working man are two different things." Newspaper stories about Rice's old union pals feeling betrayed, though, may have undermined his point (Smith 1989f) and cost him as much support as he gained.[35] Linda Arey also experienced difficulties in wooing labor votes with statements (in front of a labor audience) that she did not trust "big labor bosses in Washington" and that some union members might resent their dues going to support presidential candidates they did not prefer. Both statements were loudly jeered (Bland 1988c).[36] These incidents illustrate how the target that best fits the rest of the Republicans' campaign message—big labor—has been problematic, particularly as many white swing votes in the district are union members. They also show that while Republicans sometimes do attack large institutions in the populist tradition, their natural targets are fewer. One lovely enemy for Republicans, of course, is big government, and inasmuch as they can harness this populist theme, they will be very effective.

That Democratic campaign managers keep returning to populist messages and other resentment issues and winning elections with them is some indication that they have resonance among white (and black) southern voters. But this evidence is only suggestive. Survey research is needed to investigate further the relation between attitudes on racial issues and attitudes on resentment issues as well as the relation between attitudes on resentment issues and the vote. Nonetheless, as these cases show, the choices offered to southern voters are shaped very much by the belief among campaign officials that these types of issues work.

Conservatism and Parochialism in Southern Elections

"Conservatism," write Earl and Merle Black (1987), "occupies an exalted ideological position in the South" (213). This, of course, gives the more conservative Republicans a decided advantage. Black and Black predict the continued growth of the Republican party given the force of conservative politics in the South: "In most southern states, . . . campaigning as a Republican is a diminishing liability, for the GOP is rapidly growing and has excellent future prospects. Our analysis has shown key sectors of the southern electorate—whites, in general, but especially the conservatives, the college-educated, and the youngest generation—either realigning in favor of the Republicans or strongly moving in that direction" (255–56). The conservative advantage in white public opinion, as Black and Black label one of their chapters, favors the Republicans more than ever, and it is little wonder that analysts of southern politics have pointed to this as an indicator of a bright Republican future.

Republican congressional candidates recognize the strategic advantage that conservatism gives them, and they borrow extensively from the presidential campaigns. They run as staunch conservatives, highlighting the issues and messages that Reagan and Bush used so effectively in the South. There is a big difference between these campaigns and the presidential campaign, however. Republican congressional candidates do not face northern liberals. Their Democratic opponents are often highly conservative, and they must approach the southern electorate somewhat differently.

First, a number of issues have offered some possibilities for Republicans to distinguish themselves from Democrats. To start, they have tried to exploit "no new taxes" pledges, as Bush and Reagan did so effectively in their presidential campaigns. In these cases, the Democrats consistently refused to sign a strict pledge put out by a conservative national taxpayers organization. The Republicans signed it with great ceremony. Still, it was hard to paint their Democratic opponents as wild-eyed liberals, even on this issue. Although Democrats did not sign the pledge, they did affirm their commitment to fighting tax increases. Sometimes, they even tried to turn their refusal to sign the pledge into something positive. Gene Taylor, for example, refused to sign the pledge because it prevented him from voting to raise taxes if a military base or an industry in the district was in great trouble.

On other issues, southern Republicans have tried to "out-conservative" their conservative opponents. Linda Arey's proposal to post the Ten Commandments in every schoolroom and Tom Anderson's declarations on school prayer, for instance, illustrate candidates trying to differentiate themselves on a specific issue. But how much room was there for Arey, Anderson, and their colleagues to the right of their Democratic opponents? Did Anderson's declaration make him the purer conservative? Did this difference matter to Mississippi voters?

Emphasizing their superior conservatism does not appear to have been enough for Republicans to win over the numbers of white southerners that are required to overcome the Democratic advantage among blacks. Mostly this has been because southern Democrats have been conservative enough, particularly on social issues like abortion, gun control, and school prayer but even on some economic issues, like lowering the capital gains tax. Moreover, southern Democrats have been greatly concerned that people will judge them by their association with the national Democratic party and thus have taken great pains to separate themselves from the national party, its more recognizable celebrities, and its leadership. "I wouldn't know Ed Kennedy if he stepped on my foot," said Gene Taylor. Whether intentional or not, his reference to Kennedy as Ed proved his point. A *New York Times* reporter wrote about the Texas Democrat Jim Chapman, "[He] has so often called himself a 'conservative Democrat' as opposed to a 'national Democrat,' that some people here say they are beginning to think he is a member of some new party" (King 1985c). L. F. Payne, Wayne Dowdy, and Glen Browder also carefully dodged association with such nationally known Democratic figures as Walter Mondale, Michael Dukakis, Edward Kennedy, Jesse Jackson, Barney Frank, and the entire national party apparatus.

The Democrats' conservative positions on the issues, their alienation from the national party, and their connections with state and local conservative Democrats are the ways they have attempted to deflect the inevitable charges of liberalism. Scattered evidence suggests that they have been successful and that southern voters do not perceive them to be liberal. An *Anniston Star* poll, for example, showed that only 19 percent of registered voters (n=606) thought of Glen Browder as a liberal despite his being barraged with this charge by the Republican candidate (Rilling 1989). A large number (34 percent) could not place Browder on an ideological spectrum (not an easy task given Browder's skilled evasiveness).

Nonetheless, among registered voters Browder clearly was not thought of as a liberal. This conclusion is in line with other evidence on southern perceptions of southern Democrats. Only 34 percent of southerners place the Democratic candidate for Congress in their district on the liberal side of a seven-point liberal-conservative attribution scale, and well over half these people (20 percent of all southern respondents) see the candidate as only moderately liberal. Of course, many respondents are unable to place themselves or the candidates on this scale, but of those who do, a large majority do not consider them liberal. This is not the case for Democratic presidential candidates. Michael Dukakis, for instance, was perceived by 54 percent of southerners as liberal, and most (38 percent of all southern respondents) did not perceive him as moderately liberal.[37]

The point is that southern Democrats have strategically and success-fully placed themselves on the right, but to the left of Republicans, to capture the votes of white moderates and liberals (few as they may be) and to compete with Republicans for the conservative white vote. In Downs-ian terms, southern Democrats have situated themselves near the center of the distribution of political opinion, a decidedly conservative location. Republicans work hard to establish themselves as the bona fide conserva-tives and to many white southerners, this matters. But local Democrats have been conservative too, and conservative enough to blunt the effect of Republican charges of being "too liberal." In the Virginia case, for exam-ple, L. F. Payne's campaign manager argued that Linda Arey thought the district was more conservative than it actually was: "Partially, this was because of Dan Daniel. She also had to run to the far right to get the nomination. Once we inoculated L.F. as a conservative, though, we were okay."

A second Republican strategy in the congressional elections of the 1980s and early 1990s was to highlight the candidates' connections with popular Republican administrations. All the Republicans in this small sample but one (Hayes Dent, who ran in 1993) ran radio and television commercials featuring Presidents Bush and Reagan. They sent out letters under the president's signature. When possible, they brought the presi-dent or high-ranking administration officials into the district. Vice president and presidential candidate Bush campaigned for a day with Linda Arey in Virginia and made a presidential appearance in the Gulfport election. These events were always good for a front-page story or two.

In addition, the Republicans adopted themes from the presidential campaigns and from the president's agenda. Liles Williams talked about Ronald Reagan's budget cuts throughout his campaign. Tom Anderson obtained and was photographed with a satchel of cocaine shortly after George Bush held up a package of drugs in a nationally televised speech. Linda Arey, dubbed by *Congressional Quarterly* "an overnight symbol of the South's Reagan-era Republicanism" (Elving 1988, 1008), supported the president's veto on the civil rights bill, even when many southern Republican congressmen were not prepared to do so. The Republicans in this sample unabashedly tied themselves to both administrations.[38] Given the overwhelming victories of the Republican presidential candidates in these districts, such a strategy seemed sensible. But the major shortcoming of this strategy is that it made the Republicans vulnerable to an effective Democratic counterstrategy.

In the Reagan-Bush years, Democrats obviously did not play up their ties to Republican administrations. They attempted to find other issues to differentiate themselves from Republicans and tended to use local issues to fill this role. Republicans have often been so enamored of conservative issues that they have failed to diversify their campaigns. Southern Democrats have, and they believe that the local angle has been an important contributor to their success in the past thirty years. Whereas Republicans have emphasized their superior conservatism and their connections with the president, Democrats have highlighted issues of service to the district and discussed opportunities to deliver federal money and federal projects to the highly dependent area. In Alabama, the Democratic consultant said, "The Republicans essentially wanted to play the presidential campaign over again. Let Rice talk about national issues, we want to talk about roads and bridges and military bases." In Virginia, the sentiment was similar. "She [Arey] emphasized Washington and we emphasized the district," said a consultant to the Payne campaign. "I'll take the district any day of the week."

This difference between Democratic and Republican campaign themes was highly evident in all of the elections observed here. While Tom Anderson talked about his relation with the president, Gene Taylor talked about his relation with the area's shrimpers. Linda Arey, though possibly less accepted in the staunchly conservative district, spoke of hard-line conservative principles like "local control" and "private enterprise." L. F. Payne spoke of the local jobs he personally brought into Nelson County with his business enterprise. John Rice made cutting taxes and federal spending the centerpiece of his campaign. So did Glen Browder, but he talked about protecting the district from cuts in the federal budget (the Dick Armey bill to close down obsolete military bases was in the news at the time of the campaign). Campaign mottos captured the local image these Democrats were trying to create: Gene Taylor was "South Mississippi's Choice," L. F. Payne's motto was "Virginia Values, Virginia Leadership," and Glen Browder's was "Alabama Thinking, Alabama Values." Compare these to their Republican opponents' taglines: "Leadership, not Politics," "A Congressman We Won't Have to Train," and "Experience Where it Counts!" The key for Democrats, insisted one media consultant, has been to "parochialize the race," to make a local connection with every issue.

Toward this end, Democratic political promises have been more locally oriented. Military installations are important to the prosperity of many southern districts. Establishing one's dedication to taking care of the district on military issues has been crucial to Democratic candidates. The best way to do this is to have a position on the Armed Services Committee, from which a congressman can bring defense pork home to the district, pork that will supply jobs and support service industries in the area surrounding a military base or a veterans' hospital. It is no accident that fifteen of the thirty-one Democrats on the House Armed Services Committee after the elections of 1988 were southerners. Running for office the first time, Democrats can promise only to ask for a seat on the committee. Democrats in the Alabama and Mississippi 5 races went somewhat further: they solicited the assistance of powerful Democrats from the state delegation, Sen. Howell Heflin from Alabama and Congressman Sonny Montgomery from Mississippi. In the days immediately preceding the election, Heflin and Montgomery announced that they would attempt to assert their institutional influence to open a spot on Armed Services for their new colleague. Montgomery even spent a day campaigning with Gene Taylor, visiting military installations and veterans' hospitals and providing Taylor with an important headline. Gene Taylor did receive an Armed Services assignment upon coming to the House. Browder did not, though he got on the committee shortly thereafter. What were the hopes and promises of the Republican candidates opposing Taylor and Browder? Anderson aimed for the Energy and Commerce Committee or the Small Business Committee, picking up on some of his experience in Washington. John Rice, whose personality and ideological fervor guided him throughout his campaign, wanted to get on the Interior Committee. "I firmly believe those are going to be the hot issues," he said, "and I want to be where the heat is" (Smith 1989e).

The Republicans have recognized the strategic advantage this local angle gives Democrats. One Republican leader attributed the narrow loss in Mississippi's Fourth District to Liles Williams's "[failure] to develop any local issues" (Broder 1981b). Yet none of the other Republicans in this small sample appeared to have learned from Williams's mistake. Part of the reason is that Republicans, as mostly rational actors, have subscribed to the idea that "Nothing succeeds like success." As sensible politicians, they have done what works. But they have looked to the wrong example, the presidential election, rather than adopting the successful strategy of local Democrats. Republicans, experiencing so little success at the local level, have fixated on Washington politics, which has inhibited the development of local campaign themes. Although Republican candidates have recognized that they must make a local connection on the stump, they also have tried to capitalize on the party's national success, to use the conservative formula that won the South for Reagan and Bush. These two goals may not be complementary. Superior Republican conservatism actually may have hindered them from taking the local angle and from identifying themselves as the district's guardian in Washington.[39] Strong (1971) argued in the early 1970s that "[Republicans] take their ideology seriously. This seriousness prevents them from being flexible enough to broaden their bases of support" (254). Things did not change much in this regard in the following two decades.

A newspaper debate between L. F. Payne and Linda Arey over transportation issues illustrates the point. In the debate, Arey said that America's interstate highway system was starting to show its age and that federal money should go toward repair and renovation. At the same time, she lambasted a spendthrift Congress and "those most special of political pork barrel plums—unnecessary construction contracts." Payne, on the other hand, talked about the plum he would like to deliver to the district, the "construction of a Danville bypass for U.S. Routes 58 and 29" (*Danville Bee* 1988). On foreign trade issues, a similar contrast emerged. Arey, supporting the free trade principles that had been championed by Ronald Reagan, came out strongly opposed to trade restrictions. Payne, on the other hand, used the issue to characterize himself as the district's guardian. He talked about "inequities against American jobs in the present world trade situation" and "[working] on behalf of our district with the U.S. trade representative to increase exports of our district's products and to be a watchdog over unfair foreign practices involving district products" (*Danville Bee* 1988). The two candidates used the newspaper forum to stress different things, Arey her support of the conservative principles of President Reagan, Payne his dedication to protecting the district.

The Alabama case is another, vivid example of a Democrat neutralizing and even capitalizing on his opponent's conservative message. John Rice declared that federal money for schools came with "too many strings attached." The message was intended to strike a conservative chord, but it left Rice vulnerable to Glen Browder's message of district advocacy. For every dollar in taxes that left Alabama, argued Browder, $1.38 was spent in the district. "I like the balance of trade we have with the federal government," said the Democrat. At another point, he said, "John Rice's philosophy would devastate this district. . . . I believe that Bill Nichols worked hard to bring federal money to the district and we ought to keep it" (Yardley 1989a). Browder also argued that Rice's proposal to cut federal spending by 50 percent would threaten $85 million in benefits for district veterans as well as other valuable programs. Rice's conservative plans—Browder labeled them Ricenomics—were irresponsible and would cost people in the district (Burger 1989a).

At another point in the race, as discussed in chapter 3, Rice's campaign manager was quoted as saying that the campaign had returned $3,000 in donations from "people we don't like" (Smith 1989b). Again, Rice's intent was to win conservative votes (particularly given that his campaign was financially strapped). But again, the comment played into Browder's campaign strategy. In the words of the Democrat's media advisor, "That business came off sounding like 'I don't want to represent everybody in the district.' It was hyperideological. Glen said he would serve all the people of the district and it made him seem more constituency oriented, which is just what we were aiming for." Browder and Rice alike attempted to tie themselves closely to the late Bill Nichols, both taking notice of Nichols's extraordinary service to the district. Nichols delivered and so long as he did, Republicans were loathe to challenge him. When the opportunity arose to replace him, Rice tried to connect himself ideologically to the conservative Nichols, which was sensible given that he had a strong case for this. Browder, however, appears to have been more effective at positioning himself as Nichols's natural successor, as the individual best able to carry on his work.

These Democrats also tried to turn the Republican candidates' connections to the president into an advantage, or at least into less of a disadvantage, again by characterizing the contest as one of home versus Washington. As noted above, their opponents tied themselves to the popular Reagan and Bush administrations as much as possible, and Presidents Reagan and Bush, intent on party building to a degree that their predecessors were not, were cooperative. In fact, Reagan, Bush, and other prominent Republicans played important roles in all of these Republican campaigns. The connection to the Republican administration, notably in places where Reagan and Bush had won by overwhelming margins, was a source of great pride for the Republican candidates. But in an observation that directly addresses one of the puzzles of the southern realignment, the Democrats often salvaged some advantage from their precarious situation, and that advantage stemmed from their outsider status.

As is good campaign practice, southern Democrats blamed Washington insiders for all of the country's problems. In the 1980s and early 1990s, the Democrats had a broad target in a federal government headed by Republicans, and these conservative southern Democrats took aim at it. In one of the more clever and far-reaching claims of the campaigns observed here, Gene Taylor took credit for balancing his budget for the previous six years, while charging that Tom Anderson had not balanced his budget in the whole time he had been in Washington. A campaign aide admitted that Taylor's budget was in fact the Mississippi state budget (Mississippi has a balanced budget amendment in its constitution) and Anderson's budget was the federal budget. Anderson tried to link himself to the administration, to characterize himself as an insider. This allowed Taylor, the outsider, to lay the problems faced by the federal government at Anderson's door. His charge was outrageous, to be sure, but it went unchallenged.

The Democrats here depicted presidential efforts on behalf of Republican candidates as outside interference. They tried to turn these visits to their favor, and the general sentiment of both Democratic and Republican officials was that it worked. "The more Washington showed up, the more it played into our hands," said the Virginia Democrat L. F. Payne. In the Mississippi 5 race, claims of outside interference were a major part of Taylor's campaign, and campaign insiders on both sides felt that Anderson was seriously damaged by them. The Republican was plagued with the problem of being perceived as a pawn of Trent Lott and George Bush. Unflattering editorial cartoons and biting disc jockey comments about what was supposed to be the most important event in his campaign, Bush's appearance in the district, only reinforced that image.

The outsider image that southern Democrats had was doubly effective as they disassociated themselves from *both* national parties. They played an us versus them game and "them" included both the Republicans and the national Democrats. Political necessity thus led to an effective campaign tactic. "I will only listen to the people of the district," said Wayne

Dowdy at a McComb rally, "not the lobbyists in Washington or either political party" (Mullen 1981). Gene Taylor's argument that his campaign was poor because he failed to meet the liberal litmus tests of national Democratic donors also illustrates the point. Anti-Washington, anti-Congress campaign rhetoric is effective in most places and is a common tactic in congressional campaigns (Fenno 1978, 163–69). It was doubly effective through the 1980s and early 1990s for southern Democrats, who took advantage of their position in the party out of office and of their minority position within the Democratic party. They were outsiders in Washington, so they claimed, which gave them currency with their future constituents.

Finally, Democrats have been able to keep a local edge in that their candidates are more likely to have risen through local and state political institutions than Republicans. That is, Democrats have been more likely to come into the race having held local office or with political experience at the state level. Republicans have been more likely to come to the race with considerably less experience. In part this is a national phenomenon. As Alan Ehrenhalt (1991) argues, the Democrats, as the party of government, are better situated to recruit able candidates for low-level offices:

> Consider two bright, glib, personable twenty-five-year-olds with a natural talent for salesmanship. One is a liberal Democrat who sees government as a benevolent instrument of social policy. The other is a conservative Republican who agrees with the national GOP leadership that government itself is a large part of the problem. Which one is more likely to put his talents to work selling himself to the voters as a candidate for public office? Which one is apt to decide that it is more respectable (as well as more lucrative) to sell insurance or real estate or computers? (224–25)

Ehrenhalt's argument is that while it is not so difficult to find high-quality candidates for high-profile positions, the Republicans have been less successful, and understandably so, at recruiting superior candidates for state legislative or city council positions. Ehrenhalt's argument is even more powerful when applied to the South, where decades upon decades of Democratic dominance have made it difficult for Republicans to recruit candidates for low office. This advantage is certainly reflected in my sample; five of the six Democratic candidates were state senators or city councilors or district attorneys. They had been elected before, if not in the entire district, then in a significant portion of it. L. F. Payne was the only Democrat who came to the race with little or no political experience.

Only one of the six Republicans in these cases came into the race with previous electoral experience. Tom Anderson and Hayes Dent (see chapter 5) were aides to Republican politicians. Linda Arey held an appointive position in the Reagan administration. Liles Williams was a former Democratic party leader, and Edd Hargett had no previous political experience. John Rice was a state senator who represented a significant part of the southern half of the Third District of Alabama. Of course, Rice had been elected as a Democrat and had switched to the Republican side shortly before the election, an event that many southern Republicans see as the most important way to build the party. The point is not that these were unattractive candidates. Well funded and with political resumes that had some appeal in these districts, they had good chances to win these elections. They were not as attractive as their Democratic opponents, however. They had not won elections in the district before and, in a couple of cases, they had built their careers elsewhere, notably in Washington. In an interesting twist, when their old Republican bosses came to town to vouch for them, their Democratic opponents all further played the populist independence theme. They asserted that the Republicans were handpicked (the nature of the special election primaries had something to do with this) and argued that "powerful folks in Washington" were interfering in the local political process. It was a minor theme in the Democratic message, but it was consistent with many of the other points they were trying to make.

The local strategy Democrats pursued in these cases is likely to be most effective when the candidates are able to disassociate themselves from the national Democratic party and national Democratic figures. In this sense, the Democratic quest for white votes becomes more difficult when a Democrat is in the White House. During the Reagan-Bush years, congressional leaders or controversial Democratic figures like Barney Frank, Jesse Jackson, and Jim Wright made inviting targets for Republican candidates. Democrats, however, easily deflected the charge that they had some tie to these people. With a Democratic president in office, southern Democratic candidates have had a new problem. The president is so much more visible to the public, and the connection between a president and members of his congressional party is so much easier to make that their ability to run independently of the national party has been diminished.

Take, for instance, a special election held in Kentucky's Second District in May 1994 after the death of the venerable Democratic congressman of forty years, William Natcher. Though Kentucky is a small reach out of the South (as most scholars define it), this district, in the rural, west-central part of the state, has a southern character. Containing a very small population of blacks (5 percent of the district), the character of the district nevertheless was such that appeals to white voters were of utmost importance to gaining victory.

Not surprisingly the winning Republican candidate, a Christian bookstore owner named Ron Lewis, emphasized his outsider status. President Clinton was weakest at the time of the election, his disapproval ratings bettering his approval ratings for only the second time in his term. As a result, Lewis's out-party campaign was certainly different from the Democratic outsider campaigns detailed here. Whereas a Democrat like Gene Taylor did not portray himself as being opposed to the Republican administration and its policies (which were popular in his district), Lewis ran against the president and his policies at every opportunity, and his campaign rhetoric tied his opponent, the state legislator Joe Prather, to the president. A television commercial showing an image of Prather slowly "morphing" into an image of Bill Clinton was widely shown. Noting that the president's legislation was winning by small, even one-vote margins, Lewis would tell crowds, "A vote for me . . . will be a vote against Bill Clinton" (Kocher 1994b). In some regards, Lewis's message was not much different from the other Republican messages I describe in these cases. His attempt to nationalize the campaign, however, carried more pungency because a Democrat was in the White House.

Joe Prather's campaign message also did not differ much from the Democratic messages discussed in this book. Prather's main appeal was local in character. He associated himself with state, not national, Democratic leaders. He painted himself as the defender of tobacco interests in the district, which were vulnerable given antismoking developments. Patterning himself after Natcher, Prather refused to take money from so-called special interests (defined as money from out of state).[40] Said the candidate, "[Natcher used to say], 'if you take their money, the minute you go there to serve they have their hands all over you.' I'm here to tell you that the hands I want on me are the hands of the people of the 2nd District" (Kocher 1994a). Prather attacked Lewis for taking money from the national Republican party and accepting help from national Republican politicians. He tried to tie the two points together after Minority Leader Bob Dole visited the district on Lewis's behalf. Dole was not interested in the people of the Second District, ranted Prather: "You know I'm not going to Congress and tell Sen. Dole that I'm going to be for taxing Kansas wheat. And I darn sure don't want him in here telling us that he's going to tax that cash crop that is the economic foundation [of the Second District]" (Kocher 1994a).

Statements like this reinforced the widely held belief that Prather was a poor candidate, which certainly contributed to his loss. Nonetheless, if his campaign illustrates anything, perhaps it is that being in the out-party is not so much an advantage for Democrats in the years of Republican presidents as being associated with the party in power is a disadvantage in Democratic years. As part of the purpose of this chapter is to explain how Democrats survived a lengthy period of popular Republican presidents, I focus here on the small things Democrats did to take advantage of their out-party status or at least to neutralize the disadvantage of not being linked to Bush or Reagan. What is striking is that whether the White House was occupied by a Republican or a Democrat, Democratic congressional candidates knew their advantage lay in running local campaigns, while their Republican opponents honed in on their national advantage. In the Texas, Virginia, and Mississippi contests, the local campaigns were quite effective. In the Kentucky case, with an unpopular Democrat as president, the Republican's national theme paid off. That the largest Republican gains in Congress in the past thirty years have occurred in the midterms of Democratic administrations is some indication that the nationalizing of the congressional election is possible if the circumstances are right.

The cases in this book illustrate that Democratic candidates have adapted to and even flourished in a hostile political environment. As the Kentucky election shows, they must be prepared to adjust to continuous changes in that environment. Nonetheless, what they have accomplished to this point, and how they have accomplished it, is impressive.

The mathematics of these elections require that Democrats win only a minority of white votes in their districts, and sometimes only a modest minority of that vote. Increasingly, southern whites, even a majority of southern whites, are supporting congressional Republicans, for racial reasons or for conservative reasons or both. By cultivating new issues and refining some old ones many Democrats have been able to attract white votes and court enough of them to keep the Republicans from taking over southern delegation after southern delegation.

5 The Majority Black District

ONE RECENT CONSEQUENCE of the Voting Rights Act of 1964 has been that southern states have created new majority black congressional and state legislative districts. The number of majority black districts in the South has gone from zero in 1970 to sixteen following the 1990 redistricting. The number of black members of the House of Representatives from the South has risen accordingly from two (first elected from 45–50 percent black urban districts in 1973 [*Congressional Quarterly* 1982]) to seventeen over this period. As of the 1990 Census, blacks comprise 19 percent of the population of the South, and, as of 1992, black representatives represent almost 14 percent of southern congressional districts.[1]

The large and growing number of these districts is only one reason I include a majority black case here. The districts are located in many of the places where race has most pervaded politics in the past. And these are the places where race is still a big and very obvious issue. Moreover, including an election from a majority black district in this book offers an opportunity to test one of the major hypotheses from chapter 2. What happens when the racial balance tips the other way? Do contests in majority black districts mirror those in majority white districts? How does partisan strategy differ in these districts, and in what ways is it the same? The election described here, pitting a black Democrat against a white Republican, allows one to broach these questions. The primary election, in which five black Democratic candidates, two white Democratic candidates, and one white Republican candidate vied to get into the runoff, also provides insight into the formation of racial-political strategy.

Mississippi 2

The election that took place in Mississippi's Second District in the spring of 1993 brings this study full circle. Like the election in Mississippi 4 discussed above, this was one of the first special elections of a new administration.[2] The districts, in fact, are adjacent, even sharing some of the same territory. Claiborne and Jefferson Counties, in the Fourth in 1980, were moved to the Second when a majority black Second District was created.

The district comprises the heavily black parts of the Jackson metropolitan area, the city of Vicksburg, the overwhelmingly black Claiborne and Jefferson Counties, and the entirety of an area of the state misnamed the Delta. The area is not a triangular piece of land at the mouth of a river, the usual definition of the term, but a flat floodplain of the Mississippi in the west-central part of the state. The river's work has defined the area geographically. Rolling hills border the region to the east and the north, and the Yazoo River defines its southern border. As the Mississippi River has flooded and receded over the centuries, the soil is rich in organic material and very fertile. As one local put it, "Spit and plant a seed and it'll grow."

The seed, of course, has long been cotton. It is said that cotton was king in the Old South and no more so than in this area. Large plantations and large-scale cotton gins dot the region, and much of the Delta's other business is dependent on a healthy farm economy.[3]

The other major "crop" of importance to the area is catfish. Although catfish have long been part of the southern diet, the large-scale farming of catfish is a rather new phenomenon. In 1970, close to six million pounds of catfish were shipped in the United States. By 1989, three hundred million pounds were shipped, 87 percent from Mississippi ponds, and Delta ponds at that (Forman 1989). The big difference between catfish and cotton is that the catfish industry is providing jobs. Technology has made unskilled labor much less necessary in the cultivation of cotton, and the farms are no longer a major source of employment. The catfish processing industry, however, is located in the Delta, and this has created manufacturing as well as agricultural jobs.

Most of these jobs have gone to poor blacks, who greatly outnumber whites in the region. Indeed, the legacy of the cotton industry is the large black population. The cotton plantations of the Deep South initially operated with large numbers of slaves and were the slowest to adopt more modern agricultural techniques that made slavery much less profitable. The region even served as a market for excess slaves from the developing Upper South (Genovese 1967, 90, 247). To this day, the Delta is the most heavily black area of the country's most heavily black state in spite of the huge migration of Delta blacks northward. Many people have returned to the Delta to retire, yet the out-migration of young blacks continues to this day and is of concern to many.[4]

Not only is the district heavily black but it is extremely poor, by some measures the second poorest congressional district in the nation. At the time of the 1990 Census, 44 percent of people in the district lived below 125 percent of the poverty line, and 61 percent lived below 200 percent of that mark. More than 20 percent of the district's residents received public assistance. More than 22 percent of people over age twenty-five had less than a ninth-grade education (U.S. Bureau of the Census 1992).[5] And, as elsewhere, it is blacks who suffer disproportionately, creating a huge racial gap that shows no indication of closing. As of 1990, the unemployment rate for district whites was 4 percent; for blacks it was 18 percent.

The mean income for whites was $33,581; for blacks, it was $15,385. Whereas 71 percent of the district's whites had graduated from high school, only 43 percent of blacks had reached that milestone. Still, the statistics do not prepare the visitor for the sheer depth of the poverty that pervades the black communities in the area.

The poor, heavily black Delta experienced some turmoil during the civil rights movement. Greenwood, Ruleville, Drew, and other towns in the area had their share of confrontation and violence in the early 1960s. The major chapter that the Delta adds to the story of black political progress, however, comes later. With the passage of the Voting Rights Act and the widespread registration of blacks, black political power in the Delta (and elsewhere in the South) should have grown. But, of course, it did not. One way the white political establishment was able to dampen the effect of new black voters, particularly in heavily black places like western Mississippi, was to redefine political boundaries. In 1960, the Second Congressional District fully embraced the Delta (as it had for the prior eighty years). A redistricting in 1966 (following the Supreme Court's one-person, one-vote decisions) carved the Delta into three separate districts by running boundaries east-west across the state. The practical effect and the all-but-expressed purpose of dividing up (or "cracking") the Delta was to dilute the political strength of blacks, to keep any one district from being majority black. This districting plan remained in effect until 1982, when the Delta was glued back together (and added to) by a federal court relying upon a new judicial interpretation of the Voting Rights Act.[6] Following this redistricting, the Delta, now part of an almost-majority black district (over 48 percent), played host to the first congressional election in the rural South in which a black candidate had a fair chance of winning. Those chances improved further when the white Democratic incumbent, weighing his chances in the new district, chose to retire.

The election of 1982 pitted a black Democratic state senator, Robert Clark, against a white Democrat-turned-Republican, Webb Franklin. Clark's victory in the Democratic primary over two better-known white candidates (one the son of a segregationist governor, the other the cousin of the powerful senator James Eastland) was a major victory in and of itself. Clark, however, was politically unsophisticated and disorganized. Though he generated an enormous amount of enthusiasm among Delta blacks, whites turned out in even greater numbers, and Clark lost a very close election marked by almost complete racial-line voting. In 1984, after the district was redrawn once again to incorporate even more black population (almost 53 percent of the district), Clark once again took on Franklin. Once again he lost, this time by a little more than three thousand votes.

In 1986, Democrats fielded a different black candidate, a younger, more sophisticated state official, Mike Espy, to run against Franklin. Espy, a superior candidate to Clark, defeated Franklin, though narrowly (52 percent to 48 percent). Although Franklin attributes his loss to Espy and not to the redistricting (Fava 1993), this contest too was marked by racial-line voting. Espy won almost all of the black vote; Franklin took 88 percent of the white vote. The key to Espy's victory appears to be a dropoff in white turnout, which went from 63 percent in 1984 to 51 percent in 1986 (Lightman 1987).

Though he started at a great disadvantage, Espy built on that narrow victory to establish himself as an invulnerable incumbent. By 1990, running against an erratic black Republican, Espy won 84 percent of the vote and, of course, much of the increase in support came from white voters. That he did not emerge from the civil rights movement and that he came from a prominent family in the region (his family owned and operated funeral homes in the Delta) made him less threatening to whites and made this increase in support possible. As a local attorney put it, "All the things were there to make him perfectly acceptable to a Greenville Kiwanis Club" (Hall 1986). But it was Espy's active courtship of whites and a conciliatory message on race that generated so much goodwill. His activities in Washington—championing the catfish industry from his position on the House Agriculture Committee and taking comparatively conservative issue positions—further cemented his standing with Delta whites.[7] At the same time, many blacks remained enthusiastic about him. One black activist, who found Espy too moderate, nonetheless greatly admired him and fully supported him: "He [Espy] broke barriers. That was a great accomplishment. He was an advocate for our feelings. He was somebody we could touch. Talk to. He called us back. We haven't had anyone else in this district or even this state in over a hundred years." Forging this black-white coalition in the Delta was a most impressive accomplishment and destined Espy for even greater things.

Mississippi 2 Primary—"They're both playin' to a racist theme"

By late December 1992, President-elect Bill Clinton had made most of his decisions on cabinet appointments, but he had yet to fill the position at the Department of Agriculture. For weeks, Mike Espy's name had been mentioned as the leading candidate for the job. Only with the last set of appointments, though, did Espy win the job he quite aggressively sought. In fact, it was reported in the *Washington Post* that he pushed too much for the position and that this almost cost him the appointment (Balz and Marcus 1992).

Espy resigned his congressional position following his confirmation in late January, thereby setting into motion special election procedures in Mississippi. Like the other two Mississippi elections described above, this was a nonpartisan election to be held in two rounds if, as is likely in these situations, no one candidate received a majority of the vote in the first round at the end of March. Should the second election be necessary, it would be held two weeks later. As in the cases above, the absence of an incumbent and the opportunity for low-level officeholders to run without having to abandon their present position made for a large and talented field of candidates.

The low-salience special election also provided Republicans with a real opportunity to win a seat that would otherwise be considered beyond their reach. "We've been on the bottom so long, you know," said a finely dressed woman at a midafternoon rally for the Republican candidate. "We really are hopeful about this one." State party officials were optimistic as well but recognized that some things could be engineered to further heighten the possibility of capturing the seat. Foremost among these was to organize a caucus well before the primary election to settle on one

Republican candidate (as they had done in the Mississippi 4 special election described above). Premised on the likelihood that the Democrats would not be able to follow suit, Republican state party officials believed that a candidate chosen by caucus would assure that a Republican made the runoff. A single Republican candidate in a large field posited even the possibility of a first-round victory. Indeed, the publisher of the largest black-owned newspaper in the district unhappily predicted this to me some weeks before the first election. Republican strategists were not that optimistic, but they felt that a bitter contest between Democratic candidates in the first round could well dampen support for the Democrat who emerged from the first election. Making this pitch, state party officials were able to get all the potential Republican candidates to participate and bound them to the decision of the caucus. The party's political director described the process: "It was open and fair. We treated everybody equally. All the candidates filed with us and we gave them the names and phone numbers of every delegate. Secret ballots, of course. It worked real well. As a party official, I felt good about it."

The Republican caucus did work well, as all six Republicans participated. The clear favorite going into the caucus was Hayes Dent, a thirty-one-year-old aide to Republican Gov. Kirk Fordyce. The other major candidate was Bill Jordan, a black attorney from Jackson. Jordan, however, was clearly at a disadvantage with the caucus delegates. According to one observer of the Republican scene, "He would have been an ideal candidate for that district, but those people [the delegates] just weren't ready for it." Yet race was not the only determining factor. Jordan lived outside of the district, albeit only a couple of blocks from the district line, and this may have hurt him. And Dent had been courting important Delta Republicans for a number of years.[8] The support of the governor, the first Republican governor of Mississippi since Reconstruction, also strengthened Dent's position with the delegates. He won the caucus with ease, and, in the next two days, all the other Republican candidates dropped out, Jordan included, and publicly endorsed him. With the Republican field cleared, Dent was able to turn to his primary goal, as a Dent aide put it, "turning out our core constituency . . . can we say that?"

As anticipated by the Republicans, the Democrats were unable to settle on one candidate. A caucus similar to the Republican one was planned, but the incentives for candidates to join the process were much weaker. Although several Democratic candidates announced their early intention to participate, some of them boycotted it from the beginning and others dropped out when it appeared that one candidate, Hinds County Supervisor Bennie Thompson, was at a great advantage. In the end, only Thompson and some minor candidates agreed to be bound by the results of the caucus. The Democrats who did not participate complained that they were unable to get lists of the delegates, that Thompson and state party chair Ed Cole were co-workers, that white Democratic leaders were not invited, and that the Jackson power brokers "conceived a black political caucus in Jackson for a Jacksonian, playing us Delta folks for dummies." Upon his inevitable victory, Thompson unapologetically touted himself as the Real Democrat and the Unity Democrat and did so at every campaign appearance and in every piece of literature. His claim to such status was disputed throughout the primary campaign, but the course of events certainly worked to Bennie Thompson's advantage. All of the other candidates complained about the process and were quite defensive about their decision to pull out of the caucus. The matter came up at many of their appearances and dominated much of the media's coverage of the election, crowding out other issues that possibly could have worked to the advantage of someone other than Thompson.

While one would not describe Bennie Thompson's career as meteoric, he had advanced steadily through several elected positions. As the first black alderman and black mayor of Bolton, a town of about eight hundred people just west of Jackson, and as one of the first two black supervisors in Hinds County (following the conversion from at-large elections to district elections), Thompson had been a "trailblazer," as his campaign literature described him. It was more than just his electoral victories that made this description accurate. Thompson had been a plaintiff and an expert witness in lawsuits aimed at opening up electoral possibilities for blacks in Mississippi, possibilities that he himself had taken advantage of. As an elected official and a director on the Hinds County Human

Resources Board, Thompson had been a strong advocate for blacks, seeking better services for the black community, a share of county contracts for minority businesses, equal funding for historically black universities, and better housing, transportation, and education for his black constituents. What is more, in his career as a black advocate, Thompson developed a more confrontational approach to whites, one that he defended as effective: "The bottom line is results. If you can get results with consensus building, fine. If you get results with confrontation, fine. But for black people in Mississippi, confrontation has been one of the main means of survival" (Applebome 1993).

Six other Democrats joined Thompson and Dent in the open primary. The most prominent of them was Henry Espy, the mayor of the town of Clarksdale and elder brother of the new secretary of agriculture. Espy entered the race as a major candidate with huge name recognition (at least surname recognition) and a considerable campaign war chest. As of the week before the election, Espy had raised $168,000, compared to $152,000 for Dent and $84,000 for Thompson. Whereas no other candidate in the race had raised more than $8,500 from political action committees, Espy had $30,000 in such donations, most of it from agricultural PACS that had contributed to his brother's campaigns (Curran 1993). Espy began the race as the frontrunner, but never entered the caucus process. Without his participation, the caucus would not have served its purpose anyway, and that may have been the reason it unraveled so quickly.

The other candidates were an interesting assortment of unknown and well-known long shots, including two icons of the civil rights movement. One was Unita Blackwell, one of the founding members of the Mississippi Freedom Democratic Party and a protégée of its leader, Fannie Lou Hamer. Blackwell, the daughter of sharecroppers, founded a model Head Start program and a low-income home ownership program. In 1976, she incorporated the town of Mayersville and became its first mayor. She later became the president of the National Conference of Black Mayors. She was a frequent advisor to Jimmy Carter and was well connected to Bill and Hillary Clinton (one of her campaign brochures showed her whispering into Bill Clinton's ear). Most recently, she had received a generous MacArthur Foundation award for "creativity in public affairs."

The second icon in this race was James Meredith, the man who thirty years earlier had integrated the University of Mississippi in one of the most dramatic events of the civil rights struggle. Meredith's civil rights experience was highlighted in his campaign. His campaign literature featured a picture of him lying wounded from a gunshot wound, and his main campaign event was a two-week "march" through the district. Meredith's peculiar past, though, was a political liability as well as a strength. He had worked for Jesse Helms in Washington ("Yes, I sure did. Since I went to OLE MISS, the only man to give me a job was him") and had endorsed David Duke in his Louisiana gubernatorial race ("I did that because twelve years ago, he called me and told that because of a speech I made at a college in Louisiana, he had decided to QUIT the KLAN because he now believes that what he had been saying and doing was wrong. Ten years later, his record was clean").[9] The centerpiece of Meredith's campaign was a call for "40 acres and a mule" for all black Americans. The reference, of course, was to an unfulfilled promise from emancipation. Though he later said that this was a symbolic statement and that what he really advocated was giving $40,000 to all black Americans, many people in the district were befuddled. As one Henry Espy supporter said to me, "Now what the heck am I gonna do with a mule?"

Three other Democratic candidates rounded out the field. Brian Neely, a young black attorney and former Marine, languished in obscurity. David Halbrook, a white Democratic state representative who had obtained biracial support in his previous campaigns, was unable to generate much enthusiasm outside his home base. Steve Richardson, a dentist who campaigned under the slogan, "I want to be your cotton pickin' congressman" and made health care his signature theme (and campaigned in a white smock to illustrate the point), was not to be taken very seriously.

Henry Espy started with a formidable lead. An internal Democratic party poll in February showed him well ahead of any of his competitors. Espy had the support of 40 percent of those with an early preference; none of the other candidates was named by more than 14 percent of the respondents. Espy led among both blacks and whites and even ran on a par with Hayes Dent among Republicans. Much of this lead had to do with the popularity of his brother. Espy did what he could to build on this, claiming his brother's strong support and arguing that he could do the most for the district with his family (and thus his administration) connections. "The commitment continues" was the tagline on his literature, and wherever possible Espy's brother, grandfather, and family were highlighted ("When Mike comes home, is he going to be sitting at the dinner table with any other candidates?" asked Espy's campaign spokeswoman of a reporter [Walton 1993]).

The themes that had worked so well in his brother's four campaigns also found their way into Espy's campaign. Targeting the same voters—moderate blacks, liberal and moderate whites, and strong Christians—Espy preached a message of racial harmony and racial healing. According to his staff and the media in the Delta, he was the only major candidate occupying this electoral space, Thompson being hostile to whites, Dent to blacks. "They're both playing to a racist theme," argued an Espy campaign advisor. "It doesn't matter if you paint it white or black." Espy's major black competitor received most of his attention on this count: "If Bennie Thompson captures enough of the black vote, he can become a black congressman. Then we [the district] will get zilch." Given the campaign's promise of using excellent connections to deliver progress to the district, this was a major point of comparison.

Espy encountered some problems with his electoral strategy, however, that cost him dearly. For one thing, his brother did not endorse his candidacy. Although Henry Espy had said, "Mike is in this campaign just as deep as you can put your hand in a cookie jar," Mike Espy denied that he was involved in the campaign the week before the election. "I've got my hands full running the ag department and I am not involved in anyone's campaign," he said in a statement released to the press, "I wish my brother well. There are many qualified candidates in the race. He is certainly one of them. The 2nd District's voters will choose the best candidate" (Walton 1993). Whatever his reasons, Mike's lack of support hurt his brother because the issue consistently came up in debates and interviews. By linking himself to his brother, Henry Espy also invited comparisons that may not have worked to his benefit, and he spent some time talking defensively about coattails. "I'm Mike's older brother," he said at a candidate forum. "I'm the first Afro-American in the Clarksdale City Council and the first Afro-American mayor of Clarksdale. It kind of looks like Mike came up on my back."

Another problem Espy faced was that he actually shared the ideological middle with Unita Blackwell. And Blackwell, unlike the other minor candidates, was well funded. She was willing to spend part of her Mac-Arthur grant on the campaign, and, having connections to Hollywood and to women's groups (including the political action committee Emily's List),[10] she raised a sizable amount of national money in the weeks preceding the primary. With this money, she was able to buy thirty-two huge billboards across the region and lots of air time for radio and television commercials featuring the sonorous voice of her friend the actor James Earl Jones. Blackwell also had a biracial campaign team, including several people who would have worked for Espy had Blackwell not run. Making statements like "Freedom is freedom and it has no color" and "I'm not tryin' to isolate black folks, white folks, green folks, or polka dot folks. Who's serving the Second District needs to serve the people who need it most," she portrayed herself as conciliatory on racial issues. Blackwell certainly had some electoral liabilities. She was not a particularly good public speaker. A laudatory *Los Angeles Times* article described her as "speaking in the rhythms of the Delta" (Mills 1992), which probably hurt her with white voters. And although she ran on her ability to get things done ("I've done somethin' with nothin' and in the Second District, we have nothin'. We have to find creative ways of doin' somethin'"), and on how she planned to do practical things in the future ("I'm thinkin' about the House Appropriations Committee, which is a very important situation that we need to do somethin' about"),[11] she was somewhat of a philosopher, which likely made her less accessible to voters. Whether or not she had a chance to win a spot in the runoff, Unita Blackwell clearly shared philosophical and electoral space with Henry Espy and posed a problem for him.

Espy's biggest problem nevertheless was self-inflicted. In response to a badgering questioner at a white taxpayers' forum, Espy said that he would consider repealing Section 5, the preclearance provision of the Voting Rights Act. Worse yet, a tape of the forum came to the attention of Bennie Thompson, who used it to fullest effect. Although Espy denied making the statement and charged that the tape had been doctored, Thompson brought it up at campaign appearances because, as his campaign manager said, the Voting Rights Act was the vehicle for black political progress: "With statements like that you bring black people out of the woodwork. Black politicians are saying, 'That's how I got elected and this man wants to repeal it?'" The black press, unabashedly allied with Thompson, excoriated Espy with even more flourish. Charles Tisdale, publisher of the *Jackson Advocate*, editorialized,

> Henry Espy is immersed in a dumb, bitter and unnecessary confrontation with voters and the media over whether or not he told a white Greenwood voter that he would oppose the Voting Rights Act. He denies that he did. Having seen the tape of Espy's conversation with that Greenwood voter, however, there is no doubt in my mind that Espy agreed to—in his words—"fight" the Voting Rights Act, thus dumping on the dreams, hopes, and aspirations of generations of African Americans long dead and as yet unborn; the dreams of Medgar Evers, Martin Luther King, and hundreds of unknown martyrs who fought for the right to vote in this state when hope unborn had died. (Tisdale 1993)

The issue received a large amount of local press coverage, in part because Thompson supporters called a series of press conferences through the district to publicize and criticize the gaffe, in part because the candidates sparred over the issue at a debate televised throughout the district. With Thompson supporters calling him "a nappy-headed white man" in the newspapers (Stewart 1993b), Espy was again on the defensive.

The effort to discredit Espy worked. As the campaign manager for Hayes Dent put it, "He dropped like lead." And Espy could not afford a drop in support because his following was less devoted in the first place.

A Republican poll taken just before the primary showed that Espy's voters were much less likely to turn out. Among the 40 percent of voters who knew the date of the election, Espy fell back to third place.

The main beneficiary of Espy's unraveling was Bennie Thompson. Thompson, who had name recognition in the heavily black Jackson area (which had been added to the district in the Voting Rights refinements of the 1980s and 1990s) and financial support from organized labor, started with a solid base. Although he did not have the backing of the religious leadership in the district, which was predominantly in Espy's camp, he had cultivated the support of other black leaders over the years. As noted above, Thompson was closely tied to the most important black newspaper in the district, a weekly based in Jackson—the publisher described Thompson's campaign manager as being "like a brother to me". He had developed relations with other black officeholders throughout the region and indeed the state. He was a founding member and past president of the Mississippi Association of Black Mayors and the Mississippi Association of Black Supervisors and the founding chairman of the Mississippi Institute for Small Towns. He was part of the active civil rights community, as a plaintiff in voting rights litigation and in the *Ayers* case.[12] In short, Bennie Thompson had developed a strong network of supporters who were opinion leaders in their various communities, and they turned out his vote.[13]

Henry Espy was not the only candidate who had to deal with damage control in the closing days of the primary campaigns. Unfortunate stories also came out about the Republican Dent, though as the only Republican in the race, he appears to have had fairly stable support. The Jackson newspaper reported in a front-page story the Friday before the election that Dent had a drunk driving conviction and had been arrested for driving with a suspended license after that conviction. Dent also had been arrested at a Jackson nightclub for belligerent behavior. Obviously intoxicated, he had thrown a bottle at an off-duty police officer. Dent's lengthy college record was also mentioned in the story (it took Dent ten years to earn his degree). His staff fumed that the story came out so late in the contest and that Dent's responses were only to be found on page 9 of the newspaper.[14] Expressing regret over the incidents, Dent said he had "sowed some wild oats" during college but argued that he had since "stepped into manhood" in the Gulf War (Mitchell 1993a). The only candidate who used this material against Dent at this stage was David Halbrook, the white state representative, who attempted to drain off the Republican's white vote. Operating under old rules that held the Republican label to be a liability, he also brought up Dent's party label. Of course, he did not take much out of Dent's vote totals.

Dent won a spot in the runoff, leading the field with 34 percent of the vote. Bennie Thompson, with strong support in Jackson, won the other spot with 28 percent of the vote. Espy took only 20 percent and even with Unita Blackwell's 7 percent would not have made the runoff. The other candidates split the remaining 10 percent of the vote, with James Meredith coming in last, receiving but 360 votes of the 101,000 cast.

Mississippi 2 Runoff—
"It's like the chicken voting for Colonel Sanders"

There was only a two-week break between the primary and the general election, so the winners had no time to celebrate their victories. Dent and Thompson had to escalate their campaigns and redirect their sights in a very short period of time. Both were up to the task. Throughout the primary, Dent's staff had predicted a race against Thompson, and Dent, possibly in an attempt to activate whites in the primary, had publicly predicted that Bennie Thompson would be his opponent (Stewart and Fava 1993). Indeed, this was wishful thinking. When it became clear that Dent was not going to win the first round outright, his staff formulated a two-campaign strategy that was premised upon his facing Bennie Thompson instead of Henry Espy. Upon hearing the final preelection poll results showing that Espy's lead had dissipated, Dent's staff celebrated. One of Dent's campaign directors instructed an underling to call the media: "Issue a statement saying, 'The king is dead. Long live the king.'"

Inasmuch as they could influence the result, Dent's prediction was quite possibly a self-fulfilling prophecy. There is evidence that the Republicans did what they could to ensure a race against the more extreme black candidate. For one thing, reporters were investigating whether Republican money was being directed toward the Thompson campaign for the first election. Thompson denied it, but there is some indication that this was in fact the case. Although there is no way to determine motivations, a review of Federal Election Commission Reports from the Thompson campaign and the most recent Mississippi senatorial elections shows that a fair number of people who gave money to Trent Lott and Thad Cochran in their previous campaigns also gave money to Bennie Thompson. More important, it was the Republicans who originally had the videotape of Henry Espy's voting rights gaffe. They managed to get the tape to Bennie Thompson, who predictably used it very effectively. An advisor to the Republican campaign, savoring the final preprimary polls and taking the luxury of looking beyond the first election, said, "I never thought we'd get rid of Henry Espy. But, damn it, we have."

The Republicans celebrated Bennie Thompson's victory because they perceived him to be threatening to whites. A Chicago-based Republican advisor compared Thompson to Rep. Gus Savage of Illinois but made a distinction: "Both have strong racial components to their campaigns. The difference is that Savage was stupid and Bennie is a smart man. It's gonna be a serious two weeks." An important Delta Republican leader also made the point that Thompson would be unpalatable to whites: "If white people know how bad Bennie Thompson is, they'll go out and vote for Hayes Dent. Bennie Thompson is not what we need in the Mississippi Delta."

The Republican project for the second phase of the election was thus to get this message out to whites. Several hours before Sen. Robert Dole was to appear at a rally in the district, the finance director of the Dent campaign was spotted at lunch at the next table. When asked if Dole's visit would make a difference, he mumbled, "Well okay, sure it'll help, but we want to make Bennie the issue. We hope that will happen and it will." How to do this effectively was tricky. Dent attempted first to portray Thompson as threatening and hostile to whites. At a "debate" in Greenwood the week before the election,[15] Dent amplified purported statements by Thompson to the effect that he did not need white farmer support (Thompson denied making the comment) and argued that Thompson was aiming to racially polarize the electorate. Copies of the column in which Thompson's comments were first reported were widely circulated among white voters (Walton and Howard 1993), and editorials throughout the Delta harshly criticized Thompson and his campaign. The managing editor of the *Clarksdale Press Register* wrote in a column that became a piece of Dent literature, "Which identifier might Bennie Thompson least care for—the 'white' or the 'farmer'? . . . It is quite possible that Bennie Thompson's idea of agriculture could well be limited to the raising of hell. . . . [He] has no interest in farmers, doesn't care much for white folks and doesn't care much for anybody else who might. Holding one's nose to vote—even for a Republican—is superior, I would suggest, to drowning within the race-baiting and divisiveness of the alternative (Mosby 1993a). "The Choice is Yours," said another piece of Dent literature, which placed an underexposed photograph of the light-skinned Thompson next to a photograph of Hayes Dent.[16] It went on to compare the two candidates. Under Thompson's scowling picture were captions such as "Bennie Thompson tied up the courts in an effort to dodge the draft," which compared nicely to "Hayes Dent is a war hero." Dent's tough stand on crime was compared to Thompson "lobb[ying] to reverse the death sentence for a savage killer."

If these types of messages were intended to bring whites to the polls, the Republicans believed as well that they could claim the mantle from Mike and Henry Espy and portray their campaign as the racially moderate one. If they were successful in doing so, perhaps they could win moderate whites and even some blacks who had supported Espy, Blackwell, and Halbrook in the first round. "Our issue," rambled a Republican strategist, "is that Bennie is no Espy. Bennie is somewhat threatening. If I were a black person, I'd think he wouldn't provide the good relations we need. We'll make race the issue in this campaign. Who is the moderate on the race issue—Hayes or Bennie?"

In fact, Henry Espy appeared to tacitly support them. He refused to publicly support Thompson and, according to Republican officials, was doing what he could to support Dent. It is not clear if this is because he was angry with Thompson over the voting rights tape or because he believed that his future political interests lay in a Dent victory (Dent likely being more vulnerable in a 1994 general election than Thompson in a 1994 primary). The Republicans also hoped that Mike Espy's support of Bennie Thompson would be lukewarm and checked to see if he had filed for an absentee ballot prior to the general. Dent, for his part, paid homage to Mike and Henry Espy at every campaign stop, lauding them for their efforts to heal racial wounds and for their nonconfrontational style. He claimed to be the racially moderate candidate battling against the extremist.

The Republican campaign argued further that Thompson was a corrupt politician, a charge that may have been more potent given that the corruption trial of a high-profile black official, Congressman Harold Ford, was taking place in nearby Memphis and receiving much attention in the media. Though Ford was acquitted a few days before the election, the corrupt black politician theme clearly was being played. "We've known about Bennie Thompson for a long time," said Dent at the Greenwood event. "He's got serious problems and they all revolve around his professional life." Dent's television and radio ads were especially hard hitting. With a newspaper masthead and damaging headline in the background and the words "indictment," "kickbacks," and "corrupt" flashing red across the screen, a deep-voiced narrator recounts some charges against Thompson and intones, "Bennie. Bennie Thompson. What makes you think at a time when people are voting corrupt politicians out of Congress [a jail door is heard to slam], they'll vote you in?"

The Republican strategy here was clever. According to one reporter, the Republicans peddled the stories around. Although this reporter's newspaper did not pick them up, two Delta papers (owned by the same person) did. One of the problems the Republicans had here was that charges were never filed against Thompson. The essence of the most damaging story was that authorities *considered* a criminal investigation into Thompson's dealings with a private gravel company, but that the Democratic state auditor (later governor) Ray Mabus failed to pursue it. The *Clarksdale Press Register*, in an article titled "Friends in high places saved Thompson," quotes Pete Johnson, Mabus's Republican successor as state auditor, as saying that "there is no question that Bennie Thompson would have been indicted (given the evidence)." The article also reported that Mabus was supporting Thompson in the election and that Mabus's former chief of staff was Thompson's assistant campaign treasurer (Mosby 1993b). Since the campaign could not attack Bennie Thompson for indictments that never happened, the two damning front-page articles suggesting that Democratic officials "fixed" Thompson's situation became the source and the backdrop for the television advertisements (the audio also played on radio).[17] The newspaper reports gave some legitimacy to the advertisement, which with the sound muted made Thompson into a convicted felon.

If the first major element of the Dent campaign was to emphasize the race issue, the second was to reframe the election as a struggle between city and country, between Jackson and the Delta. The Republicans argued that Thompson was urban and unconcerned with the problems of the rural areas that comprised most of the district. They highlighted Dent's experience in agriculture, and Dent indeed appeared to have picked up some valuable agricultural expertise in working for Governor Fordyce. He spoke impressively about agricultural problems and solutions. The campaign even compared the politicians brought in to campaign for the candidates. Minority Leader Robert Dole and Mississippi's Thad Cochran, both on the Senate Agriculture, Nutrition, and Forestry Committee, stumped for Dent. Thompson, noted Dent, hosted "those noted agricultural experts" Tipper Gore and Rep. John Conyers of Detroit. Dole and Cochran made appearances in the district, one of them at the Stoneville Agricultural Research Center. Tipper Gore (and Democratic party Chair David Wilhelm) came to a fundraiser in Jackson, but "they never stepped foot in the district."

The third major element of the Republican strategy was to establish and publicize Dent's conservative credentials. Bringing Robert Dole into the campaign was part of this effort. Dole, who was involved in a filibuster of President Clinton's economic stimulus bill at the time, flew in with Thad Cochran for a few hours to campaign with Dent. Dole clearly did not know Dent very well (in an interview with a local print reporter, he strongly urged people to vote for Dent Hayes), but, being experienced at this type of campaigning, he learned a lot about him in the car going from the first event to the second. At the second event, he saluted Dent's military service in the Gulf War and his Bronze Star and talked about him more specifically. With Dole and Cochran vouching for him, Dent gained some credibility with white conservative elites.[18] Not surprisingly, the visit got a lot of press coverage throughout the district.

Dole's visit also played into the Republicans' attempt to link their campaign to the national political scene. Dole (and Dent in almost every appearance thereafter) railed against various aspects of Clinton's initial program. Clinton's BTU tax (Dole called it the big-time unemployment tax), an economic stimulus bill filled with pork ("a live hog wouldn't stand a chance in the U.S. Senate"), and Labor Secretary Robert Reich ("He's an aggressive fellow and very close to the President . . . and Mrs. Clinton") all were targets of Dole's sharp wit. "Don't give Teddy Kennedy any more help up there," Dole urged a well-heeled Republican crowd at the Greenville airport. "As you can see from this filibuster effort, every single vote counts. It could mean the difference between higher and lower taxes or bigger and lesser government." Had Dent run against Henry Espy, President Clinton would have been an even larger target for the Republicans as the race issue would have been diluted. Dent still spent a great deal of time and energy attacking a Democratic president who was not popular among whites in the district. Clinton's poor performance in the district was brought up by almost every Republican I talked with.

Other conservative issues were prominent in the Dent campaign as well. Abortion was brought up to win conservative and Christian fundamentalist votes, although Dent was not a hardliner on the issue. Commercials highlighting Thompson's support for abortion on demand and "the radical Freedom of Choice Act" were narrowcast on Christian radio. The advertisement bluntly offered its instructions: "It's your civic obligation and Christian duty to vote on Tuesday for Hayes Dent. . . . Vote as if millions of babies' lives are at stake. They are." Raising abortion served not only to activate white votes but to raise volunteers, according to a Washington-based Republican consultant. In his general experience, right-to-life activists were excellent campaign workers and in this case, much better than "the old southern ladies who are more concerned with making their gumbo than with stuffing envelopes." Dent also berated the spendthrift Congress, the bloated budget deficit, environmental over-regulation, and big government in general. His proposal on the budget deficit, to cut congressional salaries by 10 percent every year until the budget is balanced, was obviously unrealistic but combined several of these conservative signature issues.

Whereas Hayes Dent tried to win moderate black votes, votes that had previously gone to Espy, Bennie Thompson made little effort to reach out to white voters. In part, he believed that such an effort was fruitless. Asked at a Lexington meeting with about thirty core supporters if he expected to get any white vote, Thompson responded, "I expect to get about as much as Mike Espy got the first time and you know that's not that much. Let's face it, black elected officials are a rarity, and whites aren't used to dealing with us. We're like blue jeans. When you first put them on, they're a little difficult to get used to. But then you get comfortable in them." Thompson's intuition was that Mike Espy's coalition of blacks and whites was not possible for him. His reluctance to pursue white votes was more than just a calculation that he would not win white votes, however. It stemmed from a belief that the interests of most blacks in the district were not congruent with those of most whites. Recognizing that there is great poverty among Delta blacks, that agriculture is no longer supplying many jobs, and that a fair proportion of blacks in the district have come to live in urban areas, Thompson promised to confront the various problems that the average black person in the district faced. "There are a lot more voters out there than just farmers. We've gotta focus on others than the farmers," he said at the Lexington meeting, a comment that probably was similar to the "white farmer" remark that the Dent campaign was feeding on.

The issues Bennie Thompson talked about on the campaign trail and those that were highlighted in his literature had to do with improving housing, water and sewage systems, rural transportation, veterans' hospitals, programs for the elderly, day care, educational opportunities, and other social programs for minorities and the poor. These were things he had done for Bolton and for Hinds County and that he would seek for the district as a whole.[19] He talked a little about improving the economy in the district and, noting that all the cotton in the district was sent to textile mills in North Carolina, advocated bringing processing industries into the district. Mostly, though, he promised to "work with elected officials to solve problems, to deal with nuts and bolts problems that people in this district have."

Thompson argued that the Republicans were hostile to blacks and would be unable to handle these problems. In a line that got such a good response he repeated it throughout the campaign, he told voters, "If you vote for my opponent, it's like the chicken voting for Colonel Sanders." He also argued that he was far more qualified to deal with these problems than Dent not just because he was black and Dent was white but because he was experienced and Dent was not: "Hayes Dent has no track record. He hasn't done anything for anybody. You know how they say an empty wagon makes a lot of noise? Well, he's makin' a lot of noise." He would be even more effective because "a Democrat can do a heck of a lot more than a Republican, especially during a Democratic administration," and he would be able to "sit down with Clinton and make some sense." Mike Espy's presence in the administration was brought up, and, much to the chagrin of the Republicans, a commercial featuring Espy's endorsement was played repeatedly over the last few days of the campaign.

Issue positions, however, were not really central to the Thompson campaign strategy. The key to the campaign was getting black voters to the polls, and it was not Thompson's stands on issues that were of crucial importance here. In this context, Bennie Thompson's stated reason for skipping the televised debate in Greenwood is interesting. When asked by the former candidate Robert Clark at the Lexington meeting to explain his rationale, Thompson responded, "There just aren't any issues left to debate. Besides, this election is based on who gets their folks out. We hope to get ten thousand votes in Jackson. I had two hundred volunteers there and they were more important." Yet his deeper reason for avoiding the forum was that he did not perceive it to be politically profitable enough to warrant meeting Dent in what he perceived to be a hostile setting. "If you look at the *Greenwood Commonwealth* and Channel 6 [the sponsors of the debate], there's always somethin' negative about somebody black and we deserve better. If you're invited to the lion's den and if you go and get eaten alive, it's your fault."

What sort of message, then, did Thompson use to get his supporters to the polls? The main way to activate voters was to emphasize race and the racial history of the area. The guiding principle of the campaign could be found on a poster pinned to the cork walls of campaign headquarters: "It's a power thing. Vote April 13." Campaign flyers (provided by the NAACP national headquarters) had pictures of small black children and messages like "Three good reasons why you should vote April 13" and "I Can't Vote April 13 . . . You Can." Thompson also spoke frequently of his involvement in lawsuits to open the political process up to blacks in the wake of the Voting Rights Act, of his effort to increase minority set-asides in Hinds County, of his involvement in the *Ayers* case, and of the right of blacks to represent the Second District. That there were no black congressmen from Mississippi, a state with a 36 percent black population, was "an indictment of our state" and necessitated that the Second be represented by a black congressman.

Sounding this message and many variations on the same theme, Thompson conducted an aggressive campaign. The only matter that put him on the defensive involved Henry Espy. The campaign was concerned that, as Espy had not endorsed Thompson, Espy's followers might stay home on election day. When Mike Espy agreed to endorse Thompson in a television commercial, however, that concern appeared to ease. In the scheme of things, Mike Espy's endorsement was much more important than his brother's.

However important Mike Espy's endorsement, Thompson's solid organization of black opinion leaders, a network that had been cultivated over a decade and a half, was his most important source of strength. This network carried Thompson to his primary success, and much of the two-week stretch run to the general election was spent reinforcing his ties to those who would represent him in a major grass-roots campaign to turn out black voters. His schedule on the Saturday before the election illustrates this well. It started with a prayer breakfast meeting with housing officials and community leaders in Tutwiler at 7:00 A.M. The leader of the meeting urged the group to get through the morning's business quickly because they had much campaign work to do. Thompson then went to Greenwood to meet with a dozen ministers, again over a meal.[20] Most of the group, including the organizer of the meeting, had supported Henry Espy in the primary, and it was important to reestablish a positive tie to Thompson. (Fortunately for Thompson, the following day was Easter Sunday, the best-attended church day of the entire year.) Traveling at ninety miles an hour, Thompson reached Grenada two hours later for a barbecue in his honor in the town square. He was quite late. A fair number of people had gathered to listen to a band playing blues and gospel favorites. An old woman introduced Thompson by singing, "Gimme that ole time religion" ("because it's good for electin' Democrats"), and the candidate gave a vigorous get-out-the-vote speech to the crowd as a small parade of police cars circled the square with sirens wailing in a salute to Thompson. After another hour's drive, the candidate held a lengthy meeting with Holmes County volunteers in which he answered questions and calculated how many votes were expected from the county. His pep talk was basic G.O.T.V.: "We got the votes if they come to the polls. At some point, we need to know who hasn't shown up. Whether they're fishin' or takin' a nap, we gotta go get'm." By six in the evening, he was in Canton, seat of Madison County. Giving a speech to party faithful, he again talked about turnout and made a public wager with the county chair. If the county produced four thousand votes, one expense-paid charter would be provided to take county volunteers to his inauguration. If the county failed to meet this goal, the county party would have to pay some other group's expenses to Washington.[21]

The final two days were devoted to maximizing black vote as well. On Easter Sunday, Thompson visited the largest church in the Jackson area, not only because of its size but because the service was broadcast over the radio throughout the district. The congregation of about three thousand listened as the Democrat gave a very humble two-minute speech, after which he was blessed by the bishop (the blessing included an admonishment, "We're prayin' for you on Tuesday. Amen. You know we'd pray for you more if you came to church more often. Amen"). On Monday Thompson toured the district with Jesse Jackson.

As election day neared, there was a marked preoccupation with ballot security, ballot integrity, voter intimidation, and the buying of votes—by both whites and blacks, Republicans and Democrats. Stories of election fraud and intimidation beyond the usual demonization of one's opponent were told by people in and around both campaigns. Republicans, party activists, and members of the rank and file were particularly worried about irregularities in the black precincts and related many stories about them. A New Jersey transplant at a Republican rally was amazed at the way elections were run in the area. "I've never seen anything like it," he said indignantly. "Here, they'll take people into the voting booth and actually vote for them." A white woman who lived in a heavily black town told of an election official watching her vote in a curtainless polling booth. After she marked the ballot for an unopposed candidate, the friendly official informed her that she did not have to vote for unopposed candidates. A Republican official recounted several instances of laxity on the part of election officials—leaving the polls open while going out to lunch, transposing vote totals, counting two boxes at the same time in the same room (leading to some double counting). He was even more concerned with ballot security. Noting that "sometimes elections are won around here after the polls close," he told of boxes disappearing, ballots being run through scantrons multiple times, and interns who were assigned to "babysit" boxes from the closing of the polls to the reporting of results.[22]

On the other side, black political operatives mostly worried about the intimidation of black voters, which, they claimed, happened when Republicans pursued ballot security measures. Democrats argued that these measures, taken almost wholly in minority precincts, are thinly veiled attempts to keep blacks from the polls. They noted that in the Robert Clark campaign, signs were posted around polling places in black neighborhoods with the warning, "Anyone posing as an illiterate and asking for help will be FINED and JAILED" (Neilson 1989, 187). In other recent southern elections, black precincts had been saturated with postcards to this effect.[23] Republican poll watchers (in suits and sunglasses) were placed in front of black precincts, a maneuver, it was believed, that was intended to scare away some black voters. In a place with a history like the Delta, such concerns were not outlandish.

Many Democrats in the Delta also were anxious about the possibility of last-minute vote buying by the Republicans. Such fraud appeared to be enough a part of politics as usual (among Democrats and Republicans alike) that even rank-and-file blacks expected it. In a most amusing illustration, the blues band at a Thompson rally sang several songs dealing with these themes. One number, "Gonna Make up Your Mind and Let Bennie Be the Man" instructed voters who were confused at the polls to get some help ("but make sure it's the right person"). In another song, voters were told, "If they put a little honey in your hand, tell'm to take their business to someone else."

If the Republicans did try to buy some votes—and I know of no evidence that they did—it did not help them much. Blacks stayed almost entirely in the Democratic camp. Whites were overwhelmingly Republican in their preferences. According to a Republican consultant, polls showed that only 1 percent of people voted for the candidate of the other race. Under these circumstances, Thompson was able to activate enough black voters to overcome a racial differential in turnout. Whites clearly were motivated to vote against Bennie Thompson. But blacks also turned out in substantial numbers, and Thompson ended up winning the election with a rather comfortable 55 percent of the vote.

Racial Politics in a Majority Black District

Race continues to dominate people's political thinking in the Delta, "the most southern place on Earth," according to a local politician. Outsiders are struck by it immediately. "Race here is like sex at a horny prep school. You can't have a conversation without discussing it," said a Washington political consultant working in the district. Those who live in the area, and especially those involved in Delta politics, are also well aware of it. It is, as various locals put it, an "obsession," a "preoccupation," an "albatross hanging around all our necks."

That race dominates politics in this territory is not terribly surprising.[24] One would most expect racial conflict to define political conflict in areas where blacks pose a numerical threat to the political dominance of whites (Huckfeldt and Kohfeld 1989). In fact, numerous studies provide evidence that racial conflict shapes whites' attitudes toward politics, above all in places where the black population is large and concentrated enough to ensure that blacks will be courted by politicians as an important constituency (Giles 1977; Giles and Evans 1986; Fossett and Kiecult 1989; Glaser 1994). The tradition of racial-line voting in this district, a tradition upheld in this election, further supports this theory and supports it with evidence of black political behavior as well as white. Precinct returns from the general election give some indication of how divided the electorate actually was. Thompson won overwhelmingly black precincts by overwhelming margins (374–4, 355–12, 516–6, 233–2); Dent won the largest white precinct 2484–87.

Assessing how group conflict shapes politics, however, involves more than simply looking at what people think or how votes fall. The virtue of this review of events in the Second District is that it illustrates the extent to which race pervades political strategy in places like the Delta. This is not to say that every election here is fought over racial issues, but rather that politicians continually seek to address concerns about group position and group power. Bennie Thompson's campaign was premised upon the right of blacks to be represented by a black. As the poster in his office declared, this election was "a power thing." Thompson also pointed to what he had done for his black constituents in the past and talked about what he would do for black people as their congressman. His oft-repeated line comparing the Republican to Colonel Sanders was only partly in jest. Dent, he argued, would not look out for their interests and indeed was hostile to them.

Much of Hayes Dent's campaign message was based upon the threat that Thompson posed to whites. The key to the campaign was not to build up Dent's positives, his connections to Fordyce, Cochran, and Dole, or his work in the Mississippi Department of Agriculture. Neither was his staff notably concerned about his negatives, his brushes with the law, or his inexperience. This campaign was about making sure whites understood what the election of Bennie Thompson meant to them. In the words of a Republican advisor, their goal was "to make Bennie the issue." They understood very well that cultivating the impression that Thompson was antiwhite would activate large numbers of white voters throughout the district.[25]

Democrats and Republicans Change Places

A recounting of events in this election gives some sense of what group conflict between blacks and whites looks like in the political arena. It breathes some life into the equations and the numbers that support this argument. But the importance of this chapter is not just to illustrate how racial conflict shapes politics in places like the Delta. From an analytical point of view, the value of this case history is also that it offers an excellent opportunity to test a central idea of this piece. As discussed in chapter 2, part of the point of this exercise is to show how political strategy is linked to the ratio of blacks to whites in a district. This case allows the most direct test of the proposition that racial balance is a determining factor in Democratic and Republican strategy. If the racial balance in a district tips the other way, with blacks representing a larger proportion of the electorate than whites, do the incentives for candidates to behave in certain ways reverse as well? Do candidates then approach the electorate differently?

The evidence from this election suggests that they do. These candidates did reverse roles in terms of their basic plans and their approaches to the black and white electorates. Bennie Thompson's campaign looks much like the Republican campaigns described above in its strategic plan. Just as Republicans in these other races made few overtures to the minority black population and ran racially based campaigns oriented toward a white audience, Bennie Thompson ran an unapologetic racial campaign oriented toward blacks and virtually ignored the white minority. This certainly is not the only way for a black Democrat to win in this district:

Mike Espy projects another model. Nonetheless, one of two mutually exclusive choices must be made. Black Democrats must either maximize the black vote and ignore the white vote or take a racially moderate approach and hope to put a coalition of blacks and whites together, as Mike Espy did. Thompson looked at the absence of white support for Espy in his first election and noted that the district had become more heavily black since the 1990 redistricting and chose the former, probably safer, course. It was a strategy to which he was better suited in any case.

Hayes Dent's campaign approached the election more like the Democratic campaigns than the Republican campaigns described in this book. Whereas Republicans in most of the above elections made little effort to court blacks, the Dent campaign did what it could, particularly given how little credibility it had in the black community. For one thing, Dent hired a black press secretary and gave him an enormous role in the campaign. The job was twofold. First, he became the other "front-man" for the campaign, appearing on the evening news if Dent did not, interacting with local print reporters, and visibly organizing Dent's appearances. Although he was the only black on the team, he represented the campaign's visible goal of biracial progress and harmony. College educated and refined, he was well received by whites, at least from the perspective of the campaign. Second, the press secretary served as the campaign's liaison to the black community. He was the one sent to meet with black groups, often by himself, to make the case for Hayes Dent. He had held a similar position in the successful Senate campaign of the Republican Paul Coverdell in Georgia in 1992 and, according to his boss, a Washington political consultant, had managed to help dampen the black vote, if not activate it behind the Republican. One difference between that race and this one, however, was that Coverdell ran against Wyche Fowler, a white Democratic incumbent who had less appeal to blacks than Bennie Thompson.

Dent too made a public effort to reach black voters, at least in his words. His attempts to claim the legacy of Mike Espy, his praise of Espy's approach to race relations and racial progress, his support of Mississippi Valley State in the controversy over the *Ayers* case, and his attempts to portray himself as a racial moderate were all part of a strategy to win the small proportion of middle-class black vote or devout Christian black vote that would provide him with a majority. Though Dent did little actual campaigning in the black community, his public message was conciliatory on the race issue.

Still, his campaign sought to activate whites by painting Bennie Thompson as a racial threat and certainly savored the prospect of running against him as opposed to Henry Espy for that very reason. "If we go against Bennie Thompson, we'll use scare tactics. Bennie Thompson won't get any of the white vote," said one of Dent's aides before the primary. This was, of course, the strategy they adopted. For all Dent's public statements of racial moderation, the Republicans did run a racial campaign. Like the Democratic campaigns described above, they had two messages: publicly claiming racial moderation while charging the opponent with extremism when they could.

The most important difference between Dent's strategy and that of the Democratic campaigns described above is that the Democrats were able to appeal more effectively to blacks and whites through separate channels. In the runoff, the Republicans attempted to establish relations with some important black leaders, notably Henry Espy and some of those who supported him. Their avenues to the black community, though, were too few and ineffective and their Bennie Thompson scare tactics too public. Lacking the ability to communicate separately, they were unlikely to cut into the majority black vote as the Democrats have been able to cut deeply into the white vote in majority white districts.

Like the Democratic races described above, the Republican campaign attempted to redefine the election on more favorable terms in its effort to win black votes. At an obvious disadvantage in a black-white election, they tried to reinterpret the race as a Delta versus Jackson election. Indeed, the other great advantage of running against Bennie Thompson instead of Henry Espy was that he was from the Jackson area. "This campaign is no longer about white and black or Democrat and Republican, it's about downtown Jackson and the Delta. That's who he wants to represent," Dent said at an airport rally. At every campaign stop, it was the Delta against the city, the problems of agriculture versus the problems of the cities, one of us or one of them. It was the tint given to every issue and event in the campaign. Dent's strategists even pointed out (time and again) that national Democratic figures visiting the Thompson campaign never even set foot in the district. And Robert Dole's visit to Greenville was planned with this in mind. Dole himself apologized for being an outsider but added that at least he had enough respect for the people of the Second to come into the district itself.

The irony of this Republican strategy is that the Delta had been split up in the 1970 redistricting so as to preserve white representation in all of Mississippi's five districts. It was put back together to create a majority black district in the 1980s, which makes Dent's redefinition of "us" and "them" so interesting. But the tactic held some possibility because the Delta is such a self-conscious and well-defined place, the type of place where outsiders could be resented.[26] This redefinition of the electorate was also without much risk because Jackson was Thompson's power base and because the area carved out of Jackson and added to the Second was almost entirely black. Dent had little to lose in attempting to attract some black votes from the Delta by painting the choice as city versus country and by tapping into resentment among blacks who supported other candidates in the first round. The hope was that these Delta voters, excluded by "the Jackson power brokers" in the caucus process or simply resenting Thompson's victory over their candidate, would support their cause.

Finally, like the Democrats described above, Dent tried to characterize himself as the local candidate, Bennie Thompson as the national candidate. He did his best to tie Thompson to President Clinton, who did not do well among Mississippi or Delta whites in the presidential election of 1992.[27] Campaigning with Robert Dole at the peak of a Republican filibuster of Clinton's economic stimulus plan, the less experienced candidate picked up some pointers on how to attack the administration as well as some good jokes.[28] Following Dole's lead, he attacked the plan as wasteful (all the more wasteful as it did nothing for the Delta) and full of pork. The president, his wife, and his economic stimulus plan became Dent's favorite targets for the remainder of the campaign. Had Dent run against Henry Espy, this would have been an even more important part of the Republican strategy because Espy did not pose as much of a racial threat as Thompson and because Espy's brother was in the administration.

Dent claimed to be not just an outsider to Washington, but an insider in the district, one who understood the local problems of the Delta far better than his opponent. He spoke of his unrelenting opposition to raising taxes and singled out an increased barge tax as an excellent example of how Clinton's tax proposals would hurt the area. Most important, he juxtaposed his agricultural experience with Thompson's. "My opponent just this week has discovered the meaning of the word *agriculture* and only at the urging of the National Democratic Party," he announced at a rally at the Stoneville Agricultural Research Center. He, on the other hand, had been intimately involved in shaping agricultural policy in the Fordyce administration.

In that Bennie Thompson highlighted his Democratic affiliation and his ability to "sit down with Clinton and make some sense," the patterns of the majority white districts appear to be reversed here as well. Bennie Thompson, like the Republicans described above, linked himself to the national party.[29] Thompson kept a local angle to his campaign, however, in making this national link. He spoke of how he intended to use his connections to "bring home the bacon," a rally cry not at the disposal of Republicans decrying the proliferation of pork. Thompson pulled his national message and his local message together as the Republicans described in the other cases were not able to do.

Moreover, Dent's attempt to raise local issues did not really put him in a position to woo the sizable number of black voters required to put him over the top. Although agriculture is a large part of the Delta's economy and identity, only 8 percent of the district's population work in "Agriculture, forestry, fisheries, and mining" (U.S. Bureau of the Census 1992), and that includes both blacks and whites. This is rather small compared to the percentage of people in the district who are on public assistance (20 percent) or who work in public sector jobs (22 percent), both heavily black local constituencies that Bennie Thompson courted. Dent's plan to make the local connection as forcefully as he could was smart but misguided because it was directed, for the most part, toward local whites and not local blacks.

The strategic considerations posed by the racial balance of the district and the particular circumstances under which the election was held were well understood by both campaigns. As a result, I would argue, this election followed the pattern described in the two previous chapters, but with a twist. The twist, of course, is that this election is a mirror image of the other elections. From a strategic perspective, Bennie Thompson pursued a southern Republican strategy. This is not to say that he articulated more racially conservative positions. Rather, he pursued a strategy that required maximizing the turnout of the majority race without attempting to build a racial bridge across the electorate. At the same time, it was the Republican who attempted to maximize his white base with racial rhetoric while reaching into the majority black vote with racially moderate appeals and a redefinition of the electorate. The difference, for Hayes Dent, was that he was not well positioned to do either of these things. And blacks were not very receptive to his message, which is generally a problem for southern Republicans.

6 Resolving the Puzzles

TO REPEAT THE WORDS OF V. O. Key with which I began this book, "In its grand outlines, the politics of the South revolves around the position of the Negro" (5). Perhaps the most intriguing element of this argument was that racial context profoundly influenced the course of southern politics. It was the concentration of blacks in a particular area that shaped white racial attitudes, political incentives to suppress black aspirations, and political dialogue in that area.

The South has undergone dramatic changes since Key analyzed the southern polity in 1949. But while the specifics are different, his argument is still compelling. Racial context continues to be a crucial variable in understanding southern politics, at least at the congressional level. In this book, I look at the relation of racial context to political strategy and find that it remains quite strong. Both Democratic and Republican political strategy are sensitive to racial context, and to a marked degree. The result is that the interplay of political campaigns in heavily black areas of the South is still predictably different from what it is in areas of smaller black concentrations.

I hypothesize in chapter 2, for instance, that Republicans, as members of the racially conservative party dependent on white votes, are more likely to introduce racial issues into a campaign in which blacks are more numerous in a district. These are the places where the political attitudes related to racial conflict are most likely to be evoked. The political rationale is that racial issues, particularly those that evoke group or racial conflict, are most likely to rally whites and to maximize the Republican share of the white vote. Democrats also should adjust their strategy to the racial balance in the district. Where blacks comprise a larger share of the population and make a potentially large contribution to victory, Democrats will focus on boosting black turnout levels, even to the point of risking some white votes. Where blacks are less numerous, the major focus should turn to taking a larger share of the white vote.

Although the small number of cases in this study compel one to draw cautious conclusions, clearly these expectations have been met. In Mississippi 4, Alabama 3, and Virginia 5, those majority-white districts where blacks made up a large proportion of the population, racial issues became central to the Republican campaign. In an effort to unify white voters, Republican campaigns introduced racial issues into the political exchange. By talking about the extension of the Voting Rights Act, *Grove City*, the Confederate flag, and vote buying in the black community, they made direct and none-too-subtle appeals to white voters. In Mississippi 5 and Texas 1, where blacks represented only about one in five people, racial issues were not used to win white votes, and other conservative themes were tapped instead.

Republicans did have a strategy vis-à-vis blacks in these two congressional districts, however, and racial issues were part of it. While neither Tom Anderson nor Edd Hargett made an effort to court blacks, both had a message directed at black voters that their colleagues in the heavily black districts did not. The message was designed to encourage blacks to "sleep in" by making their Democratic opponent look bad or by confusing the election. The major racial issues in these Republican campaigns, Reverend Appleberry's charge that Gene Taylor was unsympathetic to blacks in Mississippi 5 and the Voting Rights controversy in Texas 1, were employed not to sell the Republican to whites but to weaken the Democrat in the eyes of the black community. Trying to make the Democrat unappealing with racial issues was not a feasible strategy in the more heavily black districts, where Republican racial conservatism designed to win white votes also activated blacks for the Democrat. Skirmishing over the black vote in less black districts was thus very different than in heavily black districts.

Democratic campaign strategy varied with changes in racial balance as well. Wayne Dowdy, in heavily black Mississippi 4, strategically courted black votes and spent inordinate resources to reach and activate them. Gene Taylor, in a neighboring Mississippi district with far fewer blacks, made only modest efforts to attract black voters, devoting scarce resources, time, and energy to winning a larger share of the white vote. The other campaigns in the majority white districts fell between these two, though none of these Democrats appealed to black votes so publicly as to jeopardize their chance to win white votes. And it was not just the relative attention Democrats paid to blacks as opposed to whites that varied in these districts, but also the tenor of their campaigns, the risks they were willing to take, and the severity of their message. Wayne Dowdy highlighted the threat to the Voting Rights Act in his campaign in order to outrage and inflame black voters and to maximize black turnout (though he still did it through separate channels to black voters). Gene Taylor's message to blacks was not much different from his message to whites. These differences, of course, were partly a function of the ammunition provided to them by their opponents' campaigns. Nonetheless, it is again clear that the dynamic of the campaign in black communities varied with change in the racial context of the election.

The election in the majority black district also fits well into this scheme. As I hypothesized, the Democratic and Republican campaigns reversed strategic places in Mississippi 2. The Democratic campaign, in this 58 percent black district, spurned coalitional politics to generate excitement among blacks, to maximize the black vote and their portion of it. The white Republican attempted to forge a racial coalition, however fruitless the task appears to have been in retrospect. Looked at together, these special elections do reveal a pattern that illustrates how racial context determines the course of southern elections. The dynamic of the campaign, premised both on the original strategies of the two camps and the responses to these strategies by their opponents, was closely tied to racial balance in the district.

Demonstrating this, however, is only one purpose of this book. The philosophy guiding this research strategy is that understanding the political strategies of candidates, that is, understanding the context of the vote choice, gives insight into the results of elections. This is not an ironclad explanation for why Democrats have been congressionally successful. There are other important explanations to consider (see below). Still, I argue here that given the strategies pursued by congressional Democrats and Republicans, Democrats have had an advantage in a great many southern districts. It is this argument that guides my contribution to the resolution of the southern realignment puzzles.

Understanding Mixed Republican Success

The evidence that more and more southerners are calling themselves Republican is irrefutable. Yet this phenomenon has been very slow to translate into electoral success below the presidential level. Why have Republican presidential candidates so dominated, while prior to 1994 Republican congressional candidates have had only limited success? Why have Republican presidential candidates been able to take advantage of a strong conservative bent in southern public opinion while southern congressional Republicans have not? Why has a partisan connection to popular presidents not been worth more? Finally, if race is so potent a force in the South, why has the "filtering down" realignment process been so slow? By all accounts, it should have occurred as Republicans up and down the ticket benefited from being associated with the racially conservative party.

The reasons for mixed Republican success are complex and multi-faceted, and it is worth reviewing them first before proceeding to my explanation. One aspect of the GOP problem is perfectly evident. Simply put, it takes time to build a party. The Republican party in the South started from nothing in the early 1960s, and many compelling explanations for the lack of Republican local and congressional success start with the very problems of building a party upon the foundation of presidential victories. "Ever try to build a pyramid from the top down?" asked one Republican campaign manager in explaining his party's fortunes in the region. The problems that vex Republican party leaders have been problems of doing just that.

For one thing, the choices that the Republicans have been able to offer southern voters simply have not been as good as those offered the Democrats. It takes more than having the right message. The right messenger must deliver it. As a general proposition, Democratic candidates have been stronger than Republican candidates. In some measure the Republicans have had a recruiting problem that Democrats did not. And the problem is self-perpetuating, for without Republicans at the lowest local and county offices, there has been no political—or electoral—training ground. In the cases studied here, the Democrats recruited stronger politicians with low-level "seasoning," candidates who had more experience at the local and state level, who had run for office before and had a sense of what it took to succeed, and who enjoyed name recognition within at least some portion of the congressional district. The Republican candidates, though able to raise money and campaign effectively, generally had shorter political resumes and less electoral experience.

A rather ironic aspect of this problem is that in the absence of some evidence of Republican success, capable conservative candidates have stayed Democratic in low-level elections. Republican party officials claim to have difficulty convincing even ideologically appropriate people to run under their banner for low-level offices. A Republican party official in

Mississippi told of bumping into a woman he had convinced to run for a local office in one Delta county. When she told him she had won, he was delighted. His pleasure was short-lived though because she had run as a Democrat. "Otherwise I wouldn't have had a chance to win," she explained. Perhaps, as Alan Ehrenhalt argues, it has been more difficult all over the United States for Republicans to recruit viable candidates for low-level offices, but it has been particularly a problem in the South. Yet there are indications of change. As recently as the early 1970s, said an official of the South Carolina Republican party, "we really had to scrape the bottom of the, um, to look everywhere to find candidates. Now we're holding competitive primaries. It's a real sign that we're healthy." Still, he and Republican party officials carry an underdog mentality when talking about recruitment.

This comment raises another recruitment problem that Republican party builders have faced. Over the time Republicans have been winning presidential contests in the South, they still have been much less likely to hold competitive low-level primaries than Democrats (Thielemann 1992, 129). Some analysts argue that intraparty competition is important to a party's health. Competition leads voters to gain an early awareness of candidates and issues and leads candidates to cultivate relations with groups of voters (Sorauf 1984). In evolutionary terms, it also may be argued that competitive situations lead to the success of candidates who develop more "adaptive" messages and characteristics. That is, running in a primary may help successful candidates to identify what works best in the district. Most important to the puzzle at hand, competitive primaries may give southerners a reason to abandon a Democratic affiliation reinforced in Democratic party primaries, which are much more likely to be competitive and thus meaningful. "The lack of primary competition means that southern voters instinctively think of themselves as Democrats below the presidential level and the GOP gives them little reason to change their minds," writes Gregory Thielemann on the Republican "stall" in Congress (1992, 127; see also Jewell and Olson 1988). In this argument, Republican party competition thus would break the last tenuous connections to the Democratic party and presumably allow many to overcome a last psychological hurdle to voting Republican in congressional and local elections. Although Thielemann's empirical demonstration of this point is unconvincing, Republicans certainly will benefit at every electoral level when they fully break the impression that the only meaningful participation in party affairs is within the Democratic party.

Yet intraparty competition has its disadvantages. Candidates must devote resources to winning primaries, resources that can be used to win general campaigns. Primary battles also bring out negative material that can be used by a general election opponent. And they may lead to bitterness between candidates that is difficult to repair and may cause problems for the victor. Glen Browder, for one, argued that his hard-fought first primary victory over a well-financed competitor with a sizable following made the ensuing campaigns quite challenging: "The question was, could I rebuild a base that had fragmented?" Mending relations with the losers became an important priority for the Alabama Democrat. Intraparty competition is thus a mixed blessing. What Republican party competition really reveals is that strategic politicians are increasingly recognizing that the Republican label is no longer the liability that it once was. From this perspective, what primary competition exists in the South is more a by-product of Republican growth than a cause of it, and situations like that in South Carolina indicate that the Republican recruitment problem is easing.

Harold Stanley (1992) points out a related Republican recruitment problem, one that has the added virtue of helping to explain the mixed-results phenomenon in the South. Having lots of opportunity for upward mobility and with fewer entrenched Republican incumbents, notes Stanley, the most successful Republican representatives have been more likely to leave the House and run for higher office than Democratic representatives. A count of retirements from the House between 1968 and 1992 shows this to be the case. Three-quarters (76 percent) of Republican retirees, but only one-quarter (26 percent) of Democrats, left the House to pursue another political opportunity (usually a Senate seat or a governorship). Congressional representatives are often the best candidates the Republicans have to offer in statewide races, and they frequently win. But this poses a problem at lower levels as Republicans have had to constantly replenish the lower ranks, which brings one back to the problems the party has had in recruiting high-quality candidates. This argument gives some insight into why the realignment has worked its way from high- to low-level offices. It does not, however, explain why this process has been so slow and difficult for the Republican party. For if it had been disadvantageous to run as a Democrat over this time, politicians would have flocked to the Republican party. The question remains, why have Democrats been perceived to be at such an advantage?

It is not just recruitment problems that Republicans suffer from. There are other problems with trying to build the pyramid from the top. Democrats have long controlled a large majority of county courthouses throughout the South, and this has given them another great advantage. The large number of Democratic mayors and sheriffs and judges affords Democratic candidates a strong, ready-made network of opinion leaders and important local officials. These networks, built on loyalty and patronage as well as a common affiliation, provide the basis for a campaign organization. Indeed the organizations of several of these Democrats were stocked with people, officials and citizens, who had some direct interest in a Democratic victory. The white organizer of a Bennie Thompson rally in the Mississippi Delta explained, "We just try to keep everything Democratic around here." He added, smiling, "We're in the construction business. That speaks for itself." The strength of the Democratic networks was noteworthy next to the weaker Republican networks, which had much less to bind them together. Linda Arey and John Rice, in particular, complained vociferously about the lack of support they received from local Republicans.

Democrats have in addition controlled electoral machinery throughout the region, which can be a great resource for keeping power, as has been demonstrated repeatedly throughout southern history. Although there is some check on election officials in the Voting Rights Act, they still make many decisions of importance. Consider the decisions of the election officials in the three Republican-controlled counties in Mississippi's Fourth District. These officials changed the order of the candidates' names on the ballot with the almost certain intent of confusing illiterate and uneducated (and most likely black Democratic) voters. It is no coincidence that these were the only counties that did not use alphabetical order on the ballot: all the other counties in the district were run by Democrats. The incident illustrates only one possibility offered by Republican control of electoral machinery, and a small one at that. But in a place where there is great concern about poll operations, ballot security, and vote counting, Democratic control of the county courthouses has made a big difference.

Given their reduced presence in the state legislatures, the Republicans also have not had much say in the drawing of district lines. Although Republicans have controlled statehouses in several southern states, in the early 1990s, while redistricting was going on, they held only four of them. This, of course, compounded the Republicans' difficulty in contributing to the line-drawing process. Redistricting can offer a growing minority party the opportunity to grow further, but unless a critical mass of state legislators is achieved, the process simply perpetuates partisan imbalance. Holding only a bit over one-quarter of all southern state legislative seats in 1990, Republicans were unable to realize that critical mass. As Republicans continue to make gains in state legislatures, this should change.

Even in 1990, though, there was a vehicle for Republican advantage in redistricting—ironically, the Voting Rights Act. Finding themselves allied with black Democrats, Republicans were greatly advantaged by the creation of additional majority black districts in several states. When heavily black areas were cut from several districts, many white Democrats lost their strategic advantage. It is not surprising that in 1992, black Democrats and white Republicans won contiguous districts in Alabama, Georgia, and South Carolina while white Democrats lost those seats. In 1994, several other Republicans claimed seats in the more heavily white districts created with majority black districts after 1990. The new districts explain part of the reason for recent Republican breakthroughs in the South. Republican presidential candidates were winning big in the old districts, however. District lines are thus not the only explanation for the lack of Republican progress in the Reagan-Bush years.

Of course, there may in fact be a relation between Republican success at the presidential level and Democratic success at the congressional level. Republicans have made their largest gains since 1964 in midterms during Democratic administrations. In 1966, 1978, and 1994, years in which southern Democrats were least able to "denationalize" their local elections, Republicans reached new plateaus of success. Where southern Democrats can run on their own game plan, proven through time to be effective, they have an advantage. I have attempted here to illustrate this advantage. With a Democrat in the White House, they lose this control. The slow filtering down of the realignment ironically may be a function of Republicans' doing so well in the presidential elections. It is nonetheless worth understanding how Democrats have prolonged their local advantage for so long.

Finally, in the days of total Democratic dominance, the Republican party was a totally impotent force in the South. Key (1946) describes Republican party leaders as politically naive and ineffective. They were interested in doling out a little patronage from the national party or in interacting with national politicians but had "only the foggiest notion where the Republican voters in the state live[d]" and "[were] overwhelmed by the futility of it all" (293). Their legacy has been devastating. Given that the party was so immature at the beginning and has worked under such a disadvantage to the Democrats, many argue that it is little wonder that a full realignment has yet to take place. Simply put, there is a strong line of argument that given the huge obstacles, all described here, it just has taken time for change to occur.

Still, the first major Republican gains occurred several decades ago, and since that time the party has almost completely dominated in presidential contests in the South and has won a share of Senate and gubernatorial contests. Add to this the advantage that race has given the GOP, and it is astounding that the forces of the past continue to make themselves felt. Other realignments have filtered down in much less time than this. Large numbers of Republican candidates in the 1850s and Democratic candidates in the 1930s, to take the two best examples of previous large-scale realignments, were elected within a few years of the large shifts in mass partisanship (Sundquist 1983, 92–98, 214). As an explanation of the southern Republican condition, the argument that it just takes time for a party to mature begs the question, why so long?

Understanding the presidential-congressional dichotomy requires analysis of the dynamics of both presidential elections and other elections. The nature of the choice is so different in these two sets of elections that it is not surprising there has been dramatic variation in Republican success. Republican presidential candidates have been able to stake a claim to the right half of the political spectrum without being crowded by their Democratic counterparts. Democratic nominees, emerging from a series of primaries and caucuses increasingly dominated by issue activists, have had to pass the liberal litmus tests of many of the Democrats' constituent groups. Although these candidates (with the exception of Carter and Clinton, northern liberals) have attempted to moderate their views during the general election, they have had few conservative credentials. Attempts to present themselves as moderate or to downplay ideological differences (such as Michael Dukakis's claim, "This is an election over competence, not ideology") were hard to accept and often futile. The choice at the presidential level has been clear-cut: A conservative faces a liberal. In the South, this is little choice.

This is not to say that race has had nothing to do with Republican success at the presidential level. Some contend that Republican tactics in recent campaigns were designed to tug at racist or racially conservative attitudes. The Republican Willie Horton television commercial in the presidential race of 1988 is a case in point. Many Democrats attacked this advertisement as a thinly disguised racial appeal. "If you were going to run a campaign of fear and smear and appeal to racial hatred you could not have picked a better case to use than this one," said Dukakis's campaign manager, Susan Estrich (Jamieson 1992, 474). In the postmortem of the election, some academic consensus has formed around the conclusion that "the Bush campaign trafficked in racially loaded stereotypes" in its use of the furlough issue (Kinder et al. 1989, 14; see also Woodward 1988; Pomper 1989; Black and Black 1992). More broadly, the Republican law and order message and Republican complaints about welfare abuse and wasteful social programs are seen through this prism (Sears and McConahey 1973; Kinder et al. 1989; Gilens 1990; Edsall and Edsall 1991). This is not to say that Democrats have not employed some of the same themes in their campaigns. But generally they have been in greater evidence in Republican presidential campaigns and party platforms.

Whether or not these appeals are racial in intention or in effect or both, I argue that the choices in recent presidential elections, in those elections since Barry Goldwater broke through in the Solid South, have been ideologically stark enough that race simply has not mattered much. There in fact may be some racial appeal to conservatism (that is the basis of another book), but when faced with a conservative and a liberal, white southerners have taken the conservative, the Republican, time after time.[1]

Southern congressional elections, however, have been different. The ideological choices offered there have not been as stark. For the most part, Democratic candidates have not paid homage to liberal constituencies. They have usually been more liberal than their Republican opponents, but not markedly so and not dangerously so. Southern Democrats have often been indistinguishable from southern Republicans on social issues like abortion and capital punishment, on defense issues, and on patriotism issues. They have presented themselves as probusiness, antitax fiscal conservatives. They have differed from their Republican opponents, to be sure, but the differences have been a matter of degree, not of kind. In southern congressional elections, Democrats have generally been moderate-to-conservative, which likely has blunted the effectiveness of the inevitable Republican charge that Democrats are too liberal.

There are several reasons to believe that Democratic congressional candidates have even been at an advantage in these elections. Ironically, Republican congressional candidates in the South, like some Republicans throughout the country, occasionally have been hampered by ideology (Barnes 1988). Democrats are philosophically consistent when they portray themselves as better able to serve the district. On the other hand, the doctrinaire conservative policy stands of Republican congressional candidates, the same ones that have served Republican presidential candidates so well, often have conflicted with the need to promise local benefits or to fight for protected markets, to name the most important examples. Such conflicts certainly make a difference in congressional elections. Indeed, Gary Jacobson (1990) attributes mixed national electoral results to differences in what voters find attractive in presidential and congressional candidates. He offers evidence that presidential candidates are evaluated according to their views on national policy while congressional candidates are evaluated on their ability to defend their district from the repercussions of that national policy. Although this is not just a regional phenomenon, the South, with its strong support of both Republican presidents and Democratic congressional candidates, has been contributing more than its share to what Jacobson seeks to explain.

In addition to their heavy use of local issues, southern Democrats have relied on an important feature of their districts to win elections. Many congressional districts in the South have large black populations. Blacks comprise 17 percent of the South's population, and, in the Deep South above all, there are large enough concentrations of blacks in most districts to give the Democrats a decided advantage. It is an advantage that Democrats must use carefully, and here is where racial issues have carried importance.

In a great many elections in the South, racial issues are raised. Racial issues do not automatically win elections for Republicans, however. In fact, oftentimes they damage Republican chances. The key to understanding this paradox lies in how the issue gets played out in the campaign. While Republicans raise the issue, Democrats often do not respond in public. If they do respond, it is in moderate tones, perhaps expressing their support for the racially liberal position but not vocally and not to the extreme. In the black communities, however, these issues play well. Democrats use the issue handed to them by their opponent in front of black audiences, in commercials on black media, and in direct mail to black neighborhoods. It is the segregated nature of many aspects of southern life that has allowed this strategy to work. Democrats can make strong appeals to blacks without losing the moderate or even the conservative white support they initially have because whites, for the most part, do not hear these appeals. So long as the Democratic candidate does not appear to spearhead black causes, he or she does not put significant white support at risk.

Democrats have been advantaged further in implementing this process because black political leaders do not expect white Democrats to be vocal advocates of black political interests. Black leaders give white Democrats considerable leeway in negotiating their tricky course. As an important official in the Alabama Democratic Conference put it, white candidates were not held to a litmus test on black issues. His organization understood the constraints that white Democrats operated under and took a pragmatic view of their campaign behavior. A black leader from Virginia also voiced this opinion, "[L. F. Payne] didn't have to come across as some big liberal on our issues [to get our support]. We knew he had to walk a tightrope. We knew that he had to maintain a core constituency." This freedom to deal with the sensitive issues of race quietly has enabled white Democrats to combine enough of the white vote with a heavy and monolithic black vote.

Democrats have won congressional elections because they take advantage of heavy support from blacks without risking a large proportion of their white support. Republicans have won congressional elections in the region, but many of their victories in the 1970s, 1980s, and early 1990s were in the traditionally Republican hill country of Tennessee, Arkansas, and North Carolina, the growing areas of Florida, and the affluent suburbs of the larger cities, places with fewer blacks than those required to make a biracial coalition viable. Throughout the rest of the region, local Democrats continued to win open seat competitive elections in the Reagan-Bush years. The racial composition of their districts and the strategies by which they pursue two separate communities have made this possible. If they are to continue to win in a very uncertain future, they must continue to to forge a racial coalition.

The Republican Future

This book is really devoted to what Democrats have done right in the South in the post–civil rights era. Analysts have been predicting for decades that the Democrats would fall, that ultimately the Republicans would break through and win at lower political levels as they have at the presidential level (Sundquist 1983; Stanley 1987; Bullock 1988b), yet Democrats have survived long odds. What of the future? How much longer can the Democrats hold out? Their dominance in the South has faded. With the 1994 elections, Democrats lost significant ground. Although they still dominate state legislatures, even this advantage has been eroding. The Republican future is bright, yet one cannot count southern Democrats out yet. Their remarkable success over the past thirty years, their winning formulas, show how adaptable they are to new circumstances. That in the 1994 House elections, 89 percent of southern Democratic incumbents retained their seats while only 83 percent of non-southern Democratic incumbents did so is some indication of their ability to weather a storm that raged against Democrats across the country.

The question thus becomes, what must Republicans do to achieve full-scale realignment. What are they doing right? What must they continue to do? What strategies hold the greatest potential for electoral payoff? This analysis offers some clues.

One possibility for further Republican growth involves Democratic politicians switching sides either in a slow trickle or en masse. The task of Republican party leaders is to make conversion attractive and to court young, conservative Democrats. Every so often the Republicans score a big coup when a congressional incumbent like Phil Gramm or Andy Ireland of Florida switches parties and is reelected as a Republican. This, however, has been a relatively rare event, and the contention here is that Republicans should be directing their attention to low-level officials, those holding the types of offices that have eluded the party. The key is to identify young, upwardly mobile politicians whose paths are blocked by senior Democrats and whose prospects improve in less crowded and less competitive Republican primaries. What the Republicans have to offer is a less cluttered career ladder. For someone willing to take the risk, there is more opportunity to achieve quickly in the Republican party in the South. Although not likely to carry large numbers of followers with them, these young politicians will improve the Republican pool of candidates, which will in turn improve the party's fortunes in the long run.

The other great advantage of converting Democratic elites is that with every conversion, the stigma carried by a Republican affiliation is broken down further. Conversion generates legitimacy for the party. When a high-profile individual makes the change, it helps dispel the idea that Republicans cannot win. That idea has been a very damaging one over the decades, and each switch makes it more likely that others will reassess the electoral consequences of doing the same.[2] Indeed, with a high-profile convert like Richard Shelby and a large number of new southern Republicans in the House and Senate in 1994, the perception may now be that the Republican label is advantageous, and this probably will lead other Democratic elites to follow suit. With each defection, with each loss of a seat, the remaining conservative Democrats also lose some cover, some comfort in their numbers, some sense of being a meaningful minority in the national party. This could inspire further defections.

Republicans have been able to convert some Democratic officeholders and other potential Democratic candidates.[3] This obviously has contributed to the growth of the party. But Republican candidates, whether they started out as Democrats or not, need to have winning campaign strategies. John Rice's campaign in Alabama (see chapter 3), shows that Democrats-turned-Republican have not necessarily been ready to run winning campaigns.

If there is a key to southern Republicans reaching dominance in upcoming years, it may be in directing their attention to the black vote in one of two ways. First, Republicans would benefit from breaking the Democratic lock on the black vote. A second possibility may be to "deracialize" their campaigns. On the first point, as is apparent from some of the cases discussed above, southern Republican strategists, even in areas where blacks do not comprise a majority, are beginning to recognize that some black votes may help Republicans win close contests. Even 20 percent of the black vote can make the difference between victory and defeat (see table 2.2).

It has taken a change in Republican leadership for this idea to be considered in party strategy. The first post–civil rights generation of leadership had no desire to direct appeals toward blacks. Nor did they think it was necessary. Their party was building, after all, on the defections of racially motivated southern whites. After nearly thirty years of stunted Republican growth at low levels, a new generation of pragmatists has begun to rethink party strategy. An Alabama campaign manager put it bluntly: "The old breed said, 'Fuck 'em. Don't pander to 'em.' We can't afford to take that attitude anymore. We want to win elections, and the reality of the situation is that we've got to win over black independents." Others, notably the late national Republican party chairman Lee Atwater, have spoken publicly about the importance of cutting into the overwhelming Democratic advantage among blacks.

If some Republican strategists now believe that the party must, in the words of a Mississippi party official, "be evangelical to blacks," they are not fully certain about how this is to be done. A Washington-based Republican consultant discussed the problem faced by the southern wing of the party: "Southern Republicans genuinely want racial harmony. And they want to do something for blacks. But they don't really know what to do." The stated desire "to do something for blacks," of course, has a certain paternalistic ring to it, but it illustrates his point well.

Part of the problem may be that many southern Republicans believe that they have a legitimate claim to at least some of the black vote, a claim that blacks do not appear to recognize. They argue that their party has been more supportive of civil rights and black progress than is commonly believed and that the Republican party was instrumental in the passage of civil rights legislation. "We cast the tough votes," said Linda Arey, arguing that historically the Republicans were the racially liberal party. Moreover, this argument goes, the Democrats, the party of segregationists, have "gotten a free ride." Complained a longtime Republican leader in Mississippi, "We had a window of opportunity in '69–'70 when blacks were grateful. I assumed they were very grateful, but they weren't grateful enough for all that we had done." He went on, "Since then, we've taken a bum rap. Sure race has been a factor in our growth but not how the liberals portray it. By the time we got on the scene, the battle was over. The Citizens' Councils, almost to a man, their leadership was Democratic. By the time we came on the scene, no one would believe you if you said, 'We gonna save you from desegregation.'" It was not that he is wrong here, but through the past two decades southern Republicans have been unable to balance this message with their appeals to whites, a finesse that requires more than just an appeal to the past.

How might southern Republicans appeal to blacks? Recruitment of black candidates is one way to break the notion that there is no room for blacks in the party. Several Republican officials talked about this as a development and noted that a few candidates were being groomed. Indeed, in Oklahoma, considered by some as having a southern political culture, a black Republican, J. C. Watts, was elected in 1994. In more heavily black places, though, such candidates invariably will be characterized as Uncle Toms, alienating rank-and-file blacks instead of attracting them to the Republican camp. Bennie Thompson's effective campaign against Henry Espy in the Mississippi 2 primary suggests that this is always a possibility.

In addition, Republicans have sought to appeal to the sentiment, either already held or easily evoked, that blacks as a group would benefit by having their votes competed for. "It would be good for blacks, the country, and the Republicans if blacks became competitive," said a resentful Republican political consultant. "The Democrats could nominate David Duke and get all the black vote." The strategy now appears to be to approach black opinion leaders who hold this sentiment and have them carry the message into the black communities. In the Mississippi Gulf Coast election, for example, the Republican campaign located a black minister from a neighboring congressional district who was unhappy with the Democratic candidate's votes in the state legislature and wished to call him to task. While this minister claimed to be a Democrat, he felt that the Democrats needed to be more accountable to the black community. "The only time they come to us is when they're running for office. We wanted to let Gene Taylor know that there's a segment out there not to forget. That's the reason we threw a little potshot at him," said the minister. He added, "Those people [the Democrats] are just usin' us to perfection."

Some Republicans assert that a number of their standard nonracial themes that work well among whites could be directed effectively toward black independents and middle-class black voters. Believing that some blacks would be receptive to "the gospel of individual initiative" and to free enterprise, antiregulation, antigovernment rhetoric, Republicans have attempted to carry this message to black audiences. Hayes Dent argued at several points throughout his campaign that the black middle class had made more progress in the 1980s than any other group in American society. "That doesn't totally absolve Ronald Reagan and George Bush," he backtracked, "but they did provide opportunity to blacks." He believed, even in retrospect, that 15 to 20 percent of the black vote could be won with the "uncomfortable" message, "You shouldn't rely on the government." Specific issues like opposing a rise in the minimum wage and welfare reform were taken to audiences of black businesspeople in Alabama and Mississippi in hope of cutting into solid Democratic support. This is possible. Both of Mississippi's senators, Thad Cochran and Trent Lott, have won portions of the black vote in their Senate races by tenaciously building a small network of black supporters. Their success in building that network has come over time, though, and southern Republicans running for Congress, at least those in this sample, have not successfully courted blacks with their conservative message.

Finally, there is some evidence that Republicans have tried to buy the support of black ministers and other black leaders in attempts to divide the black vote or at least to discourage the idea (among blacks) that their leadership is so unanimously behind the Democrats. Either by contributions to black churches or by making direct payments to individuals, the Republicans have made efforts to reach black leaders with money. One Republican campaign manager told of several instances in which Republicans had solicited black ministers in their campaigns. His most vivid example of vote buying involved a campaign official who, not trusting his new allies to deliver their congregations, gave them only half the promised money up front: "It was literally half the money 'cause he took a paper cutter out and sliced all those bills in half. Man, their eyes were about poppin' out of their head."

A second grand Republican strategy vis-à-vis blacks would direct itself not to attracting blacks to the party, but to demobilizing them. As things stand, Republicans recognize that, Lott and Cochran notwithstanding, they have little to no support from the black community. Even campaigning in the black community appears to be fruitless to Republican candidates, which is a source of great frustration. Linda Arey's comment that, even after marching in a Martin Luther King Day parade, she had only enough black votes "to fill five phone booths" illustrates this point. She believed that her public support of the parade, moreover, was part of the reason she lost so much of the white vote in Danville. John Rice argued that it did not really matter what he did, there was no way he could win any black votes: "It all came down to, 'Are you willing to lay money on the table?' . . . We went into Hobson City, a 100 percent black town, and had a blast. Played basketball. Had a parade in the downtown. A barbecue. I got no votes out of that town. My philosophy and my voting record were out the window. Meant nothing." The public opinion polls and electoral statistics show that Rice was right. He did not get any support from blacks in his election, and he was probably correct in his belief that such support was not possible. Many southern Republicans have been unable to win black votes within the confines of their present electoral strategy. Their message to whites has been incompatible with a message that would be appealing to blacks.[4] Moreover, in reaching whites, they are heard by blacks.

Perhaps because of this reality or because of the Republican perception of this reality, previous efforts to demobilize blacks have had a "low road" quality to them. Twenty-five years after the civil rights movement, there are still accusations that Republicans attempt to discourage black voters by intimidation and deceit. Most commonly, it is charged that the Republicans place people or threatening signs (offering rewards for those documenting voter fraud) outside black precincts to scare off prospective voters. Black leaders have become increasingly vigilant and active in responding to these tactics, a Texas state legislator threatening even to send out "big, black and burly" ex-convicts to watch Republican poll watchers being sent to minority precincts in a coordinated campaign (Davidson 1990, 236). Still, it is clear that these programs help keep the black vote down and that some Republicans continue to engage in them. This is not to say that Republicans are the only ones responsible for fraud and intimidation. They, in fact, respond that the Democrats violate election rules so frequently that it has become necessary to station observers at the polls, particularly in black precincts. Their list of such violations is long and varied, and many southern Republicans vehemently defend their right to try to keep fraud in check, notably in those areas where they expect to do worst. Perhaps most important here is that the accusations from both sides relate to how the parties treat the black vote. This, of course, says much about how southern politics has changed as well as how it has stayed the same.

Although intimidation may in fact work, it is problematic in many ways. And it is surely not a tactic upon which to build a party. A more attractive route for dealing with the black electorate may be to deracialize the Republican campaign. If the campaigns described in this book are any indication, introducing race into the campaign introduces a problem. It mobilizes the opponent's base. It also relieves a white opponent of having to make an affirmative case for himself or herself before the black electorate. As I have noted, the racial issue offers the Democrat a vehicle through which to approach black voters.

Racial conflict has without doubt brought many southern white voters into the Republican party. Race issues have taken the party from nothing to something (and something substantial). Republican candidates have continued to rely on them. I argue that at this point, perhaps racial appeals are counterproductive, especially in places with large black populations. The racial balance in many districts in the South has led Republicans to believe that generating group conflict is to their benefit, and herein lies part of the pattern of campaign behavior illustrated in this book. The ability of Democrats to turn these racial appeals around in the black community and to overcome them with a large enough minority of white voters to win indicates that Republicans may benefit when they adjust their perceptions of the costs and benefits of racial issues. Having other conservative populist themes in their quiver, Republicans, I argue, could abandon racial issues with little cost.

It is certainly not time to read the Democratic party its last rites in the South. The Solid South has given way to a decidedly two-party system. The Republican party has been invigorated. Yet even as a majority of whites have turned Republican, southern Democrats have continued to win much more than their share of congressional elections by sticking to a formula that has kept them on top in recent decades.

What is ultimately remarkable is that the Democrats in the South have a long history of survival and dominance. At the turn of the century, Democrats were challenged by a surging populist party and were able to beat back that challenge with Jim Crow laws and virulent racial rhetoric. What is more, they established a system of politics that they completely dominated for almost six decades.

In the past several decades, Democrats have again survived a challenge to their superiority. This time, they did not have much in their favor except perhaps a little momentum from the past. With the Republicans holding the race card that Democrats had played successfully throughout the previous regime and holding a conservative advantage in public opinion, Democrats have had to manage to survive in a hostile new political world. Through tough times, their dominoes remained standing.

In hindsight, 1994 may be viewed as marking a transition to a new era in southern politics. If this is the case, the thirty years following the Voting Rights Act constitute a period in southern political history marked by a surprisingly resistant and resilient Democratic party, a period in which race continued to matter in southern politics and matter a lot, but not in the way most expected it to. The lessons here are thus analytical as well as political. Race, racial issues, racial conflict may affect political thought and behavior in some predictable ways, yet not yield predictable electoral results. It is by looking at political campaigns, at the context within which political choices are made, that such choices make more sense.

Notes

Chapter 1 The Puzzles of the Southern Realignment

1 The South is defined by Key and many other analysts of southern politics as the eleven states of the former Confederacy: Alabama, Arkansas, Florida, Georgia, Louisiana, Mississippi, North Carolina, South Carolina, Tennessee, Texas, and Virginia. This is how I define the region as well. The South covers a large area, one that is geographically, demographically, and politically diverse. Much of what is to follow is an analysis of "the politics of the South." As such, it highlights what is common to the various parts of the region and downplays some intraregional differences. This is not to say that such differences do not exist, only that they do not fall within the scope of this research.

2 The black belt is a wide strip of rich land that runs across the Deep South. It is the part of the South where plantation agriculture was most practiced and slaves were most relied upon. It is, to this day, the area with the heaviest nonurban concentration of blacks in the South.

3 Like Democratic dominance in the region, Republican success in hill country also

goes back to events of the Civil War. These areas were not suited to plantation agriculture, and the poor white farmers who lived there generally did not own slaves and were unwilling to join the Confederacy in the Civil War. This area comprises eastern Tennessee and western North Carolina and Virginia.

4 Neither of them was that much of an exception when it came to the use of race in their campaigns. Long, writes his biographer, "more frequently than has been supposed, [did] indulge in race baiting. He never did it very well, however, and obviously did not enjoy doing it when he felt . . . that he had to" (Williams 1969, 327–28; see also Brinkley 1982; Hair 1991). Watson abandoned his populist goal of a black-white coalition and supported the disenfranchisement of blacks when it became apparent that this was politically necessary (Woodward 1938, 370–72).

5 The data for this exercise come from the American National Election Studies and were made available by the Inter-University Consortium of Political and Social Research through the archive at U.C. DATA of the University of California, Berkeley, and through Computer Services at Tufts University. The data were originally collected by the Center for Political Studies of the Institute for Social Research, the University of Michigan, under a grant from the National Science Foundation. Neither the original collectors of the data nor the Consortium bears any responsibility for the analysis or interpretations presented here.

6 Although 1994 was certainly a bad year for Democrats in the South, it was no better for Democrats outside the South. Almost 13 percent of all southern seats went from Democratic to Republican hands; 12 percent of nonsouthern seats were taken from the Democrats.

7 This open seat analysis is based upon data extracted from the biennial *Almanac of American Politics*.

8 Elections from the 1992 cycle are not included in these percentages because major redistricting often made it difficult or impossible to designate an incumbent. Seats created after the 1980 redistricting are not included here either.

9 These figures also do not include the 1992 elections because of major changes in district boundaries.

10 Republicans have picked up some ground by defeating incumbents. Nineteen Republican challengers defeated Democratic incumbents between 1980 and 1992, while only thirteen Democratic challengers unseated Republican congressmen.

11 The data upon which this discussion are based come from various editions of the *Statistical Abstract of the United States*. The data for 1994 were supplied by the National Conference of State Legislatures.

12 All these data are from American National Election Studies surveys conducted in the 1980s. These surveys have been pooled to maximize the number of cases.

13 It is instructive to look at congressional votes because even though they may not perfectly reflect a representative's personal sentiments, they do represent his political stands. A member of Congress may not be called upon by his next electoral opponent to defend his vote, but he must always be prepared for this eventuality. Roll call votes

are thus useful quantitative data on the public positions of members of Congress. Of course, there are ways for them to hide their actual positions by voting one way on procedural questions and another on the substantive issue. I have chosen to look at the more substantive votes, as I am most interested in the positions a congressman might have to defend in public.

14 Again, these data come from the American National Election Studies (1980–90 pooled).

15 Empirical tests of this idea have not all been confirming. Petrocik (1981), for example, argues that white backlash may have led to changes in the southern party system but has not sustained them. See also, Stanley (1987).

Chapter 2 The Case for Context

1 Turnout in these special elections varied but was usually rather low. In the elections studied here, turnout averaged 31 percent of the voting age population. For ease of presentation, the calculations in this table are based on the assumption that a normal turnout in special elections is 33 percent, though this is simply a convenient base. The general principles being discussed here are applicable whether normal turnout is 20 percent or 50 percent.

2 Many of the observations I make about the effectiveness of various strategies and tactics require inferences based on fragmentary evidence. Such is the nature of this type of research. Some of my conclusions are based on what people have told me in the course of interviews, how they have viewed the effectiveness of various issues. At several points in this book, I am able to test propositions with survey data. For the most part, however, where such data existed, they were almost impossible to obtain. Where they were obtained, they rarely offered the relevant variables to test my hypotheses. Aggregate data from these elections also offered limited ability to test hypotheses. I have resorted to using these data in places, if only to get a partial confirmation of my expectations.

3 This man drove his car off a bridge on election night. His injuries were minor.

4 In spite of the fact that candidates are inevitably dissatisfied with their coverage, not one of the candidates discussed here was ignored by the media. Indeed, what is striking was how much of their message got into the newspapers as intended and even unfiltered. Many of the press reports and television stories as well were very uncritical pieces on the candidates. Others came right from press releases.

5 In the pages to follow, numerous people are quoted. Most of these quotes come from personal interviews with participants in the campaign. As the names of these people are of no import to the story being told here, I have identified most speakers by their role in the campaign, for example, "Democratic media consultant" and "Republican campaign manager." Where names have been used, the person involved is one of the candidates or the quote came attributed from a newspaper or both. Quotes not followed by a newspaper citation come from personal interviews.

6 The six cases studied here do not conform to Sigelman's findings. In these special elections, turnout averaged 31 percent of the voting age population. This is certainly much lower than turnout in presidential elections, and the average turnout for the 1988 presidential election in these six districts was 52 percent. But turnout in the 1986 elections, a better comparison because it was an off-year, also averaged 31 percent in these districts (see table 2.3). Indeed the average turnout in all southern congressional districts in 1986 (not including uncontested Louisiana elections) was only 34 percent. Clearly these special elections were not unique on this count. They generated as much turnout as elections held on the regular cycle.

7 This is the average margin of victory for victorious incumbent congressmen who faced major party opposition. Those who did not face major party opposition are excluded here (seventy-two congressmen—17 percent of all congressmen—fell into this category). These numbers were calculated from data provided in Duncan (1989).

8 Jacobson and Kernell's (1983) important "strategic politicians theory" is yet another way to conceive of how national forces impinge on congressional elections. They argue that national conditions many months prior to the election influence the decisions of politicians to run for office and lead party elites and supporters to donate money to or withhold it from campaigns. These decisions determine the relative strength of Democratic and Republican candidates running for Congress and the "local choices" offered to voters in various districts.

9 The finding that fifteen of twenty turnovers went against the president is of somewhat limited value because Sigelman does not give information on how many seats the president's party and the opposition party defended in this time (he gives only the total number of contests in which there was no change in party control). The more relevant statistic would be the percentage of seats successfully defended by the president's party and by the opposition party. Although presenting the findings this way would likely show that the president's party has been somewhat less successful at defending its seats than the opposition party, it would still be quite evident that both defend their seats much more frequently than they lose them.

10 Studlar and Sigelman actually look at both British by-elections and American special elections in their research note. They are unable to test their time-passage hypothesis for special elections, however, given the poor quality of some of the American election data.

11 As Mark Westlye (1991) argues, margin of victory is not a particularly good measure of campaign intensity, and indeed, "the two concepts are theoretically distinct" (18). By his criteria—quantity of news coverage, paid advertising, campaign expenditures—these cases could all have been expected to be, and in fact were, "hard fought campaigns."

12 There were five other special elections won by Democrats in the South in the period from Ronald Reagan's first victory in 1980 to the early months of the Clinton administration. They were held in northwestern Georgia (Georgia 7; 1983), central Louisiana (Louisiana 8; 1985), Nashville (Tennessee 5; 1988), Houston (Texas 18; 1989), and Fort Worth (Texas 12; 1989).

Seven special elections were won by Republicans over this period—in the corridor between Dallas and Houston (Texas 6; 1982), western North Carolina (North Carolina 10; 1986), northwestern Louisiana (Louisiana 4; 1988), Knoxville (Tennessee 2: 1988), Miami (Florida 18; 1989), Dallas (Texas 3; 1991), and north-central Virginia (Virginia 7; 1991).

13 These percentages apply to the district at the time of the election. The 1990 redistricting changed some of the districts in marginal ways. Mississippi 4 even has gone through two changes. Nonetheless, the districts remain recognizable in the 1990s.

Chapter 3 Racial Issues in the Congressional Campaign

1 The district's boundaries changed shortly after the 1981 election looked at here. In an effort to create a majority black district in the Mississippi Delta, several predominantly black counties on the Mississippi River were taken out of the Fourth. Following the redistricting, the district became 37 percent black. Nonetheless, this description remains pretty accurate, even following the 1990 redistricting.

2 In 1964, the Third District elected a Republican congressman who was unable to defend his seat in 1966.

3 Cochran also benefited from an independent black candidacy in his first run for the Senate. Cochran beat his Democratic opponent 45 to 32 percent, while Charles Evers, the brother of the slain civil rights leader Medgar Evers, won 23 percent of the vote.

4 Robert Wheems, the former grand chaplain of the Klan, attacked the Democrat Wayne Dowdy as "a scalawag who wilfully aid[s] and abet[s] the Black Power Movement," and Liles Williams as a member of the "sinister Common Cause." "Can we afford less moral courage in 1981 than in 1964?" he asks in a *Jackson Clarion-Ledger* advertisement. In a crowded field, Wheems received less than 1 percent of the vote. "I was hoping the race would come down to me and a Negro," he explained to the *Clarion-Ledger* (1981a). In fact, Wheems miscalculated. No blacks were in the field.

5 Dowdy had a different concern vis-à-vis whites. He avoided bringing up the homosexual scandal because Hinson also was from the southern part of the district, and he feared offending any rural whites who might have connections to the political Hinson family.

6 These data were compiled from Putnam 1981b.

7 Such an arrangement, Parker (1990) notes, makes it extraordinarily difficult for minorities to win nominations (74).

8 This difference is actually a bit understated because Browder ran in two primaries and Rice ran in one. Under campaign finance laws, this allowed Browder to accept larger donations from the national party. Browder's connections to labor allowed him to raise more money overall. In their final Federal Election Commission reports, Browder reported spending $679,000 to just $443,000 for Rice (Barone and Ujifusa 1989, 15).

9 Browder himself agreed that he was not comfortable campaigning in churches, but that went for all churches, black and white.

10 Unfortunately for Ford, this opportunity did not arise. Although a majority black district was carved out of the black belt running across the central part of the state in the 1990 redistricting, it was in the western part of the belt. In 1992, the Third District remained roughly intact, and two white Democrats lost their seats to black Democrat Earl Hilliard and white Republican Spencer Bachus.

11 Browder did not receive an appointment to the Armed Services Committee upon his arrival in Congress; he was assigned to the Public Works and Transportation Committee, another fine place for congressmen interested in bringing home federal money for their districts. Later in 1989, however, Browder switched to the Armed Services Committee, where a seat became available when the Arkansas congressman Tommy Robinson defected to the Republican party.

12 Heflin was not the only statewide Democratic figure brought into the district. Browder tried to build on the district's traditional Democratic ties with highly publicized endorsements from Jim Folsom, Jr., and George Wallace, Jr., the sons of two major Alabama political figures. Even George Wallace, Sr., despite being ill, appeared in a Browder radio ad.

13 Browder's campaign manager became a little concerned when a scare over a pesticide used on apples (alar) became newsworthy during the campaign.

14 The two candidates, who both came to the Alabama House of Representatives in 1982, voted together twelve of twenty times on key votes between 1982 and 1986. They took the same side on issues like gambling, abortion, and tort reform, but diverged on taxes (allowing the public to vote in referendums for various tax increases) and education reform. On Browder's legislation to create a merit pay system for teachers, Rice had been a major and vocal opponent. He had argued that the AEA would control the teacher evaluations and that teachers' raises would cost the state millions of dollars (White 1989).

15 What was most interesting about this particular mailing is that it, unlike the other two, was not sponsored by the Republican National Campaign Committee. Their decision was likely informed by David Duke's election to the state legislature in Louisiana, which was considered an embarrassment to the national party.

16 Elite political behavior is almost as effective as a public opinion survey in assessing the direction of a campaign. In this case, the national committee's representative to the Rice campaign spent the closing weeks of the election working in Florida (Yardley 1989d).

17 The authors acknowledge that racial conservatism may simply be "racism dressed up, made respectable" (191), but they refrain from tackling the question of whether or not this is the case.

18 Rice, as noted, also called his support of the Confederate flag an act of courage, an indication that he acted on what he believed was right. The courage headline on his campaign literature again illustrates how these appeals are made less directly than in

years past. It also indicates that candidates often require a justification for taking such a stand. Rice's campaign manager said, "The issue is courage. John Rice had the courage to stand up and be counted. Everybody knows John Rice isn't a racist" (Yardley 1989d).

19 Both figures are from the American National Election Studies and represent validated vote.

20 Other radio stations often are used to reach specific groups with well-honed messages. Evangelical Christian and Spanish-language radio stations, for example, also offer excellent opportunities to narrowcast.

21 The political scientist and former congressional candidate Sandy Maisel (1986) reports that he and many other congressional candidates found the coverage of their campaigns to be unsophisticated and skewed toward bigger, local events (119).

22 Occasionally, a Republican campaign will be able to make Democratic radio advertisements a campaign issue. In the North Carolina Senate race in 1990, for example, the Republican candidate, Jesse Helms, attacked his Democratic opponent, Harvey Gantt, for using "racial ads" on black radio. His commercial accuses Gantt of running a "secret campaign": "Why doesn't Harvey Gantt run his ad on all radio stations, so everyone can hear it instead of just on black stations? Doesn't Harvey Gantt want everyone to vote?" (Toner 1990). This race was unusual, however. Gantt, running against a nemesis of liberals, had a large campaign fund and was able to advertise widely before the election, thus giving Helms the opportunity to attack him. Moreover, Helms, who was waging a racially charged campaign of his own, knew what was coming and had a ready response. In most elections, Republicans are not able to respond to the black campaign ads because they come so late in the campaign.

Chapter 4 Courting White Voters

1 Even the Republican who held the seat in 1870 did so for less than one term (King 1985a).

2 Because Republicans called great attention to the election and because little else was going on, the election attracted a lot of national attention. Even the national press paid a great deal of attention to developments in East Texas. And because the Republicans defined the situation so clearly, the election did become an important test of southern realignment in numerous reports in the *New York Times* and the *Washington Post* and in columns by various political analysts such as Mark Shields (1985), Jack Germond and Jules Witcover (1985), Michael Barone (1985), and Rowland Evans and Robert Novak (1985).

3 Gramm, after a highly publicized fight with the Democratic leadership in the House, renounced his Democratic affiliation, resigned his office, and won a 1983 special election for his congressional seat as a Republican. His bold move and the publicity surrounding it positioned him to run for and win in 1986 the Texas Senate seat vacated by the retiring Republican John Tower.

4 In 1968, as Edd Hargett was leading Texas A&M to its first Cotton Bowl victory in twenty-seven years (and first appearance in twenty-six years), Phil Gramm was teaching in the Economics Department at the university. In 1985, Texas A&M had not yet returned to the Cotton Bowl. Needless to say, Hargett's stature among alumni was great.

5 To give some perspective, in 1986, the average major party campaign raised close to $180,000 for both primary and general election activity (Stanley and Niemi 1988, 94).

6 Howard refused to endorse Chapman after the primary.

7 Hargett made his Aggie connection a major part of his campaign. His campaign speeches were peppered with Aggie jokes and his yard signs and bumper stickers were maroon and white, the school's colors. Most important, the Texas A&M alumni network proved to be a major source of his campaign funds (Watson 1985).

8 Indeed, the state Republican party officially defined homosexuality as "an abomination before God" and "indicative of a society's moral decadence" (Shields 1985).

9 Big labor was a particular bogeyman in this election. Responding to charges that he was beholden to "East Coast labor bosses," Chapman pointed to a one-thousand-dollar donation to Hargett from the Teamsters and argued at a debate that "Hargett's support is coming from some of the most crooked unions in the country" (Germond and Witcover 1985).

10 "Frequently" is perhaps not strong enough. Chapman's pollster contended that they used the trade advertisements on radio almost constantly with "700 grps [gross rating points] a week." Seven hundred gross rating points translates into almost 100 percent of the listening audience. This amount of advertising, according to a radio station account executive, is astounding for a political campaign.

11 County-level electoral results give some indication that Chapman's trade appeals were effective. The Democrat won 59 percent of the vote in Morris County, home of the steel plant and struggling under a 33 percent unemployment rate. The neighboring counties also had high unemployment rates and, with the exception of Hargett's home county and Bowie County (Texarkana), went into the Chapman column. Turnout in these counties was three points higher than in the rest of the district. Except for one county that is 36 percent black, blacks comprise about one-fifth of the population of these counties. It is thus fair to conclude that rural whites in this depressed area (near Hargett's hometown) were voting for Chapman. Their reasons for doing so cannot be determined with these data (public opinion data would be much more effective in assessing the impact and import of the issue), but these findings suggest that the "Japan bashing" may have had some effect. All these data were compiled from results reported in the *Dallas Morning News* on August 4, 1985.

12 The Justice Department, later in 1985, sought to codify the requirement to preclear special elections in some revisions of procedures for the administration of Section 5 of the Voting Rights Act. In oversight hearings before the Subcommittee on Civil and Constitutional Rights, a staff attorney for the Mexican American Legal Defense and Educational Fund , based in Texas, supported the provision with reference to the elec-

tion in the First District. Noting the Gramm election in 1983 and arguing that the Department of Justice had filed suit here because the Democrat was likely to win, she concluded that the lesson was that enforcement of Section 5 was arbitrary and selective. "I think what it clearly demonstrates is if you give the Department of Justice room to move, room to make selective decisions, they will make selective decisions on such enforcement. And we can't afford ambiguity in these regulations" (U.S. Congress 1985, 127).

13 This figure was calculated for the counties and cities comprising the Fifth District of the 1980s, which has slightly different boundaries from the district of the 1960s. These data were compiled from Scammon (1970).

14 His last contested election, in fact, was in 1970.

15 Jim Wright served as an all-purpose villain for Arey throughout the campaign. At one point, she told a reporter, "My mother always said that there's a little good in everybody; I just haven't been able to find it in Jim Wright. I think he's an archliberal, interested in power, not the people, and that is reflected in his leadership" (Bland 1988d). In reality, Jim Wright was not particularly liberal. His ADA scores were always quite moderate (between 40 and 50), which is what one might expect from a Texas Democrat. It is unlikely that the voters of the Fifth would have known this, however, and Wright was a high profile target because he was getting particularly bad press at the time of the campaign. Just under way was a probe of his financial dealings, which ultimately led to his resignation.

16 Arey's position on this issue was not even in the mainstream of the Republican party. House Republicans originally voted 124 to 29 on the issue, with less than half of the southern Republicans voting against it (see table 1–1).

17 Arey's manager said that Arey herself had called Bush to request his assistance, but it was also reported in the Danville paper that Virginia congressmen and the Reverend Jerry Falwell had appealed to Bush to visit the district.

18 Arey told of a letter received after the campaign relaying a barbershop conversation about her candidacy. When asked what he thought of Arey, one man responded, "Is she the widdah? No. What business does she have then running for the seat then?"

19 Public speaking was not Payne's strong suit. One reporter described him as being "shy" and "uncomfortable" giving a speech and noted that "he put some people to sleep" (Bland 1988a).

20 Another problem her campaign faced was hemorrhaging within her own campaign. Arey had four campaign managers and had difficulties with all four of them. She also fired a campaign consultant and a press aide (Eure 1988a).

21 Arey's deep disappointment at losing, particularly in her hometown and own neighborhood, led her to burn her political bridges. At her election night party, Arey blamed her Republican rival, Onico Barker, for her defeat, saying that he should have endorsed her (Stanbury 1988). She also resigned the Republican nomination for the congressional election to take place the following November. The next morning, she moved back to Washington, where her husband was a corporate lobbyist.

22 Arey also tried to reach black voters through the churches. It was an effort black leaders appreciated, though her position on *Grove City*, according to one prominent black leader, "raised a red flag" and made it difficult for blacks to support her.

23 The national Democratic party kept both stories alive by filing multiple complaints with the House Ethics Committee at different times. As anticipated, a high-profile story in the Gulfport newspaper followed.

24 In 1988, the Jackson paper published a story on the businessman who had provided Anderson and others with the free travel. In an investigative piece, the story raised questions about some low-interest Farmers Home Administration loans he had received, implying some sort of deal. The businessman lost a libel suit against the paper, and the records used as evidence in the suit detailed Anderson's free rides.

25 Taylor never explained his position on the first vote. His rationale for the second vote was that black-only schools were no longer needed because blacks could attend any state college. Why not consolidate the resources?

26 Reverend Appleberry became involved in the Anderson campaign because of the hospital and school issues. His organization produced more than a hundred thousand petitions from all over the state prior to Gov. Ray Mabus's veto of a bill to help the Charity Hospitals. Although one of the three Charity Hospitals in the state is in Meridian, none are located on the Gulf Coast. Appleberry's organization vowed to remember the governor and his legislative allies at the next election. Said Appleberry, "There's got to be a reckonin' day. We've got petitions from every county and we're gonna let them know there's a segment out there not to forget." Appleberry's support of the Republican was clearly motivated by his dislike of Taylor, not by any particular attachment to Anderson.

27 The events surrounding the injunction are not exactly clear. Reverend Appleberry claimed that, in fact, no injunction had been issued and that the whole thing was a Democratic ploy.

28 He not only looked bookish, he was bookish. Upon graduating from college, Anderson did graduate work in English (Brownson 1982).

29 The television and radio phone-in show have become an important part of southern campaigns. This is not only because they offer free media time (and lots of it), but because they are situations that can be controlled by the campaign. Friends and supporters are encouraged to phone in and even members of the campaign staff will call with questions that the candidate wants or needs to answer.

30 This press conference at a veterans' hospital illustrated who the most important player was. The television cameraman was about one half-hour late, leaving a half-dozen print journalists waiting patiently. Taylor and Montgomery took a second tour of the facility rather than start without him.

31 Taylor was successful in keeping the plant in the House budget, but the appropriation was stricken in the Senate.

32 Taylor's preoccupation with his local roots angered some of Anderson's supporters, who also were fixated on who was and was not local. As I watched the taping of a de-

bate with some Anderson supporters, several of them complained to me that Taylor went to high school and college in New Orleans. "And his company [the company he worked for] is based there too. Can you imagine?" exclaimed one woman.

33 Many southern politicians rail against nonracial out-groups as well. Homosexuals are a particularly vulnerable target. Although they are not a visible group in these districts, the stereotype politicians can call upon in their campaigns is accessible to most people. Both Democrats and Republicans try to link their opponents to gays and declare themselves against such things as affirmative action for gays, as Edd Hargett did in Texas and Gene Taylor in Mississippi 5. Their hostility to gays is astounding given the invisibility of the group in these areas. But again, they make an excellent target.

34 The vote was taken on April 29, 1987, and reported in *Congressional Quarterly Almanac*.

35 Rice had been a dues-paying member of the United Rubber Workers of America, an AFL-CIO union, for several years in the early 1970s.

36 Arey's positions on labor issues generated some hostility. The Virginia Republican opposed some legislation pending in Congress requiring a sixty-day notification to workers before a plant could be closed down. She believed in retrospect that her position on the issue made her appear more antagonistic to labor than she actually was and required "two-step reasoning" to generate support from the public. That is, its virtue was not apparent on its face and needed too much of an explanation to be effective. It was her biggest regret in looking back on the campaign.

37 These percentages come from the American National Election Studies. The House figures come from the 1986 survey (n=338). The Dukakis figures come from the 1988 survey (n=441).

38 Southern Republican congressional candidates sometimes find themselves pursuing a peculiar strategy with regard to their national party. In some places, like southern Mississippi, the resentment against Republicans has worn away. In other places, as in East Texas, it is still a liability to run as a Republican, and the party's candidates do not try to evoke party ties. Yet, these Republican congressional candidates do all they can to link themselves to national Republican figures if not to the Republican label. The great irony of the Texas case is that Republicans before the election and Democrats after the election claimed it was a test of southern realignment, yet neither candidate fully embraced his affiliation in the campaign.

39 This has been a problem for many doctrinaire conservative Republicans, southern and nonsouthern. The Indiana congressman John Hiler, who beat minority whip John Brademus on Reagan's coattails in 1980, is one example. Upon reaching Congress, Hiler did nothing to bring pork to the district, rebuffed the mayor of South Bend, who was seeking a federal loan guarantee, and stood by while South Bend's largest employer left for the Sunbelt ("Capital should be allowed to move freely," he explained). After some very close elections, Hiler swallowed his conservative principles and became a much stronger advocate for his district (Barnes 1988).

40 Natcher refused campaign contributions from any source (Barone and Ujifusa 1991). Prather was not quite so principled, accepting contributions from Kentucky interests.

Chapter 5   The Majority Black District

1 While the Supreme Court's ruling in *Shaw v. Reno* may put some of these districts in jeopardy,—at this writing it is not clear how this decision will play out—some if not all of these majority black districts will survive.

2 There were several other special elections pending at the time of the election, though all were scheduled for the following months.

3 When one crop feeds so much money into an area's economy, it is little surprise that it becomes important to the identity of the area. In an incident that illustrates the Delta's attachment to cotton, when the Greenville newspaper reported that Sen. Trent Lott's wife modeled polyester for a congressional wives' charity fashion show, it caused a furor. "All hell broke loose," said the reporter who wrote the piece. "That story brought in more letters to the editor than any other issue this year."

4 A striking number of middle-class blacks are returning to the area to retire, citing the difficulty of urban life up North and the lower cost of living in the region. These people have had a profound effect on the politics of the area because they have the skills and the time to volunteer in campaigns as well as some previous experience in politics.

5 As a point of comparison, in Mississippi as a whole, 32 percent of residents lived below 125 percent of the poverty line and 50 percent below 200 percent of the poverty line. Almost 13 percent of households were on public assistance. Sixteen percent of adults had less than a ninth-grade education.

6 *Jordan v. Winter*, 541 F. Supp 1135 (N.D. Miss. 1982) *vac'd and remanded sub nom. Brooks v. Winter*, 461 U.S. 921 (1983), 604 F. Supp. 807 (N.D. Miss. 1984), *aff'd sub nom. Mississippi Republican Executive Committee v. Brooks*, 469 U.S. 1002 (1984).

7 Espy is conservative compared to other black members of the House. Before the election of the Republican Gary Franks in Connecticut in 1990, he was consistently the most conservative member of the black delegation. Americans for Democratic Action gave him a rating of 67 in 1990. The average score for black members of the House that year was 91.

8 Dent told me, for instance, that while serving in the Persian Gulf during the Gulf War he made sure to write letters to Republican activists back home in order to "stay in the loop." He also had worked on numerous Republican campaigns, which he cited as the reason it took him so long (ten years) to get his college degree.

9 Both quotations are from the prepared text of a speech Meredith gave at the Democratic caucus.

10 Emily's List, in addition to the endorsement, sent a freelance campaign consultant to assist the campaign. Though she was able to raise money through women's groups, Blackwell perceived her sex to be a liability in the election: "Sometimes I think we got a menfolk-womenfolk problem more than a black-white problem in this state of Mississippi," she said in a televised debate.

11 These quotes come from a personal interview and from comments made at a candidate forum.

12 The *Ayers* case involved the unfair distribution of resources between "white" and predominantly black educational institutions. The victory of civil rights forces in the case may have been a Pyrrhic one as the state of Mississippi responded by proposing to close some historically black institutions (including the Delta's Mississippi Valley State University) to resolve the issue. Thompson's involvement in the case tied him closely to those defending the school from closure as well as the administration and faculty of the school. Indeed, a few days before the primary election, a peculiar rally on Thompson's behalf was held during a huge sociology class at Mississippi Valley State. The speaker, who had argued the *Ayers* case before the Supreme Court, gave an alarmist speech in which he endorsed his friend Bennie Thompson as students took notes. Thompson won 49 percent and Espy won 37 percent of the vote at the Mississippi Valley State precinct; he won 16 percent of Leflore County (home to Valley State) while Espy took twice that countywide.

13 The Republicans underestimated how connected Thompson was with the black leadership in the district. One official expressed surprise that the moderate black political leadership in the district had lined up almost completely behind Thompson in the first campaign.

14 A *Jackson Clarion-Ledger* reporter defended the timing of the story by noting that it took a long time to locate the policeman involved in the incident.

15 Bennie Thompson refused to debate Dent, and the televised forum thus occurred with Dent facing a panel of three reporters while sitting next to a conspicuously empty chair.

16 "The Choice is Yours" literature came from previous congressional elections in the Second District. In both of the Robert Clark–Webb Franklin elections, Republicans produced literature that used the same format and the same heading, though the original Franklin material also had a not-so-subtle tagline, "He's one of us" (Neilson 1989, 95).

17 The front-page treatment of these allegations makes it quite apparent that coverage of the election by the media in the Delta was extraordinarily tilted. That Hayes Dent's brushes with the law merited only brief mention (mostly on the editorial page) further illustrates the biased reporting of the Clarksdale and Greenwood papers. The Jackson paper appeared to tilt the other way, though. It did not run any news stories on Thompson's legal problems but did highlight Hayes Dent's problems on the front page.

18 Dole was actually the second choice of the campaign. Jack Kemp, however, had turned down an invitation, saying he was philosophically opposed to a white person representing a majority black district. Dent's top campaign staff were bitter and Dent introduced Dole with "Ladies and gentlemen, I bring you the man who's probably going to be the next President of the United States." It was supposed to be a dig at the absent Jack Kemp.

19 The Republicans excoriated Thompson for his tenure in Bolton, where, they claimed, the number of city employees went from fewer than ten to more than seventy during his tenure. The town has about eight hundred residents.

20 It helped that the good-sized Thompson had a good-sized appetite. Thompson stood in front of the brunch buffet at the ministers' meeting and told me that in the past two days he had eaten six catfish meals.

21 Madison County gave forty-five hundred votes to Thompson on election day.

22 Republicans also tell of poll watchers being intimidated by precinct officials. In an extreme example, one Republican official described being locked in a closet for several hours in a black precinct in Tennessee.

23 In the North Carolina senate race in 1990 between Jesse Helms and Harvey Gantt, postcards informing voters that "it is a federal crime, punishable by up to five years in jail, to knowingly give false information about your name, residence or period of residence to an election official" were sent out to voters in heavily black areas. Though the state Republican party promised not to use residence information obtained from returned mail, they argued that the postcards were legitimate. While the Republican National Committee had pledged by consent agreement in federal court in the early 1980s to "refrain from undertaking any ballot security activities in polling places or election districts where the racial or ethnic composition of such districts is a factor," it was argued (and accepted in federal court) that this was solely a state party effort (Edsall 1990; Ayres 1990).

24 Some argue that this is not the case. "I hope you haven't come in here with any racial predispositions. That business is over and done with here," said one Republican official to me before talking about political strategy in almost exclusively racial terms. Others pointed to Mike Espy, who courted and won over many whites during his moderate tenure as the Delta's congressman and, by this argument, "deracialized" politics. But they overlooked the fact that his first victory came without white support and also that the Republicans did not seriously challenge him after that.

25 The idea that Bennie Thompson was hostile to whites was pervasive among Delta whites, even among some of his white friends. A white Democratic activist who was deeply involved in the Blackwell campaign said, "Bennie is less antiwhite than people think he is." Though it was part of her rationale for working in the general election for the Thompson campaign, her phrasing illustrates that she clearly believed there was something to this characterization.

26 At least this was the belief of the Republican campaign. "Yankees" from the Republican National Committee staff were not allowed to answer the campaign telephone.

27 Clinton did not do particularly well with southern whites in general. In a *New York Times*/CBS News exit poll, 34 percent of southern whites reported voting for Clinton, while 49 percent reported voting for Bush and 18 percent for Perot. Mississippi whites and especially Delta whites were hostile to the Democratic nominee.

28 Although Dent was quite polished, especially given that he had never run for office before, his lack of experience was most apparent when he tried to tell a joke. Whereas Dole could tell the same joke to great effect at two consecutive functions, Dent had trouble remembering his good punch lines.

29 This, of course, is not so much a function of racial balance as of timing. All the Demo-

crats in the other cases described here were able to run against Washington during the Reagan and Bush years.

Chapter 6 Resolving the Puzzles

1 White southerners have voted for the Republican candidate over the Democratic candidate in every presidential election since 1964. From 1952 to 1964, the white vote was split about evenly.

2 Not every high-profile conversion of a southern Democrat has provided the desired demonstration. For every Andy Ireland, there has been a Bill Grant, another Florida congressman who switched parties in the middle of his term. Though Grant ran unopposed as a Democrat in 1986 and 1988, he announced his conversion in 1989 and was defeated resoundingly in the 1990 election by an opponent who made the switch a major issue of the campaign. For every Phil Gramm who left the Democratic party after feuding with Democratic leaders, there has been a Tommy Robinson, who also switched parties after many conflict-ridden years in the Democratic party. Robinson, like Gramm, tried to parlay the publicity into a run for higher office (the Arkansas governorship). Not only did he fail to win his party's nomination for governor, but the Democrats recaptured his congressional seat.

3 A survey of partisan switching among officials in 1993 reveals some variation state to state. In Arkansas, Florida, Georgia, Louisiana, and South Carolina, for instance, two or three elected officials changed parties in this calendar year. In Mississippi, twelve Democratic officials (state legislators, county supervisors, municipal aldermen, and a mayor) changed their affiliation. The state party of Tennessee reported no switches in 1993. Several state parties did not gather such information. Data were compiled by the state Republican parties of all these states.

4 This is not just because of racial issues in the campaigns. Tying themselves so closely to Reagan and Bush does not appear to be a fruitful way to appeal to blacks. As Katherine Tate persuasively shows, attitudes toward Ronald Reagan further bolstered Democratic attachments among blacks (1993, 65–70).

References

Apple, Jr., R. W. 1989. "House Race in Alabama Takes on a Biting Tone," *New York Times*, March 31.

Applebome, Peter. 1993. "Racial Lines Seen as Crucial in Mississippi Runoff," *New York Times*, April 12.

Attlesey, Sam. 1985a. "Wright criticizes GOP campaign," *Dallas Morning News*, June 4.

——. 1985b. "Candidates in 1rst District race make their last-ditch maneuvers," *Dallas Morning News*, June 27.

——. 1985c. "Hargett, Chapman in Runoff," *Dallas Morning News*, June 30.

——. 1985d. "Hargett, Chapman camps plot runoff tactics," *Dallas Morning News*, July 1.

——. 1985e. "1rst District runoff race focussing on jobs, trade," *Dallas Morning News*, July 28.

——. 1985f. "1rst District candidates target key groups in campaign," *Dallas Morning News*, June 29.

——. 1985g. "Democrat Chapman edges Hargett in runoff," *Dallas Morning News*, August 4.

———. 1985h. "Volunteers credited for Chapman win," *Dallas Morning News*, August 5.

———. 1985i. "Chapman says he's ready to go to work," *Dallas Morning News*, August 5.

Ayres Jr., B. Drummond. 1990. "Judge Assails G.O.P Mailing in Carolina," *New York Times*, November 5.

Baker, Donald P. 1988. "Two vie for conservative title, house seat in Virginia's 5th," *Washington Post*, June 9.

Balz, Dan, and Ruth Marcus. 1992. "Clinton Said to Fill Last Four Cabinet Jobs," *Washington Post*, December 24.

Barnes, Fred. 1988. "The Unbearable Lightness of Being a Congressman," *New Republic*, February 15, pp. 18–22.

Barone, Michael, Grant Ujifusa, and Douglas Matthews. 1979. *The Almanac of American Politics, 1980*. New York: E. P. Dutton.

Barone, Michael, and Grant Ujifusa. 1985. *The Almanac of American Politics 1986*. Washington, D.C.: National Journal.

Barone, Michael. 1985. "Running in the 'East Texas Tradition,'" *Washington Post*, June 25.

———. 1987. *The Almanac of American Politics 1988*. Washington, D.C.: National Journal.

———. 1989. *The Almanac of American Politics 1990*. Washington, D.C.: National Journal.

———. 1991. *The Almanac of American Politics 1992*. Washington, D.C.: National Journal.

Bartley, Numan V., and Hugh D. Graham. 1975. *Southern Politics and the Second Reconstruction*. Baltimore: Johns Hopkins University Press.

Beck, Paul Allen. 1977. "Partisan Dealignment in the Postwar South," *American Political Science Review* 71:477-96.

Berelson, Bernard R., Paul F. Lazarsfeld, and William N. McPhee. 1954. *Voting: A Study of Opinion Formation in a Presidential Campaign*. Chicago: University of Chicago Press.

Black, Earl, and Merle Black. 1987. *Politics and Society in the South*. Cambridge: Harvard University Press.

———. 1992. *The Vital South: How Presidents are Elected*. Cambridge: Harvard University Press.

Bland, Laura E. 1988a. "Payne nomination: How did he do it?" *Danville (Virginia) Bee*, March 28.

———. 1988b. "Democratic candidate stresses views of defense, education," *Danville (Virginia) Bee*, April 21.

———. 1988c. "Union members jeer Arey, but may not support Payne either," *Danville (Virginia) Bee*, May 27.

———. 1988d. "Payne takes pro-choice stand; Arey stresses anti-abortion position," *Danville (Virginia) Bee*, June 1.

———. 1988e. "Democrats tout virtues of being in majority party," *Danville (Virginia) Bee*, June 7.

———. 1988f. "Trible says a vote for Arey important to Virginia," *Danville (Virginia) Bee*, June 7.

———. 1988g. "Daniel's son counter claims in 5th," *Danville (Virginia) Bee*, June 8.

———. 1988h. "Arey draws on D.C. experience," *Danville (Virginia) Bee*, June 8.

———. 1988i. "Dole says Arey understands how Washington works," *Danville (Virginia) Bee*, June 8.

———. 1988j. "Democrat Payne 'regular guy,'" *Danville (Virginia) Bee*, June 8.

———. 1988k. "Bush urges vote for Arey, criticizes Wright inquiry," *Danville (Virginia) Bee*, June 13.

Branch, Taylor. 1988. *Parting the Waters: America in the King Years, 1954–1963*. New York: Simon and Schuster.

Brinkley, Alan. 1982. *Huey Long, Father Coughlin and the Great Depression*. New York: Vintage Books.

Broder, David S. 1981a. "Democrats, Cheered by a Victory, Leery of Disciplining Renegade," *Washington Post*, July 9.

———. 1981b. "Party chiefs launch post-mortems of Miss. election upset," *Washington Post*, July 10.

Brownson, Charles B. 1982. *1982 Congressional Staff Directory*. Mt. Vernon, Virginia: Congressional Staff Directory.

Bullock, III, Charles S. 1988a. "Regional Realignment from an Officeholding Perspective," *Journal of Politics* 50:553-74.

———. 1988b. "Creeping Realignment in the South," in Robert H. Swansbrough and David M. Brodsky, eds., *The South's New Politics: Realignment and Dealignment*. Columbia: University of South Carolina Press.

Burger, Frederick. 1989a. "Browder, Rice off to a spirited start," *Anniston (Alabama) Star*, March 9.

———. 1989b. "2 more rally for Browder," *Anniston (Alabama) Star*, March 22.

Carmines, Edward G., and James A. Stimson. 1989. *Issue Evolution*. Princeton: Princeton University Press.

Cassreino, Terry R. 1989. "Republicans clear the way for Anderson," *Gulfport (Mississippi) Sun Herald*, September 3.

Clymer, Adam. 1981a. "Mississippi to choose successor to Hinson today," *New York Times*, July 7.

———. 1981b. "Mississippi loss: 2 warnings for GOP," *New York Times*, July 9.

Congressional Quarterly. 1988. "Review of Congressional Election Winners," November 12.

Congressional Quarterly Almanac. 1981. "House Passes Bill to Extend Voting Rights Act," 415–18.

Congressional Quarterly's Guide to Congress. 3d ed. 1982. Washington, D.C., Congressional Quarterly.

Converse, Philip E. 1966. "On the Possibility of Major Political Realignment in the South," in Angus Campbell, Philip E. Converse, Warren E. Miller, and Donald E. Stokes, eds., *Elections and the Political Order*. New York: John Wiley and Sons.

Curran, Tim. 1993. "Henry Espy Tops Field in Race for Brother's Seat Tuesday, But Delta Contest Now Tight," *Roll Call*, March 25.

Danville (Virginia) Bee. 1988. "Issues and Answers: 5th District '88," June 1.

Danville (Virginia) Register. 1988. "Payne fund lead helped with 5th win," July 22.

Davidson, Chandler. 1990. *Race and Class in Texas Politics.* Princeton: Princeton University Press.

Dockins, Metric, and Patrick Peterson. 1989. "Diverse crowd shows democracy in action," *Gulfport (Mississippi) Sun Herald*, October 13.

Duncan, Phil, ed. 1989. *Politics in America: Members of Congress in Washington and at Home.* Washington, D.C.: Congressional Quarterly.

Edsall, Thomas B. 1990. "Helms Makes Race an Issue," *Washington Post*, October 31.

Edsall, Thomas Byrne, and Mary D. Edsall. 1991. *Chain Reaction: The Impact of Race, Rights, and Taxes on American Politics.* New York: W. W. Norton.

Ehrenhalt, Alan, ed. 1983. *Politics in America: Members of Congress in Washington and at Home.* Washington, D.C.: Congressional Quarterly.

——, ed. 1987. *Politics in America: Members of Congress in Washington and at Home.* Washington, D.C.: Congressional Quarterly.

——. 1991. *The United States of Ambition.* New York: Times Books.

Elving, Ronald D. 1988. "GOP Sees New Day in Southside Virginia," *Congressional Quarterly*, April 16, pp. 1008–09.

Erikson, Robert S. 1988. "The Puzzle of Midterm Loss," *Journal of Politics* 50:1011–29.

Eure, Rob. 1988a. " 'High energy' helps GOP candidate," *Roanoke Times and World News*, May 29.

——. 1988b. "Fifth District's Campaign Subtlety Faces Media Age," *Roanoke Times and World News*, June 1.

Evans, Rowland, and Robert Novak. 1985. "Realignment at the Cuthand Fish Fry," *Washington Post*, August 2.

Fava, Al. 1993. "Franklin sees race with inside point of view," *Greenwood (Mississippi) Commonwealth Delta Advertiser*, March 24.

Fenno, Jr., Richard F. 1978. *Homestyle: House Members in Their Districts.* Boston: Little, Brown.

——. 1990. *Watching Politicians: Essays on Participant Observation.* Berkeley: IGS Press.

Forman, Gail. 1989. "Catfish Achieve Upward Mobility," *New York Times*, February 1.

Fossett, Mark A., and Jill K. Kiecult. 1989. "The Relative Size of Minority Populations and White Racial Attitudes," *Social Science Quarterly* 58:412–17.

Genovese, Eugene D. 1967. *The Political Economy of Slavery.* New York: Vintage Books.

Germond, Jack W., and Jules Witcover. 1985. "1rst District campaign as test of Dixie realignment a phony," *Dallas Morning News*, July 27.

Gilens, Martin. 1990. "Racial Attitudes and Opposition to the American Welfare State." Unpublished paper, Department of Sociology, University of California, Berkeley.

Giles, Michael W. 1977. "Percent Black and Racial Hostility: An Old Assumption Revisited," *Social Science Quarterly* 30:469–85.

Giles, Michael W., and Arthur Evans. 1986. "The Power Approach to Intergroup Hostility," *Journal of Conflict Resolution* 30:469–85.

Glaser, James M. 1994. "Back to the Black Belt: Racial Environment and White Racial Attitudes in the South," *Journal of Politics* 56:21–41.

Glazer, Amihai. 1990. "A Formal Model of Group-Oriented Voting." Paper presented at the conference, "Modeling the Links between Race and U.S. Electoral Politics," University of California, Irvine, May 19.

Grofman, Bernard. 1990. "One Dozen Easy Ways to go Wrong in Modeling Race and Politics." Paper presented at the conference, "Modeling the Links between Race and U.S. Electoral Politics," University of California, Irvine, May 19.

Gulfport (Mississippi) Sun-Herald. 1989a. "Candidates work Lucedale crowd," September 10.

———. 1989b. "Anderson: Free rides overlooked," September 24.

Hair, William Ivy. 1991. *The Kingfish and His Realm: The Life and Times of Huey P. Long.* Baton Rouge: Louisiana State University.

Hall, Carla. 1986. "Espy's Mississippi Milestone," *Washington Post*, December 19.

Harris, Art. 1981. "Hinson's memory haunts his Mississippi district," *Washington Post*, June 17.

Hillman, G. Robert. 1985. "White assails suit in First District race," *Dallas Morning News*, July 25.

Huckfeldt, Robert, and Carol Weitzel Kohfeld. 1989. *Race and the Decline of Class in American Politics.* Urbana: University of Illinois Press.

Jacobson, Gary C. 1990. *The Electoral Origins of Divided Government.* Boulder: Westview Press.

Jacobson, Gary C., and Samuel Kernell. 1983. *Strategy and Choice in Congressional Elections.* 2d ed. New Haven: Yale University Press.

Jackson Clarion-Ledger. 1981. "Williams, Dowdy to meet in runoff," June 24.

Jackson Daily News and Clarion-Ledger. 1981. "We back Williams," July 5.

Jamieson, Kathleen Hall. 1992. *Packaging the Presidency.* 2d ed. New York: Oxford University Press.

Jaynes, Gerald David, and Robin M. Williams, Jr., eds. 1989. *A Common Destiny: Blacks and American Society.* Washington, D.C.: National Academy Press.

Jewell, Malcolm, and David Olson. 1988. *Political Parties and Elections in American States.* Chicago: Dorsey.

Judis, John B. 1988. "Black Donkey, White Elephant," *New Republic*, April 18, pp. 25–28.

Kernell, Samuel. 1977. "Presidential Popularity and Negative Voting: An Alternative Explanation of the Midterm Congressional Decline of the President's Party," *American Political Science Review* 71:44–66.

Key, Jr., V. O. 1949. *Southern Politics in State and Nation.* Knoxville : University of Tennessee Press.

Kinder, Donald R. 1986. "The Continuing American Dilemma: White Resistance to Racial Change 40 Years after Myrdal," *Journal of Social Issues* 42:151–72.

Kinder, Donald R., and David O. Sears. 1981. "Prejudice and Politics: Symbolic Racism versus Racial Threats to the Good Life," *Journal of Personality and Social Psychology* 40:414–31.

Kinder, Donald R., Tali Mendelberg, Michael C. Dawson, Lynn M. Sanders, Steven J. Rosenstone, Jocelyn Sargent, and Cathy Cohen. 1989. "Race and the 1988 American Presidential Election." Paper delivered at the annual meeting of the American Political Science Association, Atlanta, Georgia, September 2.

King, Wayne. 1985a. "Texas G.O.P. Seeks to Win U.S. House Seat Today," *New York Times*, June 29.

——. 1985b. "U.S. Court Says Texas Erred But Doesn't Delay Election," *New York Times*, August 2.

——. 1985c. "Texans Pick a Congressman Today," *New York Times*, August 3.

——. 1985d. "Democrats Cheer Results in Texas," *New York Times*, August 5.

Kocher, Greg. 1994a. "2nd District race takes off," *Owensboro (Kentucky) Messenger-Inquirer*, May 21.

——. 1994b. "Lewis makes a final sweep of 2nd District," *Owensboro (Kentucky) Messenger-Inquirer*, May 24.

Kurtz, Howard. 1985. "Texas to Obey Election Edict," *Washington Post*, August 2.

Lightman, Allan J. 1987. "Racial Bloc Voting in Mississippi Elections: Methodology and Results." Trial exhibit presented in *Martin v. Allain,* 658 F. Supp. 1183 (S.D. Miss. 1987).

Lubell, Samuel. 1966. *White and Black: Test of a Nation.* Revised edition. New York: Harper Colophon Books.

Matthews, Donald R., and James W. Prothro. 1966. *Negroes and the New Southern Politics.* New York: Harcourt, Brace and World.

Maisel, Louis Sandy. 1986. *From Obscurity to Oblivion: Running in the Congressional Primary.* Revised edition. Knoxville: University of Tennessee Press.

McKenzie, Danny. 1989. "Some people tired of Taylor getting fat on 'humble pie,'" *Jackson Clarion-Ledger*, October 2.

McNeil, Robert B. 1989. "Atwater pats Rice on back, but won't predict victory," *Anniston (Alabama) Star*, March 30.

Mills, Kay. 1992. "Unita Blackwell: MacArthur Genius Award Caps a Creative Political Life," *Los Angeles Times*, August 2.

Mitchell, Jerry. 1993a. "Assault 'mistake,' Dent says," *Jackson Clarion-Ledger*, March 26.

Mosby, Ray. 1993a. "Dent seen as preferable to Thompson," *Clarksdale (Mississippi) Press Register*, March 3.

———. 1993b. "Friends in high places saved Thompson," *Clarksdale (Mississippi) Press Register*, March 8.

Mughan, Anthony. 1986. "Toward a Political Explanation of Government Vote Losses in Midterm By-Elections," *American Political Science Review* 80:761–75.

Mullen, Bill. 1981. "Candidates Williams, Dowdy share platform in McComb," *Jackson Clarion-Ledger*, July 4.

National Republican Congressional Committee. 1988. Report in *The Presidential Hotline*, December 14.

Nelson, Mark. 1985. "Candidates rely on congressmen," *Dallas Morning News*, July 25.

Neilson, Melany. 1989. *Even Mississippi.* Tuscaloosa: University of Alabama Press.

New York Times. 1985. "Democrat Wins Congressional Race in Texas," August 4.

Nie, Norman H., Sidney Verba, and John R. Petrocik. 1979. *The Changing American Voter.* Cambridge: Harvard University Press.

Parker, Frank R. 1990. *Black Votes Count: Political Empowerment in Mississippi after 1965.* Chapel Hill: University of North Carolina Press.

Peterson, Patrick. 1989a. "Liberal language flies in 5th District," *Gulfport (Mississippi) Sun Herald.* September 21.

———. 1989b. "Environmentalists, Bush jump in fray in 5th District," *Gulf Coast (Mississippi) Sun Herald*, September 30.

———. 1989c. "Taylor HQ takes town by the horns," *Gulfport (Mississippi) Sun Herald*, October 12, 1989.

Petrocik, John R. 1981. *Party Coalitions: Realignments and the Decline of the New Deal Party System.* Chicago: University of Chicago Press.

Phillips, Kevin P. 1969. *The Emerging Republican Majority.* New Rochelle, N.Y.: Arlington House.

Pomper, Gerald M. 1989. "The Presidential Election," in Gerald M. Pomper, ed., *The Election of 1988: Reports and Interpretations.* Chatham, N.J.: Chatham House.

Putnam, Judy. 1981a. "Dowdy beats Williams by paper thin margin," *Jackson Clarion-Ledger*, July 8.

———. 1981b. "Dowdy sworn in; Final tally shows 912-vote margin," *Jackson Clarion-Ledger*, July 10.

Rilling, Paul. 1989. "Poll shows hefty lead for Browder," *Anniston (Alabama) Star*, March 28.

Sanders-Castro, Judith A. 1985. Prepared testimony before the Subcommittee on Civil and Constitutional Rights of the Committee on the Judiciary, House of Representatives

(99th Congress, 2nd Session). *Proposed Revisions of Procedures for Administration of Section 5 of the Voting Rights Act of 1965.* November 13.

Scammon, Richard M., ed. 1970. *America Votes 8.* Washington, D.C.: Congressional Quarterly.

Scammon, Richard M., and Alice V. McGillivray, eds. 1986. *America Votes 16.* Washington, D.C.: Congressional Quarterly.

Schuman, Howard, Charlotte Steeh, and Lawrence Bobo. 1985. *Racial Attitudes in America: Trends and Interpretations.* Cambridge: Harvard University Press.

Sears, David O., and J. B. McConahey. 1973. *The Politics of Violence: The New Urban Blacks and the Watts Riot.* Boston: Houghton Mifflin.

Shields, Mark. 1985. "East Texas Wind," *Washington Post,* August 2, p. A17.

Sigelman, Lee. 1981. "Special Elections to the U.S. House: Some Descriptive Generalizations," *Legislative Studies Quarterly* 6:577–88.

Simon, Herbert A. 1985. "Human Nature in Politics: The Dialogue of Psychology with Political Science," *American Political Science Review* 79:293–304.

Smith, Christopher. 1989a. "Rice hits Browder on home turf," *Anniston (Alabama) Star,* March 10.

——. 1989b. "Rice: A far journey to Congress," *Anniston (Alabama) Star,* March 15.

——. 1989c. "Rice on taxes: 'Never,'" *Anniston (Alabama) Star,* March 19.

——. 1989d. "Browder's war chest is fattest," *Anniston (Alabama) Star,* March 24.

——. 1989e. "Rice dedicated to conservatism," *Anniston (Alabama) Star,* March 26.

——. 1989f. "Work ethic strong in Rice background," *Anniston (Alabama) Star,* March 29.

——. 1989g. "Rice workers all but write off black vote," *Anniston (Alabama) Star,* April 1.

Sniderman, Paul M., and Michael Gray Hagen. 1985. *Race and Inequality: A Study in American Values.* Chatham, N.J.: Chatham House.

Sorauf, Frank. 1984. *Party Politics in America.* Boston: Little, Brown.

Souther, Sharon. 1989a. "Goal is balancing nature, economy," *Gulf Coast (Mississippi) Sun Herald,* September 28.

——. 1989b. "Taylor, Anderson make run-off," *Gulf Coast (Mississippi) Sun Herald,* October 4.

——. 1989c. "Anderson: U.S. must 'get rid of Noriega,'" *Gulfport (Mississippi) Sun Herald,* October 11.

——. 1989d. "Anderson, Taylor air their differences," *Gulf Coast (Mississippi) Sun Herald,* October 12.

——. 1989e. "5th District candidates work to keep from being stereotyped," *Gulf Coast (Mississippi) Sun Herald,* October 14.

——. 1989f. "Democrats attack ads by Anderson," *Gulfport (Mississippi) Sun Herald,* October 15.

Stanbury, Beth. 1988. "Barker will not run for 5th, calls Arey's charges 'absurd,'" *Danville (Virginia) Bee,* June 16.

Stanley, Harold W. 1987. *Voter Mobilization and the Politics of Race.* New York: Praeger.

———. 1992. "Southern Republicans in Congress: Fallen and Can't Get Up?" *Social Science Quarterly* 73:136–43.

Stanley, Harold W., and Richard Niemi. 1988. *Vital Statistics on American Politics.* Washington, D.C.: Congressional Quarterly Press.

Stewart, Steve. 1993b. "Loss may not be end for Espy," *Greenwood (Mississippi) Commonwealth,* March 31.

Stewart, Steve, and Al Fava. 1993. "Dent, Thompson prevail in primary," *Greenwood (Mississippi) Commonwealth,* March 31.

Strong, Donald. 1971. "Further Reflections on Southern Politics," *Journal of Politics* 33:239–56.

Studlar, Donley T., and Lee Sigelman. 1987. "Special Elections: A Comparative Perspective," *British Journal of Political Science* 17:247–56.

Sundquist, James L. 1983. *Dynamics of the Party System.* Revised edition. Washington, D.C.: Brookings Institution.

Tate, Katherine. 1993. *From Protest to Politics: The New Black Voters in American Elections.* Cambridge: Harvard University Press and the Russell Sage Foundation.

Taylor, Paul. 1985a. "GOP Hopes to Undo East Texas Tradition," *Washington Post,* June 26.

———. 1985b. "Dispute Settled, Texas House Race To Be Held Today," *Washington Post,* June 29.

———. 1985c. "Anger over Imports Fuels Texas Campaign," *Washington Post,* August 1.

Thielemann, Gregory S. 1992. "The Rise and Stall of Southern Republicans in Congress," *Social Science Quarterly* 73:123–35.

Tisdale, Charles. 1993. "Tisdale's Topics: Elect Bennie G. Thompson," *Jackson Advocate,* March 25–31.

Toner, Robin. 1990. "North Carolina Senate Contest Down to Wire," *New York Times,* October 31.

Treyens, Cliff. 1981a. "Dowdy takes seat in capitol today," *Jackson Clarion-Ledger,* July 8.

———. 1981b. "Surge in black, rural turnout put Dowdy over top," *Jackson Clarion-Ledger,* July 8.

U.S. Bureau of the Census. 1967. *County and City Data Book 1967.* Washington, D.C.: U.S. Government Printing Office.

———. 1983. *Congressional District Profiles, 98th Congress* (Supplementary Report PC80-S1-11).

———. 1986. *Statistical Abstract of the United States 1987.* 107th ed.. Washington, D.C.

———. 1992. *Population and Housing Characteristics for Congressional Districts of the 103rd Congress (Mississippi).*

U.S. Congress. 1985. Oversight Hearings before the Subcommittee on Civil and Constitutional Rights of the Committee on the Judiciary, House of Representatives (99th Congress, 2nd Session). *Proposed Changes to Regulations Governing Section 5 of the Voting Rights Act,* November 13 and 20.

Walsh, Edward. 1981. "Reagan Assists GOP Candidate for Hinson's Seat," *Washington Post,* June 23.

Walton, Steve. 1993. "Will Espys build empire on politics?" *Jackson Clarion-Ledger,* March 21.

Walton, Steve, and J. Lee Howard. 1993. "Feathers flying, 2nd District fight enters final round," *Jackson Clarion-Ledger,* April 11.

Washington Post. 1981a. "Democrat Wins Race for House in Mississippi," July 8.

——. 1981b. "The Message from Mississippi," July 18.

Watson, Tom. 1985. "Hargett Faces Chapman in Texas 1rst Runoff," *Congressional Quarterly,* July 6, p. 1336.

Weiss, Nancy J. 1983. *Farewell to the Party of Lincoln.* Princeton: Princeton University Press.

Westlye, Mark C. 1991. *Senate Elections and Campaign Intensity.* Baltimore: Johns Hopkins University Press.

White, David. 1989. "Some issues find Browder, Rice on the same side," *Birmingham News,* March 19.

Williams, T. Harry. 1969. *Huey Long.* New York: Vintage Books.

Woodward, Comer Vann. 1988. "Referendum on Reagan," *New York Times Review of Books,* December 22.

Wright, Gavin. 1986. *Old South, New South: Revolutions in the Southern Economy since the Civil War.* New York: Basic Books.

Yardley, Jim. 1989a. "It's Browder against Rice," *Anniston (Alabama) Star,* March 8.

——. 1989b. "Campaign charges escalate," *Anniston (Alabama) Star,* March 16.

——. 1989c. "Campaign is 'sleazy,' 'sickening,'" *Anniston (Alabama) Star,* March 17.

——. 1989d. "Browder, Rice clash on funding," *Anniston (Alabama) Star,* March 21.

——. 1989e. "Candidates charge each ducked votes," *Anniston (Alabama) Star,* March 24.

——. 1989f. "Browder targets the middle class," *Anniston (Alabama) Star,* March 26.

——. 1989g. "Heflin wants military committee for Browder," *Anniston (Alabama) Star,* March 29.

——. 1989h. "House race foes visit opponent's home field," *Anniston (Alabama) Star,* April 2.

Index